Urban Policy Issues

307
.76
097 I
Urb

Urban policy issues : Canadian perspectives / edited by
Richard A. Loreto, Trevor Price. -- Toronto :
McClelland & Stewart, c1990.
246 p. : ill.

Includes bibliographies and indexes.
04444310   ISBN:0771053460 (pbk.)

1. Urban policy - Canada. I. Loreto, Richard Anthony,
1949- II. Price, Trevor, 1931-

12610   90OCT30   06/go   1-00956041

Urban Policy Issues:
Canadian Perspectives

Edited by

**Richard A. Loreto,
Trevor Price**

Canadian Cataloguing in Publication Data

Main entry under title:

Urban policy issues: Canadian perspectives

Includes bibliographical references.
ISBN 0-7710-5346-0

1. Urban policy - Canada. I. Loreto, Richard
Anthony, 1949-   . II. Price, Trevor, 1931-

HT127.U72 1990   307.76'0971   C90-093768-8

Diagram of landfill site, p. 130, courtesy Victoria Primicias.

McClelland & Stewart Inc.
The Canadian Publishers
481 University Avenue
Toronto, Ontario
M5G 2E9

Printed and bound in Canada

Contents

Urban Policy Issues: An Overview

Reasons for This Collection

We live in a country in which we elect representatives to three levels of government: a federal parliament over the entire country, a provincial legislative assembly over a significant region of the country, and a local or municipal government over our immediate community. As part of our democratic tradition we regard all three levels as necessary, although it undoubtedly has brought about a complex network of intergovernmental relationships that can baffle all but the most diligent students of government.

In a general way it is probably safe to claim that the local level of government is the least understood and the most neglected in terms of scholarly analysis. This is partly due to the fact that we have ten distinct provincial systems and two territorial systems of local government and many thousands of individual units of local government. To encapsulate such diversity is a rather formidable task. Local government has a lesser role in our governmental system because it lacks a distinct constitutional foundation of its own and is placed by our constitutional allocation of powers under the jurisdiction of the provinces. The provincial influence over local government in Canada is pervasive and dominating, but it is not so overwhelming that local government lacks political resources to assert its will.

When we talk about local government it is also important to make clear the distinction between "local" and "municipal" government.

Municipal government is a general-purpose elected government responsible for guiding local development and implementing key local services. Under its administration municipal government does not have complete authority over the full range of local services. Alongside municipal government there also exists a wide variety of appointed and elected bodies with major responsibilities for many important services, sometimes in partial autonomy and sometimes in complete autonomy from the elected municipal council. This complete collection of local authorities and their services could be referred to as local government. They include such functions as policing, education, public health, urban transit, and the provision of utilities such as water and electricity. Since each province has some variations there is no constant pattern across the whole country by which these autonomous boards relate to their municipalities.

The general literature on local government has focused mainly on the broad financial and legal relationships between municipalities and provinces, the structures and organization of local government, and internal political processes. The specific functions of local governments have been given scant attention in Canada except by specialists writing within their own fields. There is, however, a lack of integrated analysis of these policies. Our central premise in bringing together the ten specially commissioned papers that comprise the volume at hand was that some form of policy analysis of all the fields involving local government was needed to fill an important gap.

It will, no doubt, be argued by some critics that the particular functions dealt with here are not exclusively, or even mainly, local government functions. This is unquestionably true, but such is the nature of contemporary public policy. The influences on public policy arise at all three levels and move backward and forward across the three levels of government. All of these functions historically emerged from initiatives at the local level, but as time went on financial necessity, the demand for equity, the need to provide uniform standards, and the dictates of provincial or federal policy preferences all brought more and more central control and influence.

The selection of the topics for this volume is based on the fact that the local delivery of these services is important in most jurisdictions. There are exceptions and these are referred to within the individual chapters.

The Approach and the Contributors

The study of current public policy is not the monopoly of any single discipline. It is pursued by political scientists, sociologists, economists, geographers, and the various specialists working in such fields as social services, education, and health. The editors realized in their early search for contributors how few specialists studied a particular function within any one discipline. It was therefore decided to solicit the interest of those scholars within a number of different disciplines who had a background of research and interest in the required fields.

Eventually we were able to contact a broad range of scholars from a number of social science disciplines who agreed to work within a very general framework of objectives established by the editors. These objectives are: (1) to examine the origins and development of the particular function; (2) to assess the involvement of various levels of government and the direction they have given to the policies in this field; (3) to analyse the current issues in this policy area and assess the direction in which they believe current policy is going; (4) to establish what, if any, is the local government role in the particular policy field.

Each of the chapters reflects the outlook and background of the contributors, and the editors did not feel that an attempt to impose a unifying framework of a single discipline would be effective or workable. Part of the value of this book is to have readers examine the particular values of the individual authors and to reflect on how this has governed their interpretation, methodology, and conclusions. As they read the various chapters students should ask themselves how the disciplines of political science, economics, geography, social work, and medicine have had their impact on the views expressed by the respective authors.

With regard to the range of topics covered the original intention was to consider all of the important functions that have a significant local presence. This goal proved to be difficult in terms of finding the necessary expertise. The coverage is, however, quite extensive and omits only the important activities related to culture, recreation, and parks. Also, public safety concentrates exclusively on policing and does not bring in fire protection. Other activities that might have been included are conservation and local government licencing activities.

Linkages Among the Policy Fields

The first chapter, on finance, is not a discrete policy area in the sense that it is a function serving a local clientele. In another sense, however, it is an important policy area since the approach adopted by provinces to the financing of local government influences the entire range and scope of local activities. As the chapter demonstrates, much of local revenue is derived from provincial transfer payments, which through the conditional grant mechanism determine the directions of local spending quite strongly. Finally, the comparative figures and charts developed by David Siegel afford a glimpse of the relative importance of local government activities and indicate which service areas local governments are actively supporting and others in which provincial and federal support counts for a large measure.

The finance chapter can also be used to show how there is a considerable provincial variation in the degree to which local government supports certain services (for example, education). An extensively urban and wealthy province, such as Ontario, has a much broader network of municipal and local government agencies than does a poorer and less urban province, such as New Brunswick or Newfoundland. In Ontario the property tax is expected to support a large part of school board expenditures, administration of general welfare assistance, and some support of public health and policing. In Atlantic Canada property taxes are much lower and generally more services are paid for directly by the provincial governments, using equalization support from the federal government.

One of the main reasons for provincial government involvement in the provision of many services is that large areas of Canada that lie outside the main urban centres are financially and administratively less able to provide basic local services than are the urban areas. Looking at the minimum provided by municipal government, we find that this amounts mainly to basic public works. The public works of roads, bridges, drainage, snow removal, and water supply, as well as the environmental services of garbage collection and disposal and sewage treatment, tend to be basic common denominators of municipal government. As we proceed up the scale of services needed and desired in urban centres, we find the urban governments are capable of handling the full range of physical, social, and protective services.

Education has strong provincial direction and support but is also deeply rooted in many parts of Canada as a distinct unit of local representation – the school board. Almost everywhere the municipal role is confined to collecting property taxes, which forms part of the revenue base. In some provinces there is no local tax support (for example, New Brunswick).

Because of the need to provide uniform standards and a mandate to pursue a national goal of equity for all citizens of Canada, redistributive functions, such as housing and social assistance, have tended to be subject to national goals. Local participation is sometimes important in the execution of local delivery, but the scope and method are a determination resulting from a federal-provincial accord.

Meric Gertler, in his chapter on economic development, also discusses the effectiveness of the municipality in terms of influencing the decisions of multinational or even national companies in locating new plants. The local role is not important in deciding broad economic policies but in facilitating the siting of industries by providing information and infrastructural services to prospective clients. The municipality provides the vital role of linkage and representation of local interests in the network of provincial, federal, and private organizations. How active a role municipalities should play is related to the values of local elites, a subject also probed by Gertler.

Canadian policing exhibits a unique blend of responsibilities scattered across three levels of government. The local component is very important where the resources are available and the need exists for a community-rooted police force. In those parts of Canada where the communities are far-flung and small the provincial or federal government has taken responsibility for the overall framework while still allowing for an appropriate level of local input. Thus Richard Loreto explains the complex web of coverage provided by local forces, two provincial forces, and the Royal Canadian Mounted Police in fulfilling a variety of roles.

If there are two disciplines with pretensions of linking and integrating all the others, they are public health and land-use planning. Public health began as a powerful force to bring some form of physical controls and regulation to the chaotic filth and individualistic disorder of rapidly urbanizing Western nations. The broad sweep of its coverage began to initiate every kind of municipal activity from water purification, drainage, street cleaning, and building code regulations to nutrition and preventive medicine. Having relegated some of its leadership in the early part of this century to newer disciplines such as civil engineering, public health is here seen by Hancock, Pouliot, and Duplessis as once more taking the lead in creating "healthy cities." The total environment and its impact on the physical and mental aspects of the citizens' lives are the focus of the new holistic public health. The emphasis is on becoming involved in all the functions that play a part, which amounts to everything in people's lives – physical, social, cultural, and emotional.

Urban planning seeks to integrate an efficient layout of urban physical services with social, cultural, recreational, and economic objectives. Apart from the substantial political obstacles preventing any single element of urban bureaucracy assuming such a role, there is the financial pressure exerted by large economic forces from without the urban centres. Kiernan discusses the aspirations and frustrations of planners in such a way as to show how effective planning could make a major contribution to many of our present dilemmas.

Other contributors, such as Gertler on economic development, Carroll on housing, Price on environment, and Kitchen on transportation, show how pressures are exerted to follow expansionist policies that urban planners have been almost helpless to control. The engine driving expansion in the above sectors is the overwhelming desire of municipal politicians to boost the tax base through commercial and industrial growth, bringing job opportunities for their communities. Thus, the caveats of planning are often easily discarded when the seductions of economic benefits are displayed before municipal councils. Planners have to accommodate these other forces more than direct them.

Two clearly basic municipal functions are roads and physical infrastructure, both of which constitute the realm of public works. The common denominator is the expertise of the engineer, which accounts for the character of this very traditional organizational responsibility and its attendant policy problems.

As Kitchen shows in his analysis of transportation, road planning and construction, traffic engineering, and transit tend to escape the overview of integrated transportation policy. In some ways this policy should be subject to national goals, which have to do with such objectives as protecting the atmosphere from pollution, conserving energy, reducing traffic congestion, and making cities more habitable. However, Kitchen demonstrates that transportation planning is not even able to create the incentives for allocating resources in the most efficient way. Much of this is due to the fragmentation of responsibilities among levels of government and different agencies operating in relative isolation at the local level.

Environmental problems are subject to broad policy objectives by both federal and provincial governments. However, when it comes to execution of environmental policies at the local level, there is a good deal of ad hocery in reacting to immediate pressures and crises. Integrated authorities with a broad overview of pollution and water planning do not exist in Canada, although as Price shows in the chapter on the environment, the federal Inquiry on Water Policy felt that some wider form of integrated planning was needed.

The editors hope the description and analysis of the major functions that have a local community impact will stimulate more investigation and research on the way in which these functions interact. It might lead to more discussion of the need for institutional reform and reallocation of responsibilities, as discussed in the Conclusion.

1 David Siegel

The Financial Context for Urban Policy

The purpose of this chapter is to provide an overview of the financial position of local government in the 1980s. It does this in four parts. The first section presents a brief historical description of the financial position of local government within the Canadian federal system. The second section discusses the sources of local government revenue and provides a discussion of some of the issues surrounding each of those revenue sources. The third section provides a brief description of local government expenditures. The fourth section presents an overview of the surplus/deficit position of local governments over the last few years.

Local Government in the Federal System

In the early years of Confederation, the federal and local governments were the most important orders of government (in terms of level of expenditure). Local governments provided education, roads, and such social assistance as was provided at that time. Provincial governments provided very few services.

The depression of the 1930s and evolving technology changed this situation. During the depression, many municipalities suffered serious financial difficulties and had to be shored up by provincial governments, which in turn were heavily supported by the federal government.

Technology also spawned some significant changes. The improved quality of the motorcar and truck and the growth of the suburbs increased the importance of inter-city highways and commuter trains. These methods of transportation were clearly in the sphere of provincial governments. The high cost of modern education caused an increasing share of this burden to be borne by provincial governments. The overall effect of this on government expenditures was that provincial government expenditure eclipsed local expenditure during the 1930s and local governments have remained in third place ever since (Bird, 1970: 15, 239, 268).

This change in the financial status of local governments had ramifications in other areas. In general, provincial control of municipal activities has become tighter over the years. A quantum leap was made in the 1930s when provinces, which had to bale out bankrupt or virtually bankrupt municipalities, strengthened provincial control over debt issuance and other financial aspects of municipal operation. There are some who would say that that provincial control has tightened considerably over the years, although this is an arguable position.

Figure 1 illustrates the trend in the relative importance – in financial terms – of the three spheres of government in the Canadian federal system for the period from 1946 to 1985. It focuses on two measures of revenue – own-source revenue and revenue including transfers from other governments.

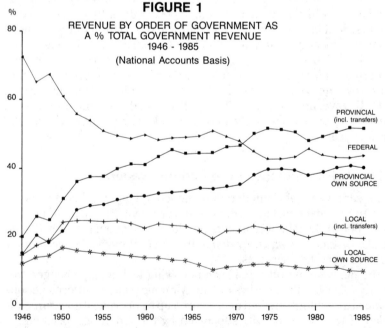

FIGURE 1

SOURCE: Adapted from Canadian Tax Foundation, *The National Finances – 1984-85* (Toronto: Canadian Tax Foundation, 1985), p. 33.

Own-source revenue consists of taxes, charges, and fees a government imposes by its own authority. *Revenue including transfers* includes all revenue received by the government – both own-source revenue and transfer payments from other governments. There is an important distinction between the two. Local governments are free to make their own decisions about raising (and spending) own-source revenue, within some fairly broad constraints established by general provincial policies on tax assessment and other matters.

Transfer payments are more problematic because these funds usually come with fairly stringent conditions attached. Also, local governments are forced to rely on the benevolence of other orders of government to provide these funds and there is no assurance about the levels of funding from year to year.

The major trends in the 1946-85 period are the declining role of the federal government and the increasing role of provincial governments. The beginning point of the graph – 1946 – is immediately after the Second World War, which was a time of strong federal dominance. The period since then has witnessed the increasing importance of such social services as health care, education, and social assistance, all of which are predominantly provincial responsibilities. Also, in the immediate post-war period, the federal government returned certain revenue sources it had used during the war (most notably, the income tax) to the provinces.

The position of local government during this period has been relatively stable. Local own-source revenue as a percentage of total government revenue declined slowly and steadily over the first part of the period but has not changed much since 1974. Revenue including transfers has been subject to greater short-term fluctuations, but has held fairly steady when viewed in the long term.

The changing financial positions of the three orders of government in the post-war period can be summed up rather quickly. The provincial governments' position has strengthened considerably at the expense of the federal government. The position of local governments has remained relatively stable.

Local Government Revenue Sources

Local governments derive most of their revenue from four main sources – property taxes and user charges (both are own-source revenues), and conditional and unconditional transfer payments. Figure 2 illustrates the changing relative importance of these four revenue sources over the period 1967-84 for the total local government domain[1] in all ten provinces. The general thrust of this figure is that the property tax is a declining, but still very important, source of revenue for local governments. Conditional transfers have been a significant and stable source of revenue. Both user charges and unconditional

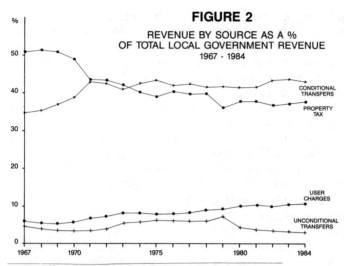

FIGURE 2

REVENUE BY SOURCE AS A %
OF TOTAL LOCAL GOVERNMENT REVENUE
1967 - 1984

NOTE: Miscellaneous revenue is not included.
SOURCE: Statistics Canada, *Local Government Finance* (Cat. No. 68-204), various years.

transfers have been relatively small and stable sources of revenue.

These total figures obscure the fact that the situation varies considerably from one province to another. Figure 3 compares per capita revenue by source for the local governments in each province for 1984. The wide variance between provinces is caused to some extent by the variance in the wealth of provinces, but mostly it is reflective of a different role for local governments in different provinces. In some provinces, local governments have a major role in providing services and this is mirrored in their need for large amounts of revenue; in other provinces, the provincial role is so significant that there is less scope for local government activity.

While the revenue per capita varies quite widely between provinces, the relative importance of the different sources of revenue really does not vary much. The property tax and conditional transfer payments are almost invariably the major sources of revenue. The only two exceptions are Prince Edward Island and New Brunswick, where the property tax is basically a provincial tax. Newfoundland and New Brunswick are the only provinces in which unconditional transfers are very important and these are the two provinces with the smallest local government sectors – measured on a revenue per capita basis.

The specific methods employed in raising local government revenue have an impact on local autonomy, on the welfare of citizens, and on the manner in which the burden of supporting local government is divided among citizens. Particular issues associated with each revenue source will be discussed below.

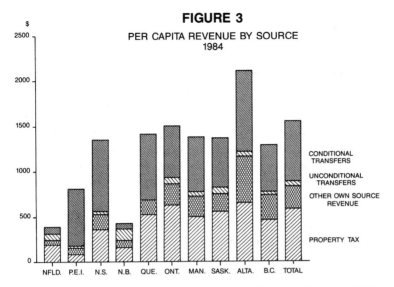

FIGURE 3

PER CAPITA REVENUE BY SOURCE
1984

SOURCE: Statistics Canada, *Local Government Finance* (Cat. No. 68-204), 1985.

Property Tax

The property tax is a major source of revenue for local governments and it has also been a controversial form of taxation in recent years. This section will first review the mechanics of calculating the tax and determining the tax base, and then proceed to a discussion of some of the controversial aspects of the property tax.

(a) The assessment system. The assignment of specific dollar values to properties (assessment) is the basis of the property tax system. This function was at one time a municipal responsibility. It has been almost universally moved to provincial governments in recent years. All provinces have a system of assessing property based either on market value or on some vaguer idea of the fair value of the land in its current use. Where provinces have used fair market value based on periodic re-assessments to establish assessed values, the system has worked fairly well. However, where provinces have allowed their systems to get out-of-date, serious problems have occurred.

The lack of a sound periodic re-assessment system causes the property tax to be less buoyant than other taxes. Income taxes are buoyant because they increase automatically as personal incomes increase. The same process *can* occur with the property tax, but only if there is systematic market value re-assessment. There are probably some benefits in depriving local governments of this automatic "inflation dividend" (Bird and Slack, 1983: 15), but weaknesses in assessment also allow problems of equity to develop in the system.

There would be no serious equity problems if all property was systematically under-assessed in the same manner. The lower *values* would require higher tax *rates*, but would not change the distribution of the tax among properties. However, poor assessment practices lead to situations in which some properties are unintentionally assessed at values closer to market than others; this causes some properties to bear more than their fair share of the property tax.

The prevailing wisdom is that buildings constructed in recent years are assessed at a value higher than those built in earlier years and that multiple-unit buildings are assessed at a higher level than single-family homes. It must be emphasized that these are not conscious decisions. The problem comes about because an assessor must examine a building completed yesterday and estimate what it would have been worth at some date in the 1960s or whenever the last complete re-assessment was performed. This makes the job of assessors so difficult that it should not be surprising that their results are often disputed.

Those owning the buildings with higher assessments argue on grounds of equity that all property should be assessed in the same manner, i.e., fair market value. Those owning older buildings argue that each owner knew what the assessed value was when the property was purchased and that, on grounds of equity, that value should not be changed.

Both sides seem to have a valid point and this discussion has generated heated debate in provinces such as Ontario, which has been slow to move to market value assessment. It usually pits the older established areas of the community, which will suffer large tax increases, against the newer areas, which will see tax reductions. There can also be significant shifts in the relative tax borne by residential, commercial, and industrial taxpayers. It is important to understand that this controversy is not just a matter of abstract theories. The method of assessment has real distributional consequences for residents and property owners in a municipality.

Another consequence of this situation is that it hampers provinces that would like to provide some form of equalization to municipalities. The principle of equalization means that the province would provide larger transfer payments to municipalities with weaker tax bases in order to equalize the ability of all municipalities to provide a basic level of services without imposing excessive taxes. The problem is that when the province cannot have confidence in the property tax assessment system, then there is no sound basis for determining which municipalities are in the greatest need.

The ideal situation is that a province would simply not allow its assessment system to fall out of date by so much that drastic changes are necessary. However, this advice is not very useful to those provinces already in that unfortunate position.

(b) Calculation of the tax. The property tax is calculated by multiplying the assessed value of a piece of property by a *mill rate*. The mill rate is expressed as a certain number of mills (one-tenth of a cent) per dollar of assessed valuation. Alternatively, some people view the mill rate as dollars per thousand dollars of assessed value. Mathematically, either view produces the same result.

Generally, this tax is imposed on the value of land and buildings. Some provinces have imposed taxes on inventory, machinery, and other personal property, but these seem to be falling into disuse (Finnis, 1979: 5). Farm land is usually assessed on the basis of its value as farm land, not on its fair market value, which could be much higher if it is located close to an urban area. This is to prevent farmers from being forced into selling their land for urban development because of a heavy property tax burden. Some kinds of property, such as pipelines, railways, and utility distribution systems, are taxed on a different basis altogether (Canadian Tax Foundation, 1986: 150-71).

In every province, the effective tax rate borne by commercial and industrial property is greater than that borne by residential property.[2] The general rationale for this is that businesses can bear a greater tax burden than individuals. The specifics of how this differential is achieved vary among provinces, but there are three general ways in which this is accomplished. First, commercial and industrial property is sometimes assessed at a rate closer to its true market value than is residential property (Boadway and Kitchen, 1984: 222-23). Second, in most provinces, commercial and industrial property attracts a higher mill rate than residential property (Canadian Tax Foundation, 1986: 165). Third, some provinces apply an additional business tax assessment that increases the assessed value of the property by some stated percentage (Finnis, 1979: 82). For example, businesses could pay a *property tax* based on 100 per cent of the assessed value of the property and a *business tax* based on 75 per cent of that same value.

(c) The benefits of the property tax. The property tax has traditionally been a very attractive tax for local governments. It is easy to administer because it attaches to the land and buildings and so is virtually impossible for taxpayers to evade. The method of computation is quite straightforward as compared to the income tax, for example.

One traditional theoretical justification for the property tax flows from a distinction between services to property and services to people. The argument is that the property tax should bear the cost of all services to property, i.e., "hard" services such as sewers, water, and roads. The rationale for this is that provision of these services increases the value of property so the cost of providing them ought to fall on the property benefited.

The difficulty with this argument is that all services are ultimately services for people. Making the distinction between services to people and services to property is not always an easy task. Education would seem to be a classic "service to people," but it is clear that proximity to a school will increase the value of a particular property.

Another argument for the property tax stems from the adage that "an old tax is a good tax." This has two complementary interpretations. One is that taxpayers have become accustomed to an "old tax" and so will offer less political resistance to it than to a new source of taxation. The second, economic interpretation of this statement is that old taxes have become built into price and market structures over time. New taxes can have unpredictable consequences on prices and markets. In short, a number of factors make the property tax attractive, but there have been some problems with its use in the last few years.

(d) Exemptions from taxation. Not all property is subject to taxation. The specific exemptions vary by province, but they generally relate to property owned and used by governments and to educational, charitable, and religious institutions. Property of the federal government is exempt from all provincial and municipal taxation because, under the terms of the Constitution Act, no other government can impose a tax on the federal government. In all provinces, except Prince Edward Island, provincial property is also exempt under terms of provincial legislation. Property owned by charitable and religious institutions and used for charitable or religious purposes has traditionally been provided an exemption because these organizations are usually considered deserving of government support.

The value of exempt property can be quite significant. A 1973 Ontario study indicated that exempt property amounted to 17 per cent of the overall property tax base. It was estimated that if this amount had been included in the tax base, the property tax bill of the average household could have been reduced by $100 per year (Boadway and Kitchen, 1984: 226).

Federal and provincial governments usually make a voluntary payment to local governments referred to as a "grant or payment in lieu of taxes." Municipalities frequently complain that this payment is not equal to the full amount of taxes that would have been imposed on the property. Charitable and religious organizations do not provide such payments.

However, exempt property does not just reduce a municipality's tax take, it can also create inefficient land-use patterns. Organizations benefiting from exemptions feel little pressure to economize on the use of even very expensive land. Municipalities have argued that the tax exemption for some organizations ought to be terminated and replaced by cash grants. If this happened, these exempt organizations would probably find ways of using less (or less expensive) land to reduce their property tax burden. In turn, municipalities would benefit from the release of new land for development purposes.

For practical political reasons, this is unlikely to occur. In many jurisdictions, providing overt subsidies to religious organizations would be such a contentious activity that politicians would rather that these subsidies remain hidden, as they currently are.

(e) Level of the property tax. A great many taxpayers complain about the amount of the property tax and its presumed escalation in recent years. However, perceptions are not always reality. Many people are keenly aware of the annual increase in the property tax, but forget that some of that increase is accounted for by inflation and some of it could be offset by increases in their incomes. Kitchen and McMillan (1985: 225) have found that property tax as a percentage of disposable income did increase from 1947 to 1971, but it has leveled off or even been reduced since then. Figure 4 shows the annual rate of change in total property taxes collected by local government *after adjustment for inflation.* The rate of change is quite erratic, but it is interesting that it shows decreases in some years when inflation is taken into account.

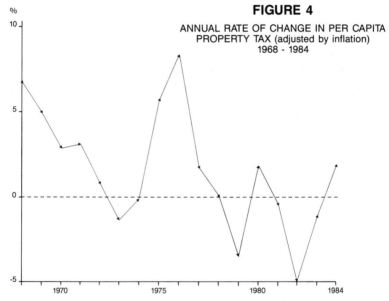

FIGURE 4

ANNUAL RATE OF CHANGE IN PER CAPITA
PROPERTY TAX (adjusted by inflation)
1968 - 1984

SOURCE: Statistics Canada, *Local Government Finance* (Cat. No. 68-204), various years.

The high levels of dissatisfaction voiced about the property tax likely stem from the fact that it is a highly visible tax that must be paid in a lump sum, unlike federal and provincial taxes, which are either hidden totally (manufacturer's excise tax) or deducted at source before taxpayers are aware they have the money (income tax). You might try an experiment with those you know who own property. Ask them if they know how much property tax they pay to the nearest ten dollars. They will likely know exactly. Then, ask them if they know how much federal income tax they pay to the nearest thousand dollars. Not many people know that because it is deducted at source.

(f) *Incidence of the property tax: regressive, proportional, or progressive?* The incidence of the property tax has been another cause of controversy. "Incidence" refers to the technical question of who actually bears the burden of a particular tax. Incidence can be very difficult to determine because the people who ultimately bear the tax are not necessarily those who pay it in the first place. For example, manufacturers must pay the federal sales tax when a good is completely manufactured, but the amount of that tax is usually added to the price of the product so that the ultimate consumer really bears the cost of the federal sales tax. In economic parlance, the manufacturer pays the tax but shifts it to the consumer.

A regressive tax is a tax that falls proportionally more heavily on low-income taxpayers.[3] Conversely, a progressive tax falls proportionally more heavily on high-income taxpayers. For example, on the surface the income tax is a progressive tax because higher incomes are taxed at higher rates than lower incomes. A proportional tax is borne equally by taxpayers in all income groups. It is usually argued that progressive forms of taxation are more desirable than regressive ones because progressive taxes involve a redistribution from the rich to the poor.

Traditionally, the property tax has been considered to be regressive because, regardless how low a person's income is, he or she must still purchase some minimum amount of shelter. The person would pay the property tax either directly to the municipality (if he or she owns the property) or indirectly when the landlord adds in the property tax to arrive at the monthly rent. In economic terms, this scenario assumes that the landlord is able to shift the tax to the renter. The argument continues that as a person's income increases, he or she spends a lower percentage of income on shelter, which is taxable, and more on such luxuries as yachts or jewelry, which do not attract an annual tax. Thus the argument goes that the property tax ought to be minimized because it is regressive.

This argument was accepted for many years and played a significant role in local politicians' rhetoric when they wanted additional money from the provincial or federal governments. However, the so-called "new view" of the property tax challenges this assumption (Bird, 1976b). The basis of the traditional view of the incidence of the property tax is that landlords are able to shift the tax by increasing rents so that tenants in effect pay the tax. The "new view" of the property tax makes the assumption that landlords are unable to shift the tax to renters because of certain market conditions, so that the tax reduces landlords' incomes. If it is assumed that landlords have higher incomes than tenants, then the tax is effectively borne by a higher-income group and so will more likely be progressive. Finally, in those provinces with geared-to-income property tax rebate systems (Canadian Tax Foundation, 1986: 154-69), any initial regressivity in the imposition of the property tax is reduced considerably by the rebate.

There have been a number of empirical studies of this question in the last few years (Bird and Slack, 1978: 53-64). The basic problem in arriving at a conclusion about the regressivity of the property tax is that no definitive answer is available about the question of shifting. A recent, comprehensive study by Meng and Gillespie (1986) suggests that if one assumes the traditional view is correct, the property tax is generally regressive over all income levels and in all regions of the country. However, if one accepts the new view, then the findings are mixed but seem to indicate that the tax is either proportional or progressive.

Boadway and Kitchen (1984: 234) summarize this debate in the following careful and tentative manner.

> What conclusions can be drawn from the evidence of the regressivity of the residential property tax? Unfortunately, there is no simple or obvious answer to this question, especially in view of the numerous conceptual and statistical problems haunting all quantitative incidence exercises. Perhaps the safest and best comment that can be made as a result of these studies is that the new view indicates that the property tax is not as regressive as the traditional view claims nor is it likely to be as progressive as some of the advocates of the new view have suggested. Empirically and theoretically, the incidence question is in an embryonic state. Further research and analysis are required before any definitive and conclusive position can be taken.

The public policy implications of this question are enormous. One of the strongest arguments local politicians have made against the property tax is that it is regressive and that society ought not rely too heavily on a regressive form of taxation. However, if the property tax is actually progressive or proportional, then it becomes a very attractive form of taxation because of its ease of administration.

(g) Sharing the property tax base. Another problem with the property tax is that a number of different units of local government must share the same tax base. In a few provinces this includes the provincial government, but more generally it would include a metropolitan or regional government, a lower-tier municipal government, several school boards, and possibly some other special-purpose bodies. Each of these bodies can have the right to impose a property tax without consulting any of the other organizations.

This problem is particularly acute for the lower-tier municipalities because they must usually collect the full tax on behalf of the other units. This creates confusion in the minds of the general public and forces lower-tier municipal governments to shoulder much of the blame for tax increases that are actually the shared responsibility of several governments.

The property tax has been the topic of much debate and criticism – not all of it particularly enlightened. There are some advantages to the use of the property tax and some of the disadvantages have been overstated. However, considering the strength of the criticism, it is not surprising that local governments have begun to search for other sources of revenue.

User Charges

User charges are fees imposed on users of services where the fee imposed bears some relation to the benefit enjoyed. The most obvious examples are transit fares, water rates, and fees to use recreational facilities. These have traditionally been a rather limited source of local government revenue, but councils seem to be turning to them more frequently in recent years as a response to financial restraint (Ridler, 1984).

The two arguments most frequently advanced in favour of user charges are that they are equitable and that they further economic efficiency (Bird, 1976a: 101-04). The equity argument holds that where specific groups benefit from a service, they ought to pay for the service. User charges further economic efficiency because they act as signalling devices to local councils to identify which services are in greatest demand. Where services are provided free, the demand is likely to be unlimited; the imposition of some price helps determine how interested people really are in a particular service.

However, there are certain negative aspects of user charges as well. User charges for such municipal services as recreational facilities can be a political minefield. In some municipalities, sports groups such as hockey and softball leagues are very well organized. They are in a good position to bring strong pressure to bear on councillors who want to increase user charges. Even picking on unorganized groups can be dysfunctional. Who wants to be responsible for beginning to charge six-year-olds to use the municipal swimming pool?

Probably one of the greatest concerns about user charges is their distributional effect. Some services are provided by government precisely because society does not like the distribution that would occur if they were provided by the private sector. For example, if families were forced to purchase education for their children, some would not be able to afford it. Most would agree that this circumstance is undesirable. There are clearly cases where the application of user charges is quite appropriate, but the distributional consequences of these charges should not be overlooked.

In sum, user charges can be desirable from both equity and

efficiency viewpoints and as a source of new funds, but they do have serious distributional consequences. Politicians have learned that they must proceed carefully in this area because of the strength of some organized groups.

Transfer Payments

Transfer payments are made to local governments by federal or provincial governments, but they are not made for the provision of any current good or service; the government providing the transfer payment is under no legal obligation to do so. Boadway (1980: 41-52) suggests that there are three main rationales for the provision of transfer payments – fiscal gap, interjurisdictional spill-over, and fiscal equity.

A significant *fiscal gap* or *fiscal imbalance* has emerged between local government expenditure and local government own-source revenue in recent years. The main source of local government own-source revenue – the property tax – has not been a particularly buoyant source of revenue in the last few years. At the same time, local governments have been forced to cope with expenditures generated by increasing urbanization and demands for improved services. These two trends have generated the fiscal gap that provincial governments have been called on to fill.

Following sound economic theory (and concern for local autonomy), a fiscal gap should be bridged by the provision of an unconditional transfer because it allows the municipality to decide which services should be funded. However, some provinces have used the fiscal gap as a rationale for the provision of conditional transfers as well.

Interjurisdictional spill-overs or *externalities* occur when expenditures made by one locality benefit other jurisdictions. Some examples are the cost of educating a young person who then moves to another area and the cost of pollution control, which benefits downstream municipalities. Municipal councillors are understandably reluctant to spend money on programs that benefit other jurisdictions. However, the provincial government is aware that these expenditures are necessary for the good of the entire province. Therefore, it provides a conditional transfer to offset this spill-over and so encourage municipalities to spend more on this service.

The third rationale for intergovernmental transfers – concern for *fiscal equity* – arises because of differences in the abilities of local governments to raise funds. Municipalities with large, stable industrial and commercial tax bases can raise sizable amounts of revenue through the property tax without imposing unduly high mill rates on residential property owners. Municipalities with weaker tax bases or higher costs are forced to impose much higher mill rates to provide the same level of service as the wealthier municipalities. Federal and provincial governments usually step in to reduce this problem by providing transfers to the municipalities with the weaker tax bases. Theoretically, transfers provided for this purpose should be unconditional, but some conditional transfers are calculated in a manner that takes this concern for fiscal equity into account.

One of the major problems with provincial transfers from the standpoint of municipalities is that the province has absolute control over the level of these payments. Thus, they can change significantly from year to year. Municipalities fear that provinces will use a reduction in transfers to save money because this does not have a direct impact on services provided by the province. This problem is exacerbated by the fact that the level of municipal transfers is sometimes not announced until the middle of the municipalities' fiscal year. This makes it very difficult for municipalities to prepare budgets.

Conditional Transfers

Conditional transfers are payments made to local governments by either the provincial or federal government to be used for a specified purpose. In most cases, these are shared-cost programs, meaning that the federal or provincial government agrees to fund a certain percentage of the cost of a program undertaken by local governments. Conditional transfers can also be calculated on the basis of a flat amount for each municipality or an amount per capita or per household. These transfers are conditional because stipulations attached to the money require that it be spent in a specified manner.

The usual rationales for conditional transfers relate to externalities and the establishment of minimum provincial standards. Because municipalities are relatively small units of government, they frequently provide services used by residents in other municipalities. For example, on any average day you might drive on roads provided by several different municipalities without even thinking about it. Equity would suggest that municipalities should be compensated for this; conditional transfers provide that compensation.

For certain services, there is a feeling that all citizens of a province should receive the same level of service or at least a certain minimum standard regardless of where the person lives. For example, Canadians feel strongly about the value of education and usually believe that a child should not be subjected to an inferior level of education just because he or she grows up in a poorer area of the province. Conditional transfers frequently come with minimum standards to ensure that this does not happen.

The largest portion of conditional transfers comes from provincial governments for programs in the areas of education, health, and transportation and communications. The federal government, through several of its departments and agencies, also supplies some funding to municipalities for transportation, communications, and environment control services.

Local governments are always pleased to receive funds, but conditional transfer payments are sometimes a mixed blessing. One of the most frequent complaints is that conditional transfers tend to skew the priorities of the recipient government. For example, where a transfer payment provides that the province will share 50 per cent of the cost of a program, the argument is usually made that the program is really spending only "fifty-cent dollars," i.e., each fifty cents of *municipal* expenditure results in one dollar of *total* expenditure on the program. This makes programs that receive conditional transfers more attractive than those that do not. But in turn, such transfers can result in municipal governments bending their priorities to attract these payments.

When this occurs, municipalities are conscious that they are vulnerable to shifts in provincial priorities. The provincial government could be very interested in a program for a number of years and encourage municipalities to develop extensive delivery systems on which local citizens become dependent. Later, provincial priorities could change, resulting in a reduction or total withdrawal of provincial funding for this service. However, the municipality cannot shift gears so easily because it has an extensive delivery system in place and a clientele that has come to rely on the service. Thus, the municipality must continue to provide the service, but without provincial assistance.

This points to another problem with conditional transfers. They can tend to muddle accountability. Stripped of all the administrative niceties, a transfer payment is basically one level of government spending money raised by another level of government. If the service is not provided properly, whose fault is it? Did the government making the transfer provide too little funding or impose inappropriate conditions? Or did the recipient government use the funds unwisely? It is difficult for a citizen to know which government should be held accountable for problems in this situation.

There can also be significant administrative costs associated with conditional transfers. Municipalities must maintain records to prove that they have spent the funds in accordance with the sometimes very detailed conditions of the program. Then, the provincial government must establish a group of auditors and program specialists to check up on municipalities to ensure that they are complying with the conditions of the transfer.

Conditional transfers have some beneficial consequences, but they also pose certain difficulties. Unconditional transfers avoid some of these problems.

Unconditional Transfers

Unconditional transfers can be used by the recipient government for any purpose. They are provided to municipalities only by provincial governments. The method of calculation varies widely by province but there is frequently some flat amount for each municipality and additional amounts based on either a percentage of total property taxes levied or on a per capita or per household basis (Canadian Tax Foundation, 1986: 210-20).

There is also frequently an equalization factor in the calculation of the transfer, which deals with the fiscal equity problem. A typical arrangement would provide extra payments to municipalities whose property value per capita fell below the provincial average. Some provinces also provide supplemental transfers to northern municipalities in recognition of the high cost of providing services in remote locations. While most provinces pay lip service to this concern for equalization, some unconditional transfers work better than others at actually accomplishing this equalization (Eden and Auld, 1987).

New Revenue Sources

Municipalities have seen themselves in a financial bind in recent years. Their own-source revenue, mostly property tax, has not been buoyant. Most municipalities have become more dependent on transfers from other governments, but these can fluctuate beyond the control of local governments. The fiscal gap has been an increasing concern.

The usual manner of dealing with this problem has not been an auspicious one from the standpoint of local government. There has been a general trend for provincial governments to take over certain functions that were previously local government responsibilities. This type of movement was seen in the 1960s and 1970s when most provinces took over responsibility for administration of justice and correctional facilities. Following the advice of the New Brunswick Royal Commission on Finance and Municipal Taxation (1963), more commonly called the Byrne Commission, New Brunswick undertook one of the most extreme programs in 1967 when it abolished many rural municipalities and took over complete control of education, health, social assistance, and some other functions (Krueger, 1970; Higgins, 1986: 183-85; Tindal, 1977: 18-20).

This reduces the fiscal problems of local governments but could make local governments hollow shells with only minimal responsibilities. A better arrangement from the standpoint of local autonomy would be to find new sources of revenue or to re-arrange existing sources to minimize both the fiscal gap and the local dependence on provincial transfers, without reducing the role of local government in service delivery.

A very innovative and extensive reform occurred in Quebec in 1979 (Lapointe, 1980). A long-standing grievance of municipal governments is that they must share the property tax with other local bodies, most notably school boards. Quebec changed this by funding school boards almost entirely through provincial transfers and allowing municipal governments to have virtually full control of the property tax. At the same time, provincial transfers to municipalities were reduced drastically. This change left municipalities with the same amount of funding they had previously but increased their autonomy by eliminating conditional transfers and providing an enriched source of taxation.

Several provinces have incorporated a tax-sharing provision into their unconditional transfer. This arrangement provides that a certain percentage of the provincial income tax is allocated to municipalities. For example, in British Columbia, municipalities receive 1 per cent of the individual income tax, 1 per cent of corporate taxable income, and 6 per cent of a large number of other taxes such as fuel and sales taxes (Canadian Tax Foundation, 1986: 219). Provincial treasurers have been slow to adopt this idea because it means that some portion of the provincial budget is earmarked and so beyond their control.

Tax-sharing is beneficial to municipalities because it allows them to estimate their future revenues (at least, as well as they can estimate future provincial revenue), and it gives them a piece of what has usually been a buoyant source of revenue. However, this arrangement means that when provincial revenue declines, municipalities share in the pain just as they shared in the gain.

Other revenue sources have been explored but the small size of municipalities eliminates some potential taxes because they can be avoided too easily. For example, a municipal sales tax would simply encourage people to shop in neighbouring municipalities with a lower tax rate or no tax whatsoever. A tax on hotel accommodation and amusements seems attractive at first because most of it would be paid by non-residents of the community. The problem is that it could cause tourists to avoid the community. Likewise, a municipal income tax could cause people to shun living in a community and also raises assessment and collection problems.

The General Trend

The trend of local government revenue has varied between provinces, but the general idea is clear. The property tax has not been a buoyant source of revenue. The reason for this is unclear and should be the subject of further research. Municipalities argue that the tax base itself is not buoyant and so their only option is to increase the tax rate on this allegedly regressive form of taxation. This might have some validity, but probably only in provinces that do not engage in periodic re-assessment. Another interpretation might be that municipal politicians simply find it easier to cry poverty and get funds from other governments than to raise taxes themselves.

The other trend has been a greater reliance on conditional transfers from provincial governments. Concern about the stability of this source of revenue has spurred a search for new revenue sources, which so far has proven fruitless. The problem is not that municipalities are facing a grave financial crisis; conditional transfers have ensured that they are not. The problem is that the increasing importance of conditional transfers will tend to erode local autonomy. Since most of the revenue problems discussed above have been created or exacerbated by greater pressure on local governments to spend, it is useful at this juncture to examine the expenditure side of the situation.

Local Government Expenditure

Figure 5 illustrates the trend of local government expenditure in Canada over the period 1967-84. There have been few significant shifts in the percentage of local government expenditure devoted to major functions during that period.

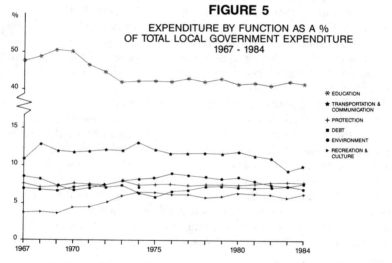

FIGURE 5

EXPENDITURE BY FUNCTION AS A %
OF TOTAL LOCAL GOVERNMENT EXPENDITURE
1967 - 1984

✳ EDUCATION
★ TRANSPORTATION & COMMUNICATION
+ PROTECTION
■ DEBT
● ENVIRONMENT
► RECREATION & CULTURE

SOURCE: Statistics Canada, *Local Government Finance* (Cat. No. 68-204), various years.

Primary and secondary education has always attracted the major portion of local government expenditure. The proportion of local expenditure devoted to this function declined somewhat in the early 1970s but has remained stable since then – in spite of declining enrolments. Transportation and communications expenditures, mostly roads and public transit, have been a consistent and distant second. Protection of persons and property (police and fire services), environment (water purification and sewage treatment), and debt charges come after that. Sometimes a lack of change can be re-assuring. At a time when debt charges are taking up ever-expanding portions of federal and provincial budgets, it is pleasing to note that local government debt charges have remained a stable proportion of total expenditure. Expenditure on recreation and culture has increased slightly over the period. All other expenditure categories take up less than 5 per cent of local government expenditure. However, these totals obscure the differences in particular provinces.

Figure 6 illustrates total per capita expenditure by province in 1984 and expenditure on the four most significant functions. The first point that stands out is the variance in total expenditure. Newfoundland and New Brunswick have much lower per capita expenditures largely because the provincial governments in both provinces have a major role in primary and secondary education. In every province where education is a local government responsibility, it is by far the largest item of expenditure. The categories after that vary so widely that it is difficult to generalize, but the usual high-price items are transportation and communications, environment, protection of persons and property, and debt charges. The remaining chapters in this book will undertake a more in-depth review of most of these expenditure items.

FIGURE 6

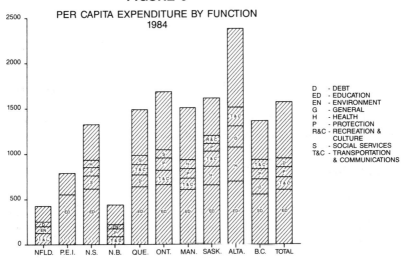

SOURCE: Statistics Canada, *Local Government Finance* (Cat. No. 68-204), 1985.

Local Government Surplus/Deficit Position

Local governments are not allowed to budget for a deficit in their operating budgets. However, they are allowed to operate at a deficit and borrow funds in their capital budgets. The capital budget consists of the purchase of tangible items that will have value in future years, e.g., parkland, highways, buildings. Since local governments operate close to the margin in their operating budgets, they are almost invariably required to borrow to undertake capital construction projects. Thus, it should not be surprising that Figure 7 shows deficits in every year except one in the 1967-84 period.

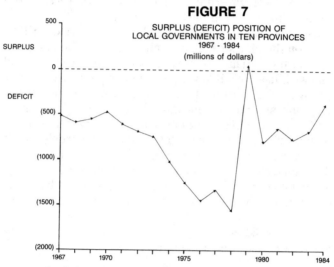

FIGURE 7

SURPLUS (DEFICIT) POSITION OF
LOCAL GOVERNMENTS IN TEN PROVINCES
1967 - 1984
(millions of dollars)

SOURCE: Statistics Canada, *Local Government Finance* (Cat. No. 68-204), various years.

Since these deficits were incurred for the purpose of acquiring assets that will produce benefits into the future, the situation is not as bad as it seems. However, an interest cost associated with borrowing obviously has an impact on annual budgets.

Conclusion

Local politicians and others concerned with local government in Canada are sometimes guilty of over-reacting to the difficult financial position in which some local governments find themselves. Yes, local governments, like all other governments, are facing a financial squeeze; no, the entire system of local government is not on the verge of bankruptcy. However, the squeeze is very tight and is likely to continue. The choice of mechanisms employed to deal with the squeeze can have significant consequences for the future development of local government.

So far, the major solution offered has been a greater provincial role both in direct service delivery and in funding local provision of services through conditional transfers. If this trend continues, we will not see the demise of local government, but we will be looking at a system of local government very much different from the one we have known.

NOTES

1. In this chapter, "municipal government" refers to the multifunctional unit usually thought of as "the city"; the phrase "local government" includes both municipal government and such special-purpose bodies as boards of education.
2. The effective tax rate is defined as the tax payable divided by the market value of the property. This could vary considerably from the stated mill rate because of differences between the assessed and market values of property.
3. Conventionally, the regressivity of a tax is measured by the relationship between the amount of the tax payable and the taxpayer's income. In the case of the property tax, an argument could be made that the more relevant measure is the relationship between the amount of the tax and the taxpayer's *accumulated wealth*. Many would say that a retired person with low current income (but significant accumulated wealth) would be better able to pay the property tax than a young family with higher current income but little accumulated wealth.

REFERENCES

Bird, Richard M. (1970). *The Growth of Government Spending in Canada*. Toronto: Canadian Tax Foundation.

— (1976a). *Charging for Public Services: A New Look at an Old Idea*. Toronto: Canadian Tax Foundation.

— (1976b). "The Incidence of the Property Tax: Old Wine in New Bottles?" *Canadian Public Policy*, 2 (Supplement): 323-34.

— (1979). *Financing Canadian Government. A Quantitative Overview*. Toronto: Canadian Tax Foundation.

Bird, Richard, and N. Enid Slack (1978). *Residential Property Tax Relief in Ontario*. Toronto: University of Toronto Press.

— (1983). *Urban Public Finance in Canada*. Toronto: Butterworths.

Boadway, Robin W. (1980). *Intergovernmental Transfers in Canada*. Toronto: Canadian Tax Foundation.

Boadway, Robin W., and Harry M. Kitchen (1984). *Canadian Tax Policy*, 2nd ed. Toronto: Canadian Tax Foundation.

Bossons, John, Michael Denny, and Enid Slack (1981). *Municipal Fiscal Reform in Ontario: Property Taxes and Provincial Grants*. Toronto: Ontario Economic Council.

Canadian Tax Foundation (1986). *Provincial and Municipal Finances – 1985*. Toronto: Canadian Tax Foundation.

Eden, Lorraine, and D.A.L. Auld (1987). "Provincial-Local Fiscal Equalization" (Department of Economics, Brock University, discussion paper 1987-2).

Finnis, Frederic H. (1979). *Property Assessment in Canada*, 3rd ed. Toronto: Canadian Tax Foundation.

Higgins, Donald J.H. (1986). *Local and Urban Politics in Canada*. Toronto: Gage Educational Publishing Company.

Kitchen, Harry M. (1984). *Local Government Finance in Canada*. Toronto: Canadian Tax Foundation.

Kitchen, Harry M., and Melville L. McMillan (1985). "Local Government and Canadian Federalism," in Richard Simeon (ed.), *Intergovernmental Relations*. Toronto: University of Toronto Press.

Krueger, Ralph R. (1970). "The Provincial-Municipal Government Revolution in New Brunswick," *Canadian Public Administration,* 13 (Spring): 51-99.

Lapointe, Jean-Louis (1980). "La reforme de la fiscalité municipale au Québec," *Canadian Public Administration,* 23 (Summer): 269-80.

Meng, Ronald, and W. Irwin Gillespie (1986). "The Regressivity of Property Taxes in Canada: Another Look," *Canadian Tax Journal,* 34 (November-December): 1417-30.

New Brunswick Royal Commission on Finance and Municipal Taxation (1963). *Report.* Fredericton.

Ridler, Neil B. (1984). "Fiscal Constraints and the Growth of User Fees Among Canadian Municipalities," *Canadian Public Administration,* 27 (Fall): 429-36.

Saskatchewan Local Government Finance Commission (1985). *Alternative Local Sources of Revenue and Utilization of the Property Tax Base.*

Tindal, C.R. (1977). *Structural Changes in Local Government.* Toronto: The Institute of Public Administration of Canada.

2 Meric S. Gertler

Economic Development

Introduction

In recent years, Canada's economy has seemed to be more open than
ever to world-scale economic change, with its traditional resource-based
sectors being buffeted by unstable commodity prices and its manufacturing industries facing stiff foreign competition. In such an era,
it is not at all surprising that economic development and job creation
have come to the forefront of daily policy issues and have permeated
the consciousness of all levels of government. In many Western
countries, this interest has been expressed in part by a greater
involvement of local governments in the mounting of economic development strategies (for a survey of recent activity in the U.K.,
Western Europe, and the U.S., see Boddy, 1984; Young, 1986; Fox
Przeworski, 1986; OECD, 1985 and 1986b; Bingham and Blair, 1984;
Goldstein, 1987). Within the Canadian context, there is also evidence
of a reinvigorated interest in these issues at the local government
level (Stankovic, 1987), induced not only by the economic climate but
by a number of recent changes in the political and institutional
environment. This development is significant, both at home and abroad,
since it represents a trespassing over what has traditionally been the
policy turf of more senior levels of government. Furthermore, such
initiatives are, by their very nature, contentious since any intervention
into the economy by the state, no matter what level, arouses ideological
debate about the appropriateness of such actions within a predominantly private enterprise system.

This chapter addresses itself to current municipal involvement in the economic development process in Canada. Given the inherent contentiousness referred to above, it begins by briefly reviewing the rationale for state involvement in economic development in general, and the major arguments for and against *local* government participation in these activities. It then proceeds to a discussion of the historical and current institutional context within which local initiatives in this policy area must be understood. This leads to a survey of current practices within Canadian municipalities, including an examination of some of the more prominent and interesting strategies being pursued by a number of cities across the country. The chapter concludes with a summary and some speculative comments about the directions future economic development initiatives at the local level might take.

If there is a dominant theme that pervades this chapter it is the set of constraints imposed by senior levels of government on the latitude of local governments to promote their own economic development, and the efforts expended by municipalities to circumvent those constraints. In this respect, its content is likely to be reminiscent of discussions elsewhere within this volume that address overlapping policy areas – notably finance and planning.

Rationales for State Intervention in Economic Development

The potential forms of intervention suggested by economic and political theory are considerable and provide a framework for organizing and understanding current policies and programs. By linking individual initiatives to the underlying political-economic ideologies or philosophies that justify their application, we are afforded both a typology of policy action and a sense of policy alternatives that remain somewhat untried within the current range of economic development policies and practices. It should be emphasized that the following categories are somewhat overlapping and are not necessarily mutually exclusive. While they may represent significant points along a spectrum of action, there are some important discontinuities in this progression.

At the most conservative end of the economic development policy spectrum are government activities that rely overwhelmingly on the market itself to create opportunities for local prosperity. Strategies emanating from this perspective consist largely of efforts to improve the local conditions for private production. As such, they are not entirely consistent with a truly laissez-faire philosophy of keeping private markets free of government intervention. They include various measures to reduce the cost of local inputs to production (capital, land, and labour): tax breaks and forgiveness, accelerated depreciation schemes, free or low-priced land offers, suspension of minimum wage laws, and passage of right-to-work legislation. These kinds of tools are frequently supplemented by the well-known efforts of community promotion and boosterism practised by many governments at all levels (but especially local and provincial), which both advertise the list of local advantages awaiting prospective firms and project an overall "pro-business" attitude on behalf of public officials in the area. Apart from these limited offerings, such conservative policies reflect the tacit assumption that the market, left to its own devices, will allocate resources both sectorally and spatially in a way that is both privately and socially optimal.

Closer to the middle of the political spectrum are a set of economic development policies whose functional logic springs from the identification of various imperfections that hinder the efficient workings of the private market. The majority of these more liberal strategies can thus be understood as measures that attempt to ameliorate or eliminate market imperfections where they arise. Hence, by definition, they are considerably more interventionist than the relatively limited conservative measures. Furthermore, they can be organized according to the nature of the imperfection they seek to correct.

Perhaps the largest number of such policy initiatives are motivated by the existence of transaction and information costs – i.e., costs incurred in the making of transactions that inhibit the smooth and rapid equalization of supply and demand in the marketplace. For example, large distances between cities or regions may prevent local labour markets from "clearing" (when local supply and local demand are equal) due to the financial and time costs for unemployed workers to determine where job vacancies exist and migrate to fill them. The liberal solution to this situation of local labour market disequilibrium would enhance the distribution of job vacancy information and reduce the costs of mobility to labour (Clark and Gertler, 1983; Saunders, 1984). Alternatively, it has come to light in recent years that a number of large, fixed costs associated with the raising of capital in public markets make it difficult for small, young, and risky enterprises to obtain the equity capital they need to survive and expand (Litvak and Daniels, 1979). Hence, liberal strategists have prescribed a number of measures to reduce the costs for potential investors of obtaining information about such enterprises, as well as mechanisms to pool and spread risk among large numbers of small businesses.

In a related vein are attempts to pool private resources in order to achieve greater efficiencies in the development and application of new product and process technologies, thereby reducing the overhead costs of production that are disproportionately onerous for small firms (Britton, 1981). In another sense, frequently numerous public regulations, approvals, and programs create time and information costs for prospective producers that may be reduced by local government "facilitators" or "red-tape cutters." These actions, too, can be understood as efforts to overcome or minimize transaction costs in the marketplace, despite the apparent similarity to laissez-faire policies they exhibit.

A second form of imperfection identified by this more liberal approach concerns the inability of the market to provide on its own the kinds of infrastructure required to enable subsequent private investment and production to occur. The elements of this infrastructure are generally regarded as public goods – i.e., goods that, once provided, are consumed jointly, may not be rejected by consumers, nor may consumers be excluded from their consumption (Musgrave and Musgrave, 1980). In practice, such goods or services as roads, sewers, water and energy systems, port facilities, or police and fire protection do not strictly conform to all of these criteria as set forth by the liberal economist (being therefore labelled "impure" public goods), but nevertheless they do possess certain of these or other attributes that make their provision by a public source more "sensible." Many development strategies, therefore, have focused heavily on the provision of infrastructure facilities that individual private-sector actors would ostensibly be incapable of financing or reluctant to install due to perceived difficulties in excluding "free riders" from their use (Hansen, 1974; OECD, 1986a). Alternatively, such facilities may be bankrolled by the public purse simply as a subsidy for private investors, or to influence the pace and form of private development in a particular area.

Externalities constitute a third imperfection in the workings of the private market that justifies a further role for the liberal state both generally and in the more restricted realm of local economic development policy. Externalities may be understood as resulting from a divergence between private and social costs or benefits – that is, some positive or negative effect created by one party and enjoyed or suffered by another without a formal transaction occurring. Traditionally, liberal economists and planners have attempted to foster or replicate the kinds of mutually beneficial growth stimuli (positive externalities) resulting from highly concentrated forms of spatial development (benefits also referred to as "agglomeration economies") when devising strategies for underdeveloped or depressed areas (Kaldor, 1970; Alonso, 1975). More recently, policy analysts have drawn attention to some of the negative externalities (high social costs) associated with ultra-rapid local development (Markusen, 1977) or the unfettered mobility of private capital (Bluestone and Harrison, 1981), prescribing public action to internalize these external costs so that the offending agents are made accountable for a greater proportion of these costs. This policy agenda includes plant-closing legislation and other restrictions on the mobility of capital whose implicit curtailment of the property rights of private producers constitutes a departure from mainstream liberal-democratic philosophy.

While liberal theorists have identified other market imperfections –

most notably the phenomenon of imperfect competition and the problem of intergenerational demand – their existence and "correction" are not central to local economic development policy. Even without considering them, the above list of liberal policy options is notably longer and more extensive than the list of conservative strategies. This is true almost by definition, as the chief distinguishing characteristic of the latter philosophy is the minimal presence of public intervention in the private market.

While the two groups of economic development policy actions just reviewed would seem to differ quite markedly, they do in fact share two underlying premises. First, they both rely on competition and the market mechanism, although with varying degrees of regulation. Second, both presume exclusively private forms of ownership in productive and job-generating enterprise. More radical strategies may be distinguished from their conservative and liberal counterparts primarily by their use of alternative forms of ownership and organization of production, even within a predominantly market-oriented economy. They are supported by a variety of rationales or assumptions: (i) that the private market is not sufficiently developed to provide a particular good or function; (ii) that the private market does not face strong enough financial incentives or certainty about future returns to provide the good or service in question (e.g., maintaining transportation links to small and remote communities along unprofitable routes); (iii) that there are significant social benefits from the provision of a particular good or service that could not be captured by private producers (e.g., job security, community stability, control over decisions affecting investment, employment, and technological change); or (iv) that private ownership of enterprise is objectionable on political, ideological, or moral grounds.

These kinds of arguments have led to the creation of various publicly chartered, owned, and capitalized organizations whose operations influence the economic development prospects of particular areas either directly or indirectly. Canadian examples have included Crown corporations (Air Canada, Petro-Canada, Canadian National Railways), publicly owned utilities (Ontario Hydro, Alberta Government Telephone), and urban public transit systems. While Canadian governments at the federal and provincial level have at times invested directly in private corporations (Canadair, DeHavilland, Suncor), these investments have usually been motivated by considerations such as technological sovereignty or security of supply, rather than some ideological commitment to public ownership *per se*. As we shall see in the following sections, local governments in Canada have generally not pursued the kinds of public investment/ownership options that have been used in countries such as Britain (Boddy, 1984), but have been limited to the pursuit of economic development strategies toward the centre and conservative end of the policy spectrum.

Justifications for Local Government Participation in Economic Development

Having now presented the major rationales for government involvement in the field of economic development in general, we have not specifically addressed the grounds upon which an explicitly *local* role might (or might not) be justified. In doing so, it is important to distinguish between the practical exigencies of prevailing institutional arrangements and arguments based on economic theory.

Beginning with theory, it is perhaps stating the obvious to say that many economic phenomena operate at a spatial scale far beyond that of any single municipal government. To return to an example raised earlier – local labour markets in disequilibrium – it makes obvious sense for a more senior level of government to attempt to facilitate the clearing of local and regional labour markets by virtue of its ability to assess conditions and co-ordinate activities in the multiple labour markets within its jurisdiction. Similar logic applies to attempts by government to influence the location of private investment if the objective is to reduce interurban or interregional disparities.

Indeed, it has been argued elsewhere that local attempts to influence the location of private investments in job and assesssment-generating activities (as is common among American municipalities) constitute a complete waste of public resources when viewed from the perspective of the entire economy in question, since such efforts merely aim to redistribute a fixed quantity of economic activity between places, at considerable cost to the system as a whole (Heilbrun, 1981; Kitchen, 1985). Such behaviour constitutes a kind of "beggar thy neighbour" approach whose operation may only cause greater levels of financial resources to be expended in the future as bidding wars between municipalities for footloose firms drive up the ante, with frequently questionable returns.

Another common feature of local development efforts attempting to influence private investment decisions is the dissemination of information about the conditions for production and amenities in particular areas. The promotion game has long been a central part of local development initiatives in many Western countries, Canada included. And yet, as Kitchen (1985) points out, because local governments are motivated by economic self-interest, they have a strong incentive to bias the kind of information they choose to propagate about their communities, so as to show themselves in the best possible light. Furthermore, they are likely to produce excessive quantities of this information in hopes of blanketing the market of potential investors. For these reasons, it might make sense for a more senior level of government to co-ordinate the gathering of standardized information about the economic characteristics and comparative advantages of its constituent municipalities, which it would then make available to all prospective firms in a readily accessible form.

Despite such logically sound arguments (arguments that assume the viewpoint of the larger collective society or "economy as a whole"), one can readily appreciate why, when viewed from their own perspective, local governments would want to engage actively in efforts to promote the growth of their local economy. With growth comes not only prosperity for its residents, in terms of employment and income, but also an expanded base for property taxation – the single most important source of locally raised revenues for Canadian municipalities (Bird and Slack, 1983). This is especially significant in the case of industrial and commercial activity that, in provinces such as Ontario, is usually taxed at a level exceeding the cost of public services provided to them (Kitchen, 1985).

Furthermore, promotion activities such as those reviewed in following sections of this chapter communicate not only basic facts about the local community but also less tangible information reflective of local government's attitude toward prospective investors (one important facet of the local "business climate"). To the considerable extent that the medium *is* in this case the message, local governments would naturally feel that a provincial or federal agency acting on their behalf could not fully disseminate their message, particularly when that senior agency is expected to be officially impartial with respect to the many competing local interests within its broader jurisdiction. It is also understandable that municipalities should want to engage in the kinds of promotional competition with other jurisdictions that they see their provincial and federal counterparts engaging in with apparent gusto, if not outright success. And yet, as we shall see in the following section, these very same senior governments have generally curtailed this kind of activity at the local level through various legislative constraints. As with other matters, "do as I say, not as I do" is not a very compelling guide to behaviour, and many municipal governments have responded by engaging in whatever implicit or explicit competitive activities are not expressly prohibited by the law.

To this point, we have only begun to touch on some of the more important dimensions of the institutional context that militate against greater participation by local governments in economic development policy-making. These are more directly and fully addressed in the following discussion of the scope and extent of past and present activity in Canadian municipalities.

Historical and Institutional Context for Local Government Economic Development

It has been a fact of constitutional life since 1867 that local governments in Canada exist solely as creatures of provincial fiat and are therefore subject to a broad range of legislative constraints that define the extent of their powers and freedom of action (see O'Brien, 1976; Tindal and Tindal, 1979; Fish, 1981). Even a cursory reading of the other chapters of this volume should convince one of this fact, and the field of economic development is no exception. Indeed, there exists a long and colourful history of attempts by local governments in Canada to enhance their own economic growth, and an equally long history of provincial measures to frustrate and control these efforts.

Canadian urban history from the nineteenth century is dominated to a large extent by the activities of local businessmen and their advocates on municipal councils trying to promote the development of their local economies. These "boosters," as they came to be known, were responsible for the earliest local economic development programs through their direct and indirect participation in civic affairs, whether the local board of trade, chamber of commerce, various trade associations, or the local council. Among the endeavours they encouraged municipalities to undertake were the underwriting of local railroad and municipal transit systems ("street railways"), the provision of loans, tax exemptions, and outright grants to individual manufacturing enterprises ("bonuses"), and the improvement of urban services for industrial purposes. This sort of activity was especially prevalent in (though by no means confined to) Ontario, where towns such as Berlin (later to become Kitchener) boasted the successes of an "industrial policy" that granted over 100 direct bonuses to private firms between the years 1870 and 1914 (see the colourful and detailed account by Bloomfield, 1986).

In many cases, the passage of time revealed that many municipalities, in their zeal to promote industrial development, had overextended themselves financially – some to the point of fiscal insolvency. In recognition of this fact, provincial governments decided for the first time to regulate more closely the financial decisions taken by local governments as a way of avoiding costly financial bailouts or the outright financial collapse of municipal governments. The provinces were also responding to the perceived abuses and inequities created by the unregulated use of municipal bonuses. This movement, reflected in the formation of the Ontario Railway and Municipal Board (later the Ontario Municipal Board) in 1906 and the passage of the Municipal Aid (to industrial or commercial establishments) Prohibition Act in Quebec in 1925, signified a crucial turning point in local-provincial relations. While provincial legislation pertaining to municipal activities and powers prior to this point was generally loose, open-ended, and laissez-faire (where it existed at all), it henceforth became increasingly restrictive (see Taylor, 1986, for a more complete documentation of the progressive erosion of local government autonomy in Canada during and after this period). The later round of municipal bankruptcies induced by the depression of the 1930s further reinforced the control of provincial governments over urban financial affairs, as local governments came to be regarded as fiscally irresponsible entities that, given the chance, would simply spend their way into bankruptcy in the pursuit of local economic self-interest.

The paternal or custodial role of the provinces with respect to local government financial dealings became firmly and chronically entrenched through the passage or amendment of municipal acts to regulate more closely borrowing activity, capital expenditures, budgeting procedures, and the conveyance of economic benefits to private businesses (Taylor, 1986). As one prominent example, Ontario's Municipal Act was amended on a number of occasions beginning in 1888 to place progressively tighter restrictions on local government bonuses to private firms (Kitchen, 1985). The current situation, in which all bonusing is expressly prohibited by Section 112 of the present Act, is a direct extension of this legacy of provincial paternalism. Furthermore, it has come to represent the state of affairs in most other Canadian provinces, with a few notable exceptions that will be described below (see, for example, the discussion of Alberta's Municipal Government Act and other pertinent legislation in Seasons, 1985, and discussion of provincial influence in Quebec in Divay, 1980). Clearly, such restrictive provincial statutes have important implications for the manner in which local governments fashion and pursue their own economic development strategies, since they are constrained from engaging fully in the kind of competitive interjurisdictional bidding for economic activity that American municipalities have developed to a fine art (Bingham and Blair, 1984).

One final aspect of the institutional environment surrounding local government economic development activities further delimits the range of local action, that is, the formal division of powers between the three levels of Canadian government has conferred on federal and provincial actors both the responsibility and the revenue-raising ability necessary to implement many of the strategies reviewed in the previous section. These powers encompass jurisdiction over labour matters pertaining to unionization, minimum wages, mobility, job placement, and plant shutdowns, plus a major presence in the areas of regional development, science and technology policy, and the regulation of capital markets.

Hence, a large part of the spectrum of potential development strategies, particularly that which falls outside the conservative realm, is *ultra vires* the municipal level of government, or beyond its scope by virtue of logistics, finances, or statutory constraint. In the following section, we conduct a selective but representative overview of the range, funding, and organization of economic development by Canadian municipal governments.

A National Overview of Current Local Government Economic Development Activities

Given the kinds of restriction under which they must operate, local governments across Canada have been compelled to find other ways, within their narrowly circumscribed range of freedom, to enhance the economic growth of their jurisdictions. Recent reviews of this policy area suggest a strong and continuing emphasis on four strategies: first, and more generally, a tendency to pursue existing firms already located elsewhere; second, a distinct preference for attracting manufacturing firms rather than service activities; third, the provision of developable, serviced industrial land, frequently within publicly planned and owned industrial parks; and fourth, the publication and dissemination of glossy pamphlets, brochures, advertisements, and other information as part of an overall promotional effort that may also include "wining and dining," limousine connections to and from the nearest airport for visiting potential investors, and other activities designed to inform and entice firm owners to relocate (Bureau of Municipal Research, 1982; Kitchen, 1985).

Economic development functions may be delivered through a number of different organizational arrangements. Most commonly, municipalities create a committee of the local council, including both elected councillors and appointed representatives of business, labour, and other relevant groups. In support of (sometimes instead of) such committees of council are departments of professional civil servants (either a separate economic development department or a division within the planning department) who provide expertise in economic analysis, planning, promotion, and liaison with existing and prospective local businesses. An alternative model involves the assembly of similar professional personnel within separate economic development commissions or corporations that usually operate at arm's length from the immediate control of municipal council. Less formal arrangements include the designation of the local chamber of commerce as being responsible for local promotion, as well as the establishment of advisory committees of qualified or concerned local citizens to provide occasional input to local government actions (Davidson, 1986; Kitchen, 1985; Bureau of Municipal Research, 1982). Of these various forms, Davidson (1986) notes that the first kind is increasingly popular by virtue of the direct control council exerts over policy and operations.

While towns and cities may be formally constrained from offering specific financial incentives to *individual* businesses on a case-by-case basis, this does not prevent them from pursuing strategies that enhance the *general* attractiveness of their area to relocating firms, such as attempting to keep their tax rates on industrial and/or commercial property lower than those in nearby jurisdictions. Of course, as Kitchen (1985) has pointed out, the costs of such a strategy may outweigh the benefits either for the entire community as a whole (if the services provided to industries cost more than the taxes those businesses actually pay), or for certain other segments of the local community, such as residential taxpayers, whose own tax rates will of necessity be higher in order to cross-subsidize industrial beneficiaries. However, as noted earlier, the most common situation in provinces such as Ontario currently finds industrial taxes assessed to be higher than the cost of services provided to industrial uses, implying a cross-subsidy in the opposite direction.

Other adaptive strategies that municipalities can pursue involve their provision of industrial land to private users. Publicly owned and planned industrial parks are particularly prevalent in smaller communities where the private industrial land market is small and not well developed (Bureau of Municipal Research, 1982). While local governments may be expressly prohibited from conveying such lands to firms at prices demonstrably below market, in a small-town setting where the major holder of vacant, serviced industrial land is the municipality itself, local officials can effectively dictate what the prevailing "market" price will be. Hence, the capacity for circumventing restrictive provincial statutes by manipulating the price of industrial land may be greater in smaller communities than in larger ones. Of course, the actual cost of the land itself may pale in comparison to the cost of servicing the land with water, sewers, and roads – a cost frequently underestimated or forgotten in the rush to attract new industry.

The above picture of the typical development strategy pursued by local governments in Canada suggests an emphasis on generally conservative options (promotion, creation of a "good business climate," reducing the cost of land), with limited forays into the more liberal realm (facilitation of approvals processing, provision of basic infrastructure and site services). Given the boosterist origins of present-day economic development activities, this should hardly come as a surprise. And yet, despite the serious limitations and constraints within which local governments must operate, some observers feel that many communities, particularly the smaller ones, have shown a tendency in the past to by-pass any serious attempt to assess the condition and context of their local economies, or to consider carefully and critically the costs and benefits of the various initiatives prior to engaging in the kinds of simple actions outlined above. What prevails instead is a kind of knee-jerk, "act now, think later" approach, where the perceived need for quick action usually precludes any serious consideration of non-traditional strategies or the seeking of community input or consensus on their economic priorities (Bureau of Municipal Research, 1982; Kitchen, 1985; Seasons, 1985).

Having laid out the basic dimensions of this "typical" local development effort, we turn now to a more systematic review of activities in different parts of the country. Basic patterns of resource allocation by municipalities within the ten provinces are conveyed in Table 1 for the period from 1976 to 1987. One is immediately struck by two things: (i) the degree of temporal and geographical variation in both the absolute level of municipal expenditures on economic development and the prominence of these expenditures as a share of total municipal expenditures, and (ii) the generally small share of total local government spending directed toward this function. With respect to the latter observation, it should be pointed out that the data shown here represent a rather conservative estimate of actual local government expenditures explicitly earmarked for these purposes and exclude other kinds of municipal expenditures that may contribute indirectly to economic development activities. These might typically include certain expenditures in categories such as planning and community development, tourism development, culture, water/sewer/waste systems, and roads and streets.

Despite this caveat, perusal of the bottom row of Table 1, showing national totals and shares, reveals that municipal expenditures on economic development have been increasing over time, both in absolute and relative terms. Overall, economic development expenditures rose from one-quarter of 1 per cent of total municipal outlays in 1976 to peak at one-half of 1 per cent in 1981. This proportion dipped in 1982 and 1983, most likely as a result of recessionary conditions that apparently influenced local government priorities in other directions, implying the rather discretionary character attached by local governments to expenditures in this area. The post-recession period from 1984 on sees a period of stability in these shares, indicating that the recessionary decline has not been reversed. This general picture would thus seem to confirm our opening observation that municipal activity in this program area has been on the upswing recently, though it is apparently quite sensitive to cyclical fluctuations of the economy and, for the nation as a whole, seems to have peaked in the early 1980s.

Of all the provinces, Ontario municipalities outspent their counterparts elsewhere, in absolute terms, throughout the observation period, with Alberta and Quebec governments alternating between second and third rank, at least until 1985 and 1986, when Nova Scotia overtook Alberta for third place. However, Ontario's expenditures appear to dip markedly in 1985, recovering thereafter. Apart from these cases, expenditures in other provinces are generally quite small, with exceptions in B.C. in the last five years.

In relative terms, the highest shares of total expenditure (in excess of 1 per cent) are found in Nova Scotia in 1982, 1985, and 1986. Although it is impossible to discern from the available data, one suspects that such high shares (also perhaps including New Brunswick

TABLE 1
Municipal Expenditures on Economic Development[*]
by Province, 1976-87
Absolute Levels and Percent of Total Municipal Expenditures
(current '000 dollars)

	1976		1977		1978		1979		1980		1981	
	$	%	$	%	$	%	$	%	$	%	$	%
Nfld.	—	—	100	.10	207	.18	96	.07	84	.05	130	.07
P.E.I.	—	—	—	—	2	—	—	—	—	—	—	—
N.S.	825	.15	381	.06	777	.12	320	.04	377	.05	1,955	.21
N.B.	305	.16	780	.44	425	.23	324	.16	693	.33	489	.21
Que.	6,523	.13	7,233	.12	8,063	.13	13,679	.21	40,547	.53	47,172	.55
Ont.	27,645	.38	29,562	.37	40,443	.46	64,267	.70	69,544	.69	73,451	.65
Man.	292	.04	200	.02	736	.08	423	.04	103	.01	137	.01
Sask.	—	—	122	.01	—	—	—	—	—	—	154	.01
Alta.	10,312	.53	20,713	.91	14,470	.54	3,283	.10	11,534	.30	33,480	.71
B.C.	490	.02	691	.03	1,097	.05	421	.02	1,465	.05	3,370	.10
Total	46,392	.25	59,782	.29	66,220	.29	82,813	.34	124,347	.44	160,338	.50

	1982		1983		1984		1985[**]		1986[**]		1987[**]	
	$	%	$	%	$	%	$	%	$	%	$	%
Nfld.	282	.13	286	.13	105	.04	229	.09	205	.08	245	.08
P.E.I.	—	—	7	.01	6	.01	29	.03	26	.02	27	.02
N.S.	11,802	1.19	6,272	.58	5,608	.49	15,358	1.28	23,921	1.81	11,297	.81
N.B.	839	.31	2,079	.71	969	.31	1,453	.44	1,409	.41	1,431	.42
Que.	18,379	.21	20,501	.22	22,600	.23	29,732	.28	32,032	.29	30,139	.27
Ont.	72,789	.56	75,821	.54	74,749	.50	54,668	.34	69,184	.40	76,153	.41
Man.	242	.02	208	.01	171	.01	351	.02	360	.02	381	.02
Sask.	—	—	451	.03	463	.03	752	.04	903	.05	902	.05
Alta.	31,151	.55	12,220	.22	11,478	.21	15,061	.26	14,414	.24	14,378	.24
B.C.	5,102	.13	7,379	.19	9,830	.25	6,515	.17	8,226	.20	8,473	.20
Total	140,586	.40	125,224	.33	125,982	.32	128,888	.31	146,558	.33	145,741	.32

[*] Excludes tourism and agricultural development expenditures.
[**] Indicates preliminary figures.
SOURCE: Adapted from Statistics Canada, Catalogue 68-204 (annual), *Local Government Finance*.

after 1982) were financed through transfers from more senior levels of government for purposes of regional development. Apart from these somewhat aberrant experiences, the highest expenditure shares are found in Alberta, although the prominence of economic development expenditures within total municipal expenditures in this province varies dramatically from year to year, with a high of .91 per cent in 1977 and a low of .10 in 1979. The prominence of economic development expenditures in the remaining western provinces is quite low, with shares ranging from .01 to .25. By contrast, Ontario shows much greater stability from year to year, with the economic development budget share beginning the period at .39 and .37, rising to a peak of .79 in 1979, declining gradually back to .34 by 1985, then rising slightly again to .41 by 1987. The relative importance of these expenditures in Quebec is surprisingly low until 1979, when its figure rises from .21 of 1 per cent to .55 in 1981, before dropping back to .21 in recessionary 1982, rising slowly again thereafter. In the Atlantic provinces, New Brunswick shows the consistently highest budget share devoted to development activities over the entire period, though all of the provinces in this region (except Prince Edward Island) exhibit the same kind of year-to-year fluctuations evident in Alberta.

In interpreting the variation evident in the figures just described, it is important to note that, almost by definition, municipalities in the more resource-based and less urbanized provinces are less likely to be concerned with the enlargement of their manufacturing base. This remains so despite the argument of politicians and others in some jurisdictions such as Alberta that such areas ought to be trying to diversify their economic structures in order to insulate themselves somewhat from fluctuations in the world prices for their primary commodities. Hence, the low figures in the West outside of Alberta are not all that surprising.

It should also be remembered that federal and provincial governments are themselves quite active in various aspects of economic development policy (for reviews of this activity, see Canadian Tax Foundation, 1983, and Doherty *et al.*, 1985). To the extent that the scale of senior governments' intervention in local and regional economies varies from province to province, their direct expenditures could tend to obviate those of local governments in places where senior governments are more active. This is especially so because the federal government has tended to spend funds for these purposes itself, rather than transferring the funds to municipal governments to be spent by them (Kitchen, 1984, p. 120, reports that the proportion of industrial development expenditures by municipal governments in 1978 that were financed from own-source revenues ranged from 65 to 99 per cent, with the average figure around 95 per cent). Given the stated objective of federal regional development programs since at least the mid-1960s to bring levels of well-being in relatively depressed regions such as the Atlantic provinces closer to the levels found in other parts of the country, then the relatively small emphasis given to municipally funded economic development in this region (at least prior to 1982-83) can be understood in part as a reflection of the relatively greater prominence of direct federal aid to industry in this area. Similar arguments would pertain to much of the province of Quebec, where federal expenditures have also been very significant over the past two decades.

While the figures in Table 1 are quite revealing, the absolute expenditures shown do not directly take into account two further possible sources of variation between provinces and over time: sheer population size and inflation. Table 2 incorporates these effects directly into our analysis by presenting municipal expenditures in per capita form, using constant (1971) dollars to remove inflationary sources of change over time. The results here are quite consistent with those patterns and trends suggested in Table 1, and serve to reinforce some of the points made earlier. Per capita expenditures have been rising, in real terms, from 1976 to 1981, with the same dip in 1982 and 1983 and subsequent stability that was evident in Table 1. Also, we now see that local governments in Ontario and Alberta dominate those in all other provinces prior to 1982, with Quebec showing the same upward trend from 1979 to 1981, Nova Scotia again high in 1982 and thereafter, and New Brunswick and British Columbia coming on strong after 1982 and 1981, respectively.

Portrayed in this manner, the most startling revelation from these figures is the extremely high per capita expenditures within the province of Alberta. Much of this may be attributable to the wave of municipal spending on basic infrastructural services for industrial park developments, which was stimulated in part by provincial government financial assistance for such expenditures (Seasons, 1985).

Having now explored some of the overall patterns of expenditure intensity and priority in the ten provinces, we are still without a sense of the attempts by some cities to deviate from the typical development effort presented earlier. Hence, by way of concluding our survey of current practice, we shall now embark on a brief and selective review of some of the more novel economic strategies and policy shifts occurring in some of Canada's urban areas.

Some Interesting Departures from the Norm

Those cities that have departed most markedly from the norm, either by pursuing innovative strategies or by testing the strength of provincial statutory constraints, have tended to be the larger metropolitan centres in Canada. This is a reflection of the generally greater level of financial resources and economic planning expertise among their professional

TABLE 2
Municipal Expenditures Per Capita on Economic Development*
by Province, 1976-87
(constant 1971 dollars)

	1976	1977	1978	1979	1980	1981	1982	1983	1984	1985**	1986**	1987**
Nfld.	—	.11	.21	.10	.07	.09	.19	.18	.06	.13	.11	.13
P.E.I.	—	—	.01	—	—	—	—	.02	.02	.06	.13	.06
N.S.	.67	.29	.53	.20	.22	.99	5.37	2.66	2.28	5.94	8.56	3.85
N.B.	.28	.71	.35	.25	.48	.30	.46	1.07	.48	.69	.62	.60
Que.	.71	.72	.74	1.14	3.04	3.14	1.09	1.15	1.22	1.54	1.53	1.37
Ont.	2.26	2.21	2.77	4.01	3.88	3.65	3.24	3.14	2.95	2.05	2.37	2.46
Man.	.20	.12	.41	.22	.05	.06	.09	.07	.06	.11	.11	.10
Sask.	—	.08	—	—	—	.07	—	.16	.16	.25	.28	.27
Alta.	3.78	6.80	4.28	.84	2.58	6.41	5.14	1.90	1.72	2.16	1.90	1.81
B.C.	.13	.17	.25	.08	.26	.53	.70	.96	1.21	.77	.89	.87
Total	1.36	1.61	1.64	1.85	2.48	2.83	2.21	1.84	1.78	1.73	1.81	1.71

* Excludes tourism development expenditures.
** Indicates preliminary figures.
SOURCE: Adapted from Statistics Canada, Catalogue 68-204 (annual), *Local Government Finance.*

staffs, which smaller communities cannot presently match. In the case of some cities, such as Winnipeg (see the chapter by Kiernan in this book, and Kiernan, 1987) and Sudbury (Ontario, 1985), it may also reflect an unusual amount of co-operation and interaction among local, provincial, and federal governments in response to clearly identified local crises. If any trend characterizes the more innovative cases, it is a general shift away from the old-style promotion, based solely on the attraction of industries from other places, toward a new emphasis on the *in situ* generation and nurturing of local (frequently small) businesses, including white-collar activities as well as traditional manufacturing industries (Stankovic, 1987).

British Columbia is one jurisdiction that has generated a number of noteworthy departures in the past several years. One such change is the recent decision of the provincial government to allow municipalities to reduce or waive their property tax charges on particular private businesses as a way of luring them to their community (Seasons, 1985). Second, and in contrast to the traditional conservative nature of the latter change, are the planning efforts being mounted in Vancouver. The city of Vancouver established its economic development office in 1978, along with the Vancouver Economic Advisory Commission (VEAC) representing the business community, labour, academics, and politicians. In 1981, then-Mayor Harcourt asked VEAC to develop a forward-looking economic strategy for the decade. A draft plan was presented to city council in May of 1982 (VEAC, 1982) and, after a period of public debate, was reformulated as a set of specific policy proposals (VEAC, 1983) that were adopted by council in June of 1983. These policies were based on an assessment of Vancouver's comparative advantages within the national and international economy and are meant to build on the city's perceived strengths. Specific objectives include the promotion of Vancouver as (i) a communications centre for the Pacific Rim, (ii) a growing centre of international finance, (iii) a tourist attraction, and (iv) an international source of specialized services, including managerial, financial, engineering, transportation, and health. Despite this strong emphasis on service activity, the city is also seeking to support small business and encourage "advanced technology manufacturers."

While the plan is still not fully implemented, specific initiatives already under way include: (i) the amendment of land-use zoning to reduce pressures to convert industrial lands to other uses and encourage multi-storey industrial buildings in the city's core area, (ii) the restructuring of the city's industrial park program, including the exploration of joint public-private ventures in order to develop land for light industrial entrepreneurs to be leased at preferential rates, (iii) conducting surveys and seminars with Vancouver employers, workers, and educators to promote the exchange of views and information on the city's emerging human resource needs, (iv) the establishment of a small business advisory office to provide referrals and facilitate licensing, permit acquisition, and other dealings with various public departments, and (v) the leading of a trade mission to Hong Kong, Singapore, and Kuala Lumpur to stimulate exports and foreign investment on behalf of the Vancouver economy (VEAC, 1984).

In Ontario, a number of communities have shown leadership in exploring and implementing new ideas and approaches in economic development. Of particular interest are recent initiatives to create public incubator facilities for the purpose of spawning and nurturing business start-ups and new ventures. This kind of action has been made possible by the efforts of cities like Toronto and Waterloo to lobby provincial officials to make the necessary legislative changes required to accommodate what, under the terms of the old Municipal Act, would likely constitute illegal bonusing. The province has responded with both amendments to the Act itself, for the express purpose of permitting incubator developments, as well as the establishment of a pilot program to create a number of these "enterprise centres" in such cities as Waterloo, Toronto, York, Brantford, London, Thunder Bay, Kanata, and Cornwall (Ministry of Industry, Trade and Technology, 1985).

Toronto itself has undertaken a planning effort similar to the one in Vancouver. This began under the mayorship of John Sewell and has continued under Mayor Arthur Eggleton (see City of Toronto, 1980; Eggleton, 1983). This process has been stewarded by an economic development committee of council created in the mid-1980s, supported by an economic development division within the (renamed) Department of Planning and Development (Economic Development Committee, 1985). The city's efforts centred initially on the preservation of existing industrial jobs and various extra-market strategies to prevent the conversion of industrial land to non-industrial uses, although many of their earlier initiatives (including a public-private "JobCorp" joint venture proposal) were ultimately abandoned on advice that they would contravene the anti-bonusing provisions of the Municipal Act (see Gertler, 1985, for a recounting of the recent history in this area). Current thrusts include the already mentioned incubator project, which had been housed on the site of the old Massey-Ferguson plant in the west central area of the city, industrial land acquisition, banking and leasing through a newly created economic development corporation, a program to support the rejuvenation of the local fashion industry (whose initiatives have included the establishment of a day-care centre for the express use of fashion industry workers), and the preparation of a number of industry studies to gauge the impact of the U.S.-Canada Free Trade Agreement on key local sectors of the economy. These are in addition to other activities that emphasize liaison between local businesses and the program activities of federal and provincial governments, and an international program with cities such as Chong-qing, China, and Amsterdam to promote trade linkages and export activity for local businesses.

Currently, the economic development division appears to be most concerned with the tremendous pressure being placed on vacant or underused industrial lands in Toronto to be converted to other uses. These pressures have been fuelled by at least three considerations. First, a chronically short supply of vacant (especially affordable) housing has led some local politicians to propose the use of such lands for residential purposes. That this is a real possibility is demonstrated in the St. Lawrence Square (later renamed Ataratiri) project announced in the summer of 1987, in which the city has allowed largely industrial lands to be used for a large affordable housing complex. Second, the local development lobby, which gained considerable clout during the 1980s, has exerted continual pressure on city councillors to permit them to maximize the revenues derived from the development of industrial lands by allowing their conversion to commercial or upper-income residential uses. Third, the creation in 1988 of a federal royal commission headed by former Toronto mayor and federal cabinet minister David Crombie to determine the future development of the Toronto waterfront has directed more attention to the future use of the extensive eastern port industrial lands, a large proportion of which remain vacant, for non-industrial (largely residential and recreational) uses. These pressures will likely make it more and more difficult for the economic development division to attract or generate new manufacturing jobs to Toronto, despite the activist stance they have defined for themselves.

In the east, the city of Halifax has also recently obtained new powers from the Nova Scotia legislature, through amendment to its city charter, which permit its Industrial Commission to engage in the sale of lands in its publicly owned industrial park at prices substantially below market value, subject to provincial approval. This action affects not only the purchase price of the land but also future taxes paid on it, since assessment values are set at the price actually paid for the property (personal communication, Halifax City Planning Department officials, 1986). While this new development certainly broadens the abilities of the city to attract and/or generate new economic activity within its borders, it brings with it the hidden cost of servicing and preparing lands, which in the rocky environment of the Halifax region can run to over $100,000 per acre.

Halifax is by no means alone in its efforts to attract industrial employers to the area. Other aggressive promoters within the region include Halifax County, which recently offered serviced land in its Aerotech Business Park to Litton Systems Canada at half its "normal" selling price (Mosher, 1986). Similarly, the city of Dartmouth owns the large Burnside industrial park and other estates, and continues to pursue an active promotion policy recently broadened to include the attraction of higher-order service employers as well as the traditional industrial firms (City of Dartmouth, 1985). Not surprisingly, the existence of this intermunicipal competition has led to the creation of an oversupply of industrial land and overconstruction of expensive infrastructure in the region, raising once again the spectre of unproductive use of public resources to fuel inter-city rivalries.

Conclusion

Given the recent character of many economic initiatives of local governments, it is still too early to tell how successful they might be. Nevertheless, these initiatives have already raised a number of questions about their potential effectiveness. Two of the more interesting are (i) the ability of the local public sector, even in large and sophisticated centres like Toronto and Vancouver, to identify and nurture growth prospects successfully outside the normal market mechanism, and (ii) the overlaps, wastage, and duplication of effort that may occur more frequently as more and more jurisdictions acquire a capability in economic development programming. In Metropolitan Toronto alone, most of the six local municipalities are now actively pursuing their own economic development strategies, and the Metropolitan council (supported by its own economic development office) has not yet been fully able to co-ordinate activities among these various jurisdictions, thereby failing to prevent a certain amount of unproductive local competition. Most recently, Metro council has adopted a proposal to expand its own presence in the economic development area, deciding to enlarge its staff from five to about twenty and to increase its annual economic development budget from $800,000 to $2.2 million (Cresap, 1988). Already, these initiatives have met with scepticism from area municipalities, which feel that Metro's recent actions, having failed to define a clear logic for Metro's role, will increase the degree of overlap with other government activities (Bruce and Todd, 1988).

In any event, all of these concerns underscore the importance of the as yet underdeveloped (and underutilized) methodologies for evaluating public actions in this general area. While traditional cost-benefit methods represent a useful starting point (Bureau of Municipal Research, 1982; Kitchen, 1985), it is likely that such tools will need to be broadened somewhat to reflect the full range of private and social impacts of economic development policies. Finally, such analyses will also have to come to grips with the difficult problem of defining the "public" interest in a way that is acceptable to the multiple levels of government in the Canadian political context.

NOTE

The author wishes to acknowledge the helpful comments received on an earlier draft of this chapter from John Britton, Cynthia Horan, Harry Kitchen, Mark Seasons, and the editors of this volume. He would also like to express his gratitude to the local officials who provided assistance and information. None of the preceding should be held responsible for any shortcomings.

REFERENCES

Alonso, W. (1975). "Industrial location and regional policy in economic development," in J. Friedmann and W. Alonso (eds.), *Regional Policy: Readings in Theory and Applications*. Cambridge, Mass.: MIT Press.

Bingham, R.D., and J.P. Blair (eds.) (1984). *Urban Economic Development.* Volume 27, Urban Affairs Annual Reviews. Beverly Hills: Sage Publications.

Bird, R.M., and N.E. Slack (1983). *Urban Public Finance in Canada.* Toronto: Butterworths.

Bloomfield, E. (1986). "Community leadership and decision-making: entrepreneurial elites in two Ontario towns, 1870-1930," in G.A. Stelter and A.F.J. Artibise (eds.), *Power and Place: Canadian Urban Development in the North American Context.* Vancouver: University of British Columbia Press.

Bluestone, B., and B. Harrison (1981). *The Deindustrialization of America.* New York: Basic Books.

Boddy, M. (1984). "Local economic and employment strategies," in M. Boddy and C. Fudge (eds.), *Local Socialism? Labour Councils and New Left Alternatives.* London: Macmillan.

Britton, J.N.H. (1981). "Innovation, industrial strategy, and the urban economy: Toronto's development options," Research Paper No. 127, Centre for Urban and Community Studies, University of Toronto.

Bruce, A., and R. Todd (1988). "Metro economic plan is called 'too timid' by labour council head," *Globe and Mail*, April 21.

Canadian Tax Foundation (1983). *Provincial and Municipal Finances 1983.* Toronto.

City of Dartmouth (1985). "Dartmouth municipal planning strategy review background paper: industrial activity in Dartmouth." Dartmouth, N.S.: Planning and Development Department, July.

City of Toronto (1980). *A Selective Economic Development Strategy.* Toronto: Planning and Development Department, July.

Clark, G.L., and M.S. Gertler (1983). "Local labor markets: theories and policies in the U.S. during the 1970s," *Professional Geographer*, 35: 274-85.

Cresap (1988). *Becoming an International Competitor: Metro's New Economic Development Strategy.* Report prepared for the Metro Industrial and Business Development Advisory Council and submitted to the Economic Development and Planning Committee of Council, Metropolitan Toronto.

Davidson, G. (1986). "Municipal economic development: an organizational overview," Centre for Rural Development, Auburn, Ontario.

Divay, G. (1980). "Le développement d'initiative locale," *Canadian Public Administration*, 23: 236-51.

Doherty, P., T.P. Muir, and R.J. Fantham (1985). *Industrial Assistance Programs in Canada*, 9th edition. Toronto: CCH Canadian Limited.

Economic Development Committee (1985). Minutes of the meeting held on December 20, City of Toronto.

Eggleton, A. (1983). *Future Directions: A Jobs and Economic Development Strategy for Toronto*. Toronto: Office of the Mayor, City of Toronto, September.

Fish, S.A. (1981). "Winning the battle and losing the war in the fight to improve municipal policy making," in L.D. Feldman (ed.), *Politics and Government of Urban Canada: Selected Readings*, Fourth Edition. Toronto: Methuen.

Fox Przeworski, J. (1986). "Changing intergovernmental relations and urban economic development," *Environment and Planning C: Government and Policy*, 4: 423-38.

Gertler, M.S. (1985). "Industrialism, deindustrialism, and regional development in Central Canada," *Canadian Journal of Regional Science*, 8: 353-75.

Goldstein, H.A. (1987). *The State and Local Industrial Policy Question*. Chicago: American Planning Association.

Hansen, N.M. (1974). *Public Policy and Regional Economic Development: The Experience of Nine Western Countries*. Cambridge, Mass.: Ballinger.

Heilbrun, J. (1981). *Urban Economics and Public Policy*, second edition. New York: St. Martin's Press.

Kaldor, N. (1970). "The case for regional policies," *Scottish Journal of Political Economy*, 17: 337-48.

Kiernan, M.J. (1987). "Intergovernmental innovation: Winnipeg's Core Area Initiative," *Plan Canada*, 27: 23-31.

Kitchen, H.M. (1985). "The role for local governments in economic development." Discussion Paper Series. Toronto: Ontario Economic Council.

Kitchen, H.M. (1984). *Local Government Finance in Canada*. Toronto: Canadian Tax Foundation.

Labour Council of Metropolitan Toronto (1983). *A Time for Leadership: Industrial Strategies for Metropolitan Toronto*. Toronto: Labour Council of Metropolitan Toronto.

Litvak, L., and B.H. Daniels (1979). *Innovations in Development Finance*. Washington, D.C.: Council of State Planning Agencies.

Markusen, A.R. (1977). *The Fiscal Crisis of American Boomtowns: An Analysis of State and Federal Policy*. Washington, D.C.: U.S. General Accounting Office.

Ministry of Industry, Trade and Technology (1985). News release: Ontario to support community small business centres. Toronto, December 4.

Mosher, M. (1986). "County administrator says: Litton got half-price deal on county land," *Halifax Mail-Star*, July 30.

Musgrave, R., and P.B. Musgrave (1980). *Public Finance in Theory and Practice*, Third Edition. New York: McGraw-Hill.

Neighbourhoods Committee (1983). Report No. 18 for consideration by the Council of the Corporation of the City of Toronto on September 19, 1983: Economic Development. Toronto City Council.

O'Brien, A. (1976). "Local government priorities for the eighties," *Canadian Public Administration*, 19: 102-11.

OECD (1986a). Infrastructure investments and their contribution to employment and economic growth. Labour/Management Programme report, March, Paris.

OECD (1986b). Revitalising urban economies. Group on Urban Affairs report, May, Paris.

OECD (1985). *Creating Jobs at the Local Level: Local Initiatives for Employment Creation*. Paris: OECD Project on Local Employment Initiatives.

Ontario (1985). Project group on urban economic development case study report: Sudbury, Ontario, Canada. Toronto: Ministry of Municipal Affairs, Community Planning Programs Division. Prepared for OECD, Paris.

Plunkett, T.J., and G.M. Betts (1978). *The Management of Canadian Urban Government*. Kingston: Queen's University Press.

Saunders, R.S. (1984). *Aid to Workers in Declining Industries*. Toronto: Ontario Economic Council, Policy Study Series.

Seasons, M.L. (1985). "Economic Development in the Calgary Region: Current Practice and Future Approaches." M.A. thesis, University of Calgary.

Stankovic, D. (1987). "An entrepreneurial approach to local economic development," *Plan Canada*, 27: 6-15.

Taylor, J.H. (1986). "Urban autonomy in Canada: its evolution and decline," in Stelter and Artibise (eds.), *Power and Place*.

Tindal, C.R., and S.N. Tindal (1979). *Local Government in Canada: An Introduction*. Toronto: McGraw-Hill Ryerson.

Vancouver Economic Advisory Commission (1984). An economic strategy for Vancouver: progress report no. 2. City of Vancouver, September.

Vancouver Economic Advisory Commission (1983). An economic strategy for Vancouver in the 1980s: proposals for policy and implementation. City of Vancouver, April.

Vancouver Economic Advisory Commission (1982). An economic strategy for Vancouver in the 1980s. City of Vancouver, May.

3

Matthew J. Kiernan

Land-Use Planning

Of all of the functional concerns of Canadian local government, none is *potentially* as comprehensive or as all-embracing as urban planning. Indeed, viewed in its broadest terms, the planning function could (and in my view, should) be regarded as virtually coterminous with the mandate of local government itself. It can and should have as its central focus nothing less than maximization of the city's economic, social, and physical potential. Interpreted this broadly, urban planning would essentially constitute the local government's central strategic planning capability and would subsume and integrate most if not all of its narrower, more functionally specialized concerns.

As we shall see, however, in practice Canadian cities rarely if ever accord urban planning a role either this broad or this pivotal. Indeed, the tendency has been precisely the opposite. Local politicians and senior administrators have tended to define their cities' urban planning mandates much more narrowly, confining them for the most part to the control of physical land use and the regulation of the height and densities of buildings. Clearly, however, both the nature and the status of urban planning are strongly derivative of its situation within the broader context of Canadian municipal government itself, a context that generally militates *against* an activist, comprehensive, and inter-ventionist role for city governments (Plunkett, 1971, 1985). Urban planning, then, simply falls heir in a more specific way to these more general and pervasive limitations on local government.

Before examining these propositions in more detail, we shall review briefly the origins and history of urban planning in Canada. We shall then examine the ideological and organizational contexts in which contemporary urban planning takes place and explore the major substantive and procedural issues with which Canadian local government planners and politicians are currently grappling. Finally, we shall conclude by sketching the outlines of some of the more compelling new trends that can be expected to shape the future direction of urban planning in Canada.

The Historical Evolution of Urban Planning in Canada

Urban planning in Canada has evolved through a number of relatively distinct "epochs," each one characterized by different ideological influences, institutional frameworks, and substantive preoccupations.

The earliest real antecedent of formalized urban planning was the Commission of Conservation of Natural Resources (Hodge, 1986). Created by an Act of the federal Parliament in 1909, the Commission was comprised of federal and provincial cabinet ministers as well as leading academics from each province. Its mandate was sufficiently broad to embrace any question related to the improved utilization of Canada's natural resources. The Commission could and did engage permanent staff, who carried out studies on topics ranging from the effects of railways on forests to problems related to public health and housing in urban centres. The Commission and its two principal staffers, Dr. Charles Hodgetts and Thomas Adams, synthesized a number of ideological influences from both Britain and the United States and created the intellectual foundations that continue to influence Canadian urban planning nearly eight decades later. Their work was strongly influenced by the countryside conservation movements in Britain and the United States, as well as by the American urban reform movement, which sought both to improve the quality of municipal services and to reduce the influence of local politicians over the delivery of those services – in short, to de-politicize local government. The American influence was also evident in the Commission's functional approach to urban planning – its strong emphasis on zoning and the orderly arrangement and separation of land uses, streets, and utilities. In addition, the Commission and its staff were heavily influenced by the British public health and housing reform movements, which emphasized governmental responsibility for the amelioration of the social conditions of the urban poor.

Adams and the Commission synthesized these divergent influences into a distinctive (and, predictably, somewhat schizophrenic) Canadian planning ideology, elements of which continue to be strongly evident even today. For Adams, planning ought properly to concern itself with a broad spectrum of both social and physical problems, although in his view both could be rectified through the proper planning and arrangement of the physical components of towns and cities. Moreover, planning was seen as an inherently rational, technical, and professional enterprise: urban problems were essentially technical in origin and therefore amenable to solution by technically trained, professional planners. Most important of all, Adams felt that government had both the right and the obligation to intervene and to take a lead role in devising and implementing solutions to urban problems,

Besides providing the ideological underpinnings for Canadian urban planning, the work of Adams and the Commission also provided its original statutory and organizational context by spawning both the drafting of the Town Planning Act and the formation of the Town Planning Institute of Canada. The former served as the model for most of the early provincial planning statutes in Canada; the latter marked the official debut of urban planning as a profession in 1919.

This dynamic and formative period of Canadian planning was followed by nearly two decades of relative quiescence. During the depression, there really existed no Canadian equivalent of the American New Deal, through which the federal government had become active in attacking housing and other poverty-related problems in American cities. Only one Canadian city (Toronto) even *had* a planning depart-ment, and those few cities and towns that did have plans and zoning bylaws at all (Vancouver, Edmonton, and Windsor, for example) had grossly outdated ones.

By contrast, however, the post-World War Two era witnessed a marked reinvigoration of planning in Canada. The federal government's Advisory Committee on Reconstruction dealt specifically with the issues of housing and community and social planning. The Committee's 1944 report (the Curtis Report) proposed a wide-ranging and inter-ventionist agenda, including aggressive federal programs to promote land assembly and slum clearance. While the government's ultimate response to the Curtis Report was considerably narrower, it did establish the Central Mortgage and Housing Corporation in 1945, with a mandate to stimulate the flow of mortgage capital and to provide low-cost housing (for further detail on housing issues in general and CMHC's role in particular, consult B. Carroll's chapter on housing elsewhere in this volume).

The pursuit of the first of these two objectives was to have a profound if somewhat indirect effect on urban planning in Canada. By increasing both the amount and the availability of residential mortgage money, CMHC not inadvertently fuelled and indeed accel-erated the explosive development and growth of the suburban areas on the periphery of Canada's major urban centres. In the metropolitan areas, housing stock increased by up to 20 per cent between 1945 and 1950 alone. This led in turn to a dramatically increased need to plan and accommodate the new suburban growth, with a concomitant increase in provincial and municipal government planning activity and legislation (Hodge, 1986).

At the same time, in the older city centres, the new legislation ushered in a focus on slum clearance and urban renewal activity, which was to last from the late 1940s until the mid-1960s. During this period, the federal government invested over $125 million in nearly fifty separate urban renewal projects across the country, projects whose twin aims were to demolish deteriorated housing and to replace it with new, modern accommodation for low-income people. By the late sixties, however, increasingly well-organized protests against the insensitivity and dislocations of the "bulldozer approach" had effectively ground the federal urban renewal program to a halt. The watershed battle in this regard had been the successful protest by the working-class residents of Toronto's Trefann Court neighbourhood (see Fraser, 1972). As a result of this experience and other similar ones elsewhere, the federal government undertook a complete re-examination of its urban renewal program. It was subsequently replaced by the Neighbourhood Improvement Program, which was predicated on radically different physical and social planning assumptions, and stressed a more physically sensitive, selective, and participatory approach.

Meanwhile, the 1960s had also marked the real beginnings of the institutionalization of urban planning within the local government system. Prior to this period, most city governments had relied on arm's-length, advisory planning commissions. These planning commissions, normally comprised of lay people, would generally prepare city plans with the assistance of outside consultants and submit them to city councils for approval. By the early to mid-1960s, however, most Canadian cities had abolished these external commissions in favour of in-house planning departments, staffed with professionals.

This situation of the urban planning function within the local government apparatus was to have major consequences for the substantive focus of planning itself. From this time forward, the concerns of planning came increasingly and understandably to be dominated by those of the broader local government system itself. Most local governments tended to view themselves as primarily apolitical and technocratic and to conceive of their principal mandate as being the prudent and orderly administration of physical services to support growth and development (Plunkett, 1971). This being the case, it was only logical that urban planners would interpret their roles within these same narrow parameters. The same profession, which in Adams's time had had a catholic range of social and environmental as well as physical concerns, found itself increasingly confined to a much narrower focus on physical land use, subdivision design, and zoning approvals (Qadeer, 1977; Page and Lang, 1977).

Until the late sixties, then, local government planners generally played the role of relatively uncritical handmaidens to suburban growth and high-rise redevelopment in Canada's downtowns and inner cities. The next decade, however, found planners squarely in the middle of the new urban politics of citizen protest. Citizen opposition to urban renewal, high-rise redevelopment, and urban expressways frequently placed planners directly at the axis of a three-cornered fight among their municipal government employers, private developers, and a concerned citizenry. It was a period of great intellectual turbulence for planners, as many of the cherished notions that had sustained their profession since Adams's time came under severe strain and critical re-examination. While the principal focus of urban planning during this period remained very much physical – on buildings and land use – a much greater stress was placed on concerns about the social and environmental impacts of development and on more participatory *styles* of planning that would involve citizens as well as professional "experts." For planners who had come to believe that growth and development were unquestionably positive, and that planning was an inherently rational, technocratic, and professional science, the decade beginning in the late sixties was a difficult one indeed.

We would argue that yet another epoch in the evolution and development of Canadian urban planning began sometime in the late 1970s and has continued to the present time. It was an era whose intellectual parameters have been overwhelmingly defined by the economic, social, and even physical consequences for Canadian cities of the global recession of the late seventies. The balance of this chapter will examine this contemporary era in greater detail – the ideological and organizational context in which planning currently takes place, the major issues with which it is grappling, and the emerging new trends that will shape its direction in the future.

The Contemporary Context for Urban Planning in Canada

The Ideological Context

Canadian urban planning has from its inception been bombarded by a variety of frequently conflicting ideological influences. Of those currently determining its nature and scope, four intellectual influences are particularly important:

- fundamentally ambivalent Canadian attitudes concerning the legitimacy of public-sector intervention in the urban land market;
- the depoliticizing consequences of the situation of urban planning within the broader local government system;

- the persistence of the notion that planning is essentially a rational, technical, professional enterprise; and
- the consequences of the macro-economic context, that is, the recession and its aftermath, for both public and professional attitudes toward growth and development.

The very existence of urban planning as a local government activity would seem to indicate a certain measure of acceptance of the proposition that the state has the right to intervene in the urban land market, notwithstanding that property is overwhelmingly privately owned in Canada. Yet provincial legislators, local politicians, and the general public have all exhibited considerable ambivalence about even this basic planning precept. As usual, we Canadians seem to have come down squarely in the middle between the British and American views on the matter, and, given the intellectual ancestry of Canadian planning, this is scarcely surprising (Gerecke, 1977; Hodge and Spragge, 1978). In British planning circles, it has long been taken for granted that land is a scarce public birthright and that its use and development are matters over which the state has extensive and legitimate control (McAuslan, 1980). The American attitude, however, is quite different. In the United States, the ownership of private property is generally seen to confer virtually inviolable rights, and government incursions upon those private rights are viewed with a jaundiced eye by legislators, courts, and the general public alike. The dominant Canadian ethos seems to be an amalgam midway between the British and American extremes. Both the Canadian planning profession itself and its local government masters retain strong ethical reservations about the legitimacy of strong public controls over the use of private property (Fainstein and Fainstein, 1971). Put more bluntly, most Canadian planners are extremely ambivalent about the very legitimacy of public-sector planning itself (Page and Lang, 1977; Baum, 1980; Kiernan, 1982a and 1982b). At the very least, this creates a rather schizophrenic set of ideological underpinnings for Canadian urban planning, and it robs its public-sector practitioners of much of both their resolve and their political support. In the absence of a strong political and professional consensus supporting forceful public interventions in the urban land market, planning will be doomed to a chronically reactive and marginal role.

The second major set of ideological influences on contemporary Canadian urban planning flows directly from its situation firmly within both the structure and the intellectual traditions of Canadian local government. Various legal, financial, and ideological constraints have combined to create a powerful ethos of apolitical, anti-interventionist minimalism in municipal government (Plunkett, 1971 and 1984; Kiernan, 1983). The dominant notion has been that local government exists primarily for the prudent, business-like provision of a limited number of "hard" services (sewer, water, fire protection, etc.), and that its role is fundamentally a narrow, passive, and apolitical one. With one or two exceptions, Canadian local governments have by and large resisted a more aggressive, pro-active involvement in such politically contentious but critical issues as low-income housing, day care, and social services delivery. Questions relating to poverty and distributional equity are almost universally dismissed as the responsibility of other better-funded and more powerful senior levels of government. Even those limited responsibilities that *are* readily acknowledged as legitimately municipal (bridge- and road-building, for example) are normally interpreted as fundamentally technical exercises, devoid of political or distributional implications. In short, the overwhelming tendency of Canadian local government has been to assume as few responsibilities as possible, and then to interpret those few it will accept as narrowly as possible (Kiernan, 1983). A current and classic illustration of this predilection is Canadian municipalities' quixotic and futile campaign to persuade the federal government to cost-share an $8 *billion* program to upgrade municipal sewers and roads. The municipalities' concerns in the proposal are exclusively restricted to the provision of hard services; there is no hint in the proposal that city governments are prepared to accept a broader set of responsibilities, even in return for additional funding.[1] Under such circumstances, it is scarcely surprising that most local government planning departments have had little incentive to move beyond a narrow reactive preoccupation with physical land use and zoning.

The third important ideological influence acting on contemporary urban planning in Canada is the persistent belief that, at bottom, planning remains a fundamentally rational and technical endeavour, undertaken by trained professionals in pursuit of incontrovertible and generally shared public goals. This comforting if naive view has sustained Canadian planners from the time of Thomas Adams until the present (Page and Lang, 1977; Spragge, 1975; Gerecke, 1977; Kiernan, 1982a). It is an ideology that, unfortunately, has been reinforced if not actually created by the academic content of most contemporary Canadian graduate planning school curricula (Page and Lang, 1977), as well as by the planners' own " professional" association, the Canadian Institute of Planners. The chief and regrettable practical consequence of these pretensions to a professional and technocratic status, however, has been to obscure from both planners and their political masters the fact that, quite to the contrary, their work almost invariably *does* involve debatable value judgements, and the costs and benefits of those judgements are rarely if ever uniformly or equally distributed (Davidoff, 1965, 1975; Simmie, 1974; Kiernan, 1982a).[2] In addition, these professional ideologies tend to reinforce similar predispositions growing out of the constraints imposed by the planning function's situation within the broader local government framework.

The net result is a planning system that tends on the whole to be reactive, overwhelmingly focused on physical land-use and zoning issues, and without the mandate, expertise, intellectual underpinnings, or political support to concern itself with broader social and economic issues.

These three preceding ideological influences on planning thought and practice have tended to be relatively constant over time and independent of fluctuations in external, macro-economic circumstances. The fourth, however, is not. One of the greatest determinants of contemporary planning behaviour has been the intellectual aftermath of the global recession of the early 1980s.

Throughout the decade prior to the recession, Canadian planners and their political masters frequently found themselves taking extremely critical and often flatly negative perspectives on proposed new developments, albeit for the most part from their familiar reactive posture. Citizen activism, "reform" politicians, and the rise of new planning tools such as environmental impact assessment all tended to impel the planner toward an adversarial posture vis-à-vis the private developer, although, as usual, most of the critiques were limited to the physical dimensions of the proposals. Within what was at the time an overall context of relative affluence and strong economic growth, however, city governments could afford to be and frequently were quite choosy about both the quantity and quality of new development they were willing to accept. Having spent the previous decade encouraging and accommodating both suburban and downtown growth, many Canadian planners spent the period from the late sixties to the late seventies doing precisely the opposite.

The recession, however, has changed all that. Global, macro-economic difficulties and collapsing world markets for Canadian resource commodities have had a devastating effect on the economies of a number of Canadian cities, particularly in the West. The result has been a remarkable transformation in both public and professional attitudes toward urban growth and development. Almost imperceptibly, new development has once again become something to be embraced and encouraged as a welcome and tangible sign of economic regeneration and vitality. In the current post-recession era, planners in most Canadian cities find themselves not only more *receptive* to new development than was the case during the previous decade, but increasingly in the business of actually trying to *catalyze* it. (See, for example, M. Gertler's chapter in the current volume.)

This represents a quantum attitudinal shift for planners, and it is qualitatively different even from the halcyon, pro-growth days of the early 1960s. In those days, as today, growth and development were generally and rather uncritically viewed as beneficial. The difference, however, is that today a good deal more intervention and encouragement are required. This forces planners to switch from their traditional passive, reactive, and regulatory mode to a much more pro-active and *developmental* role. It is a transition that urban planning departments, and indeed local governments generally, have found extraordinarily difficult to accomplish (Kiernan, 1983). Indeed, on the whole they have been unable to accomplish it at all, and as we shall see, the major urban development projects of the 1980s have taken place outside the aegis of not only the local *planning* departments, but outside the framework of local government altogether.

The Organizational Context for Canadian Urban Planning

Of equal importance to its ideological context is the organizational context within which urban planning takes place. That organizational context is comprised of two principal dimensions: the enabling legislation creating the arsenal of powers that planners and politicians may potentially use, and the organizational structures through which those powers are actually exercised. The enabling legislation is generally the prerogative of the various provincial governments, while the actual organization of the planning bureaucracy is usually left to the discretion of the local government.

Under the Constitution Act (originally the British North America Act), all planning powers exercised by local authorities must first be delegated to them by acts of the provincial legislatures to which local governments are legally subordinate. In Canada, "local planning authorities" may be anything from regional planning commissions and planning districts, through metropolitan or regional governments, to single-tier city governments such as Calgary, Edmonton, Vancouver, or Winnipeg. In cases such as Toronto and Montreal, where both lower- and upper-tier municipal governments co-exist, planning legislation attempts to divide responsibility between what are deemed to be regional issues on the one hand and "local" ones on the other. In practice, however, these divisions tend to be considerably less neat and precise than they sometimes appear on paper!

Notwithstanding a certain degree of variation among provincial jurisdictions, the planning powers that each confers are broadly similar (Rodgers, 1976). Virtually all local governments can pass zoning and planning bylaws, which control land use, height, lot coverage, and density. Many jurisdictions also have development control powers, which are usually comparable in substance to zoning bylaws but have the important distinction of allowing municipalities to control development on a case-by-case basis at the time of development, rather than setting out detailed ground rules, often years in advance, through zoning bylaws. A number of cities (Victoria, Vancouver, Edmonton, Regina, Toronto, and, latterly, Winnipeg) have a hybrid of the two systems known as design control, which gives the local authority the opportunity to scrutinize the detailed design features of a project even if it conforms to the general height and bulk requirements of the existing zoning regulations. Finally, most local governments have the authority to regulate the subdivision of land (usually though not always suburban) and thereby control the timing, servicing, use, and density of development. In addition, most municipalities also have powers enabling them to transcend a purely passive, regulatory role and become more aggressively involved in stimulating development. While the actual *use* of such powers varies widely, most cities have at least the legal *capacity* to assemble and lease land for development, to create and operate local housing corporations, and to recycle the monies raised through developmental levies to help generate further development.

There is, however, one critically important restriction on the urban planning powers of Canadian local governments. Not only do provincial statutes normally prescribe *which* planning powers a municipality may use, but they also generally reserve for the provincial government a substantial voice in *how* these powers are actually exercised. This is generally accomplished by requiring that major municipal planning decisions be provincially approved, either by appointed boards such as the Ontario Municipal Board or, more directly, by provincial cabinet ministers. Needless to say, this situation creates an endlessly fertile source of municipal-provincial political conflict, as the ethos of local autonomy collides head-on with the often compelling necessity for provincial governments to protect their own interests on major planning issues. And regardless of the relative merits of the municipal and provincial arguments, at the end of the day the bald legal and political reality remains that the provincial government almost invariably has the final say. This municipal-provincial tension is one of the most powerful underlying motifs of contemporary Canadian urban planning, and it is virtually ubiquitous.[3]

While provincial governments normally set the overall legislative framework for planning and frequently intervene in particular cases, city governments are almost invariably free to organize their own planning departments as they see fit, and there is a remarkable similarity in how they have chosen to do so. Most cities of sufficient size divide their planning departments into at least two distinct divisions – one concerned with forward planning, the other with the day-to-day administration of current development permits, rezonings, inspections, zoning and development agreements, and so forth. The forward planning function is itself frequently divided into separate branches, one concerning itself with long-range, city-wide strategic planning and the other focusing on small area and neighbourhood planning. Larger, more sophisticated planning departments such as those in Vancouver and Toronto have specialized branches dealing with their downtown and waterfront areas.

In recent years, several Canadian cities have also become more actively involved in planning and administering incentives for economic development, although it is significant that for the most part this function does *not* take place within traditional city planning departments or even central agencies (see the chapter on economic development by M. Gertler in the present volume). Toronto's planning department, arguably the largest and most sophisticated in the country, is one of the few exceptions. It includes a small economic development branch, as well as a unit within its policy and research section that explicitly concerns itself with social planning issues.

Despite such occasional exceptions, however, the overall pattern that emerges is one of a local government planning system overwhelmingly preoccupied with physical land-use and development issues. As we have seen, many of the reasons for that preoccupation are derivative of the legal, financial, and ideological limitations of Canadian local government itself. Others are related to the training and ideological predispositions of the planners (Page and Lang, 1977). Having reviewed the ideological and organizational context within which most Canadian urban planning takes place, we shall now examine the major substantive issues that currently dominate the planning and development agendas of most most major Canadian cities. What is particularly striking if somewhat disconcerting about this examination is its revelation that these issues, while absolutely central to the planning and development of our cities, in most cases involve local government planning *departments* only peripherally.

Current Issues in Canadian Urban Planning

While every city is physically, socially, and politically unique, a number of contemporary planning issues tend to cut across these distinctions and are common to most if not all Canadian cities. By far the most dominant of these issues in recent years has been the revitalization of Canada's downtown and inner-city areas.

Downtown, Waterfront, and Inner-City Revitalization

A number of contemporary factors have combined to create the impetus for the major downtown redevelopment efforts currently under way in nearly every Canadian city. For most cities, the post-war years were a period of rapid suburban growth and expansion. Low-density suburban housing was built and massive public investments were made in the infrastructure required to support the new growth – roads, sewers and water lines, schools, parks and recreation facilities, and so on. Suburban shopping centres proliferated to service the new communities, and thousands of industrial jobs were moved to suburban locations where cheap, abundant, and accessible land could accommodate the new production technologies. In short, for nearly three decades following World War Two the focus of both governmental and private-sector capital and attention was squarely on suburbia.

None of this took place, however, without significant and deleterious consequences for the downtowns and inner neighbourhoods at whose expense much of this growth was occurring. Downtowns lost substantial portions of their retail market shares and became less active and attractive places for workers, residents, and visitors. Inner neighbourhoods became physically run-down and came to house ever-greater concentrations of the poor, the elderly, single-parent families, and ethnic and other special-needs groups.[4]

By the late seventies, however, there began to emerge a fortuitous convergence between the *problems* of downtown decline on the one hand and some significant *opportunities* for downtown revitalization on the other. For many local governments, downtown and inner-city deterioration was fast becoming a major issue. The downtown tax base was eroding, while the costs of maintaining and servicing a downtown inhabited and used by fewer and fewer people were increasing. There were growing questions about both the economic and environmental viability of continued suburban development. The downtown, the one part of the city that really ought to define its character and quality for all its citizens and for tourists, was in deep trouble. However, help was on the way in the form of demographic and attitudinal changes. For middle- and upper-income consumers, for example, a combination of demographic changes (two-income families, fewer and later children, marital breakups), mounting concern about energy costs, and increasing dissatisfaction with commuting time began to make downtown living a serious option for the first time. Yet the neighbourhood preservation battles from the mid-sixties to the mid-seventies effectively placed many inner-city neighbourhoods off-limits for any redevelopment more intensive (or affordable) than the "whitepainting" of a single-family or row house.

So how could this growing market demand be satisfied while still revitalizing (and not destroying) downtown? The answer in many Canadian cities was to reclaim derelict downtown industrial land for new development and thereby kill at least two birds with one stone – the removal of an unsightly liability on the one hand and the creation of a positive new urban element on the other. The first generation of these major downtown redevelopment projects has tended to take place on obsolescent industrial land, much of it on formerly neglected urban waterfronts. The second generation of the major projects, still in its infancy in the late 1980s, will unquestionably take place on the strategic but increasingly underutilized urban landholdings of the major railways.

By the mid-1980s, one could cite examples of massive downtown redevelopment projects in various stages of implementation in virtually every major Canadian city. While the scale and scope of the projects differ substantially in reflection of local circumstances, all share several critical distinguishing features. By far the most important of those features is that in nearly every case the project was spearheaded by a publicly established, publicly funded development corporation. The emergence of the public corporation as a dominant player in the urban redevelopment game clearly has been one of the defining characteristics of the Canadian planning scene in the 1980s (Kiernan and Artibise, 1988).

In nearly every major city, arm's-length, special-purpose corporations have been established by one or more levels of government to undertake prescribed development mandates. Their establishment rested on three basic propositions. The first was that public resources would have to be concentrated and focused through both an extraordinary effort and a cross-departmental co-ordination mechanism; the ongoing mandates and resources of the existing line departments would simply not be equal to the task. The second was that resources of government alone would not be adequate to the magnitude of the urban redevelopment challenge; a way had to be found to attract substantial private capital as well. And thirdly, if one of the principal tasks of the new public corporations was to be the catalyst of private-sector investment, the new public corporations would need to be able to deal with private developers on a reasonably equal footing. They would require at a minimum the ability to move with the same confidentiality and speed that normally give private developers an enormous advantage in their dealings with government. In short, the new corporations would need to pursue public-sector objectives, but with many of the capabilities of a private corporation. This necessitated the creation of public development corporations with a considerable degree of arm's-length operational independence from their governmental creators.

As we shall see, however, the creation of these new public corporations has raised an exquisitely difficult public policy question: just how far removed from the arms of government should these corporations be? What is a politically sustainable balance between the corporations' requisite freedom and independence from the normal constraints of government, on the one hand, and the necessary political and public accountability and responsibility for the corporations' activities, on the other? The evidence suggests that, if anything, the corporations have tended to err on the side of *excessive* independence, particularly when viewed from the standpoint of *local* government and the local planning process. And, while the track records of these new corporations in radically reshaping and regenerating Canadian urban centres have been truly impressive, they have, unfortunately, exacted a rather steep price: the evisceration of much of the urban planning capability of local government.

The *real* planning in Canadian cities today tends not be done by city planning departments at all but by the new public corporations, which are generally not even creatures of *local* government in the first place. Instead, almost without exception, the new corporations are arm's-length agencies of one or the other of the senior governments, most often the federal. Moreover, the public corporations enjoy three critical resources historically denied to traditional planning departments: enormous capital budgets, a mandate actually to *develop* land rather than simply to plan and regulate it, and broad public and political support. This leaves local planning departments in the unenviable position of scrambling, from a distinctly disadvantaged position, for whatever influence they can bring to bear on the major projects.

In Vancouver, for example, the two most dramatic waterfront redevelopment projects have both been driven, at least initially, by public-sector corporations established by senior governments. The mixed-use Granville Island revitalization project was spearheaded by the federal government through its Canada Mortgage and Housing Corporation. It has transformed forty acres of derelict industrial land into a vibrant industrial area including a major market, theatres, restaurants, and shops, and this has become a major tourist attraction in its own right. Yet the input of the Vancouver planning department has been virtually non-existent, inasmuch as the federal government chose to invoke its constitutional prerogative and treat the site as a federal enclave, immune from municipal jurisdiction.

Even more ambitious is the planned redevelopment of the north shore of False Creek in Vancouver, a project initially launched by B.C. Place Ltd., in this case a provincial Crown corporation. Among other things, the corporation has assembled 224 acres of strategic urban land, including the site of Expo '86 as well as the $125 million B.C. Place Stadium. More recently, in mid-1988, the provincial government auctioned off the site as a part of Premier Vander Zalm's privatization drive. The winning consortium, headed by Hong Kong billionaire Li Ka-Shing, has an extraordinarily ambitious plan that will quite literally reshape the Vancouver waterfront and a goodly portion of its inner city as well. The plan (now known as Pacific Place) contemplates over three million square feet of office space, 10,000 new housing units, and over forty acres of park space. In all, the project will involve over $2 billion in direct capital expenditure and can be expected to generate roughly 28,000 person-years of employment and $6 billion in further spin-off investment. The full build-out of the project will require at least fifteen years to complete, and, at least in its early stages, it can be expected to engender some vitriolic debates with Vancouver's planning department, as the developer's commercial imperatives for profit maximization inevitably collide with the department's traditional concerns regarding excessive densities, obstructed view planes, traffic problems, and the like. As always, however, the crucial determinant will be the level of support the planning department receives from its political masters on city council.

When one examines both the department's historical track record in this regard and the current ideological composition of council, one would be hard-pressed to be overly sanguine about the department's potential influence. Once again, the key force shaping the urban environment will *not* be the planning department but a development corporation, in this case a private one.

In Toronto, the redevelopment of ninety-two acres of formerly derelict industrial waterfront land is being undertaken by the Harbourfront Corporation, a federal Crown corporation. The Harbourfront project began moving in earnest around 1976 and today represents well over $300 million in combined public- and private-sector investment in housing, shops, theatres, and office space. The Harbourfront Corporation has been a major force in a complete transformation of the Toronto waterfront, and yet it, too, until very recently, has operated virtually completely independent from the city's planning department and machinery.

As it happens, however, in this case the Harbourfront Corporation's exclusionary strategy has recently backfired rather spectacularly. Late in 1987, a public outcry began building against the Corporation, fuelled largely by the view that it had sacrificed "good planning principles" and "the public interest" on the altar of excessive and poorly designed private development. So vociferous did the outcry become that in March of 1988 the Prime Minister appointed a Royal Commission to investigate the planning and jurisdictional issues involving Toronto's waterfront. The Prime Minister named David Crombie, former cabinet minister and also a popular former mayor of Toronto, to head the Commission. Regardless of its outcome, however, one thing is already abundantly clear: once again the key planning and development decisions have been taken by a public, *senior* government development corporation, with precious little input from the local planning department. Indeed, Harbourfront represents (at least so far) one of the more dramatic examples of the evisceration of the power of the local planning apparatus by a public development corporation completely external to the entire local government system.

In Halifax, the provincial government has created the Halifax Waterfront Development Corporation, which has undertaken a $185 million, mixed-use development on twenty acres of publicly assembled waterfront land. Once again, however, although the WDC's board of directors initially included federal as well as provincial representatives, the WDC's activities were pursued in virtually complete isolation from the city government and its planning department. Among other things, this cost the project an important opportunity to develop a local political and popular constituency, and slowed its progress considerably.

In both Montreal and Quebec, the federal government has also established public development corporations to redevelop major under-utilized waterfront sites (130 and 72 acres respectively). To its credit, this time the federal government has, in both cases, included local government representatives on the corporations' boards of directors, although financial and therefore operational control will effectively continue to reside with the federal government. Nonetheless, the active involvement of local government during the planning phases is likely to increase the level of local political and public "ownership" and acceptance of the eventual development programs.[5]

Waterfront projects have also been pursued in Saint John, New Brunswick (the Market Square project), and Charlottetown, Prince Edward Island (Harbourside). It is interesting to note that, while the initial political and financial impetus for both projects came, as usual, from senior governments, local governments were active decision-making and financial participants.

Thus the reclamation and rejuvenation of the urban waterfront has proven to be one critical vehicle for downtown revitalization across the country. But it has not been the only one. Unquestionably the most conceptually ambitious of the recent Canadian urban revitalization efforts has been Winnipeg's Core Area Initiative (Kiernan, 1986, 1987). The Core Area Initiative is a tri-governmental partnership which, over its first five-year term, used its $96 million core budget to generate nearly three-quarters of a billion dollars worth of public- and private-sector investments in the physical, economic, and social revitalization of Winnipeg's downtown and ten square-mile inner city. The breadth and scope of the CAI's activities is without precedent in either North America or Europe: over 1,000 projects have been implemented in policy areas including health, social services, employment and training, housing, neighbourhood improvement, small business, industrial development, heritage preservation, and joint-venture commercial development. One relatively minor dimension of the CAI has been the creation of a spin-off, tri-governmental public corporation: the North Portage Development Corporation, which is currently constructing a $300 million, mixed-use development on ten acres of prime, publicly assembled downtown land.

Over the next several decades, the next generation of major Canadian downtown revitalization challenges will likely occur on hundreds of acres of strategically located but obsolescent railway lands. Technological and economic factors are currently encouraging the national railway companies to relocate substantial portions of their operations to the urban periphery, thereby creating tremendous development opportunities on their former downtown sites. In Toronto, for example, the redevelopment of 190 acres of prime downtown railway land is deservedly *the* major planning issue in town. The eventual development of the full $2 billion plan would essentially recreate another downtown Toronto and would rival Vancouver's B.C. Place as the largest downtown redevelopment project in North America. Similar although more modestly scaled opportunities for downtown rail relocation and redevelopment are under active discussion in Regina, Edmonton, and Windsor.

In Winnipeg, work has already begun on the redevelopment of eighty acres of obsolescent downtown rail lands at the junction of the city's two rivers. This multimillion-dollar, mixed-use redevelopment is being spearheaded by a tri-governmental development corporation, the second such spin-off from Winnipeg's Core Area Initiative.[6] All of them will require excruciatingly difficult and complex negotiations among the railways, several levels of government, and, subsequently, other private development interests. But whether its particular focus is on the urban waterfront, obsolete rail land, or elsewhere, the importance of downtown development as an urban planning issue can only increase in the foreseeable future.

There is at present an inexorable shift in the centre of gravity of Canadian urban development away from suburbia and toward downtown. The causes of this phenomenon are many and complex, but they include structural economic and demographic changes, shifting consumer preferences, and a growing inclination on the part of various levels of government to take the lead in redeveloping their increasingly strategic downtown land positions (Kiernan and Artibise, 1988). Moreover, this shift from suburbia to downtown is likely to intensify as we continue our societal "mega-shift" from an economy predicated on natural resources and manufacturing to one based on knowledge, information, and services (Shannon and Cohen, 1985). These commercial activities tend to concentrate in the central city rather than in the suburbs, and they also tend to have a parallel and magnetic effect that draws housing and service industry demand along in their wake.

All of this suggests that not only was downtown development the number-one planning issue in Canada for the 1980s, but it is likely to remain so into the 1990s and perhaps even beyond.

Citizen Participation and Neighbourhood Renewal

While downtown redevelopment is unquestionably the primary contemporary issue in Canadian urban planning, it is by no means the only one. Of the others, perhaps the most important and pervasive are the interrelated issues of neighbourhood revitalization and citizen participation. While neither of these issues remain as prominent today as they both were in the mid-1970s, both have established themselves as virtually permanent items on the contemporary urban planning agenda.

The two issues emerged in tandem in the late 1960s. As we have seen, a substantial public backlash arose at that time in response to the "bulldozer approach" to urban renewal that had previously prevailed. Public objections centred on the substantive issue of the physical insensitivity and dislocation inherent in the new projects and on the procedural issue of the general lack of consultation with the residents directly affected by the schemes. As a result of both the cogency and the vociferousness of the public criticisms, the federal government completely rethought its entire approach, essentially abandoning the old-style urban renewal and replacing it with a series of programs designed to rehabilitate rather than demolish existing neighbourhoods wherever possible. As well, this shift in thinking effectively empowered residents to have a significant role in the planning of projects affecting them. A number of seminal "citizen victories," such as those in Toronto halting an urban renewal scheme in Trefann Court in the late sixties and the Spadina expressway in the early seventies, helped to create a virtual revolution in both the substance and the procedures of planning.[7] Planning efforts became increasingly small in scale, neighbourhood preservationist in substance, and participatory in style.

The zenith of the intertwined neighbourhood preservation and citizen participation movements in Canada was probably reached somewhere around 1978, when the federal government ended its nation-wide Neighbourhood Improvement Program. Since then, both issues have declined in relative importance. The absence of an adequately funded national program has hampered neighbourhood revitalization efforts in most cities,[8] and the increasingly pro-development climate engendered by the recession has, somewhat unnecessarily, robbed the citizen participation movement of much of its coherence and power. Nonetheless, both movements deserve mention here because they have permanently altered the way in which planning is done in this country, in matters of both substantive concern and procedural style. If they are not today the dominant issues they once were, neighbourhood revitalization and citizen participation have nonetheless firmly established themselves as fundamental factors that must at least be reckoned with in nearly every Canadian city. And from the standpoint of the local planning systems, they have the further redeeming feature that at least they do tend to involve the city planning departments in a very central and fundamental way.

Heritage Conservation

If the citizen participation and neighbourhood renewal movements are currently in a state of relative decline themselves, they have nonetheless given birth at least indirectly to a third and what is at present a far more potent planning issue: heritage building preservation. A logical intellectual and political outgrowth of the neighbourhood renewal and citizen participation struggles of the 1970s, heritage conservation surfaced as a major issue in virtually every Canadian city during the 1980s. And, while the level of popular and political support for the preservation of historic buildings varies considerably from city to city, as a general rule it has increased markedly over the past several years (Jamieson, 1984).

Initially, private owners and developers had tended to view the preservation and recycling of heritage buildings as both intrinsically uneconomic and an unconscionable confiscation of their private property rights by government. Municipal and provincial attempts to preclude private owners from demolishing their buildings through prohibitive legislation were vigorously resisted, and indeed were frequently half-hearted in the first place because of the fundamental governmental ambivalence we have already observed about the legitimacy of state interference with private property rights.

By the early 1980s, however, two emergent trends had begun to converge and add extra impetus to the heritage preservation movement. Arguably the more important of the two was the belated realization on the part of private owners and developers that, at least in certain sub-markets, the recycling of architecturally meritorious buildings could be exceptionally profitable. In large part this was due to dramatically altered consumer tastes, which had begun to place a much higher premium on both the architectural charm of older buildings and their generally greater proximity to the downtown. At the same time, municipal governments were becoming increasingly sophisticated and balanced in their own approaches, and began to supplement their earlier reliance on purely negative prohibitive legislation with positive financial incentives, ranging from property tax abatements to direct grants. One of the most impressive examples of the effectiveness of this latter approach can be seen in Winnipeg's Historic Warehouse Area, where a combination of grants from the Core Area Initiative and property tax incentives from local government has helped to stimulate the recycling of some twenty-five privately owned heritage buildings. Other successful Canadian heritage districts have involved varying mixes of public- and private-sector initiative: Vancouver's Gastown, Saint John's Market Square, Toronto's St. Lawrence Historic District, Old Quebec, and Old Montreal.[9]

For Canadian planners, the heritage preservation movement has represented both challenge and opportunity. The opportunity derives from the fact that heritage planners have generally found themselves right in the thick of whatever efforts their political masters happen to be making to encourage heritage conservation in their respective cities. As we have seen, planners have by no means always been privileged to play such a central role in urban policy-making or implementation. The challenge associated with this opportunity has been that, until recently, planners have often found themselves in the unenviable position of being left on the ramparts of the heritage preservation battle totally unarmed: caught between an unwilling and resentful building owner on the one hand and a local government that has failed to equip him/her with either the carrots or the sticks necessary to get the job done. Happily for Canadian planners, however, such situations are becoming increasingly rare, and the heritage conservation issue is one of the few from which they can derive both satisfaction and credibility.

Future Directions for Canadian Urban Planning

As we have seen, the present contours of the Canadian urban planning system have been largely defined by historical, ideological, economic, and structural imperatives, the net effect of which has been to narrow and circumscribe its purview. Indeed, one could go further and argue that this has been occurring at a time when Canadian local governments and their planning departments ought to be moving in precisely the *opposite* direction, becoming *more* comprehensive and more aggressively involved in centrally co-ordinated strategic planning and implementation. And, while it is difficult to predict the future of Canadian urban planning with much certitude, what *is* clear is that a number of emerging but compelling trends will powerfully affect it. To the extent that planning departments can anticipate and adapt to those trends, they could finally play the central and pivotally powerful role in local government that has heretofore escaped virtually all of them. If they do not, however, their current drift toward a reactive and peripheral role will only accelerate. In short, the new trends have the capacity either to invigorate contemporary Canadian planning or to marginalize it entirely. In our view, the most critical of these emerging new trends are the following:

- an increase in the importance of the quasi-autonomous development corporation as a dominant instrument of urban public policy;
- an increased reliance on public/private-sector partnerships to undertake major urban development projects;
- the dramatically increased importance of intergovernmental affairs in urban planning and development; and
- a growing public and political acceptance of more aggressive and comprehensive approaches to urban problem-solving.

Public development corporations have played a dominant role in Canadian cities such as Toronto and Vancouver for much of the past decade, and their importance will undoubtedly continue to grow across the country. Indeed, over the past few years alone, new public development corporations have been established in downtown areas in Montreal, Quebec City, Edmonton, Winnipeg, Saint John, and Charlottetown. In most cases, these corporations have been equipped with a substantial and strategic land base, a multimillion-dollar capital budget, or both. They have already wrought dramatic and, for the most part, positive physical and economic changes in the fabric of our cities. The corporations' implications for local governments' urban planning functions, however, are much more ominous. Perhaps ironically, the one hope for revitalizing the planning departments may rest with what is at present only an incipient phenomenon – a backlash against the new development corporations. In cities such as Toronto, for example, the Harbourfront Corporation is coming under increasing criticism as something of a public-sector Frankenstein, not perceptibly more sensitive to public policy concerns than the avaricious private developers it was originally designed to supersede.[10] As we have already observed, this public criticism has recently culminated with the virtually unprecedented measure of the establishment of a Royal Commission to investigate the development of Toronto's waterfront.[11] Similar rumblings can be heard in criticism of Winnipeg's $76 million North Portage Development Corporation. Should these types of concerns grow strong enough, municipal councils and even senior governments may decide that the arm's-length corporations aren't the answer after all, and thus will begin searching for yet another vehicle, one more directly amenable to local government control. Should this happen, the day may finally dawn when local planning departments find themselves functionally integrated with the city's development capability (and budgets) in a new "mega-department" at the centre of the city's strategic planning function. At present, however, this prospect admittedly seems somewhat remote.

The second major urban development trend is a corollary of the first: the increased use of public/private-sector development partnerships. Invariably, the new arm's-length corporations rely on private developers to finance and build many components of the new complexes, usually through some form of joint venture with the public corporation. Each side brings some unique gifts to the marriage. Government brings: a large chequebook; the unique legal capacity to undertake large land assemblies, against landowners' wishes if necessary; the ability to supply subsidized financing, tax incentives, training programs, and other financial inducements; the capacity to contribute major public facilities such as subway links, schools, office space, or museums to the project; and the ability to set an authoritative overall planning context and thereby reassure all private investors that their projects will be fitted into an overall pattern that makes sense and protects their investments. For the investors' part, the private developer contributes substantial additional capital (and financial expertise) and a capacity to construct, market, and manage the project that is on the whole superior to that of a public agency.

The question for planners is again: where do *they* fit into this litany of contributions? As we have seen, the "public" half of these new public/private partnerships is almost invariably handled by the development corporation; indeed, that was precisely their *raison d'être* from the beginning. The training and experience of most planners, however, simply does not equip them with the knowledge, contacts, or credibility to contribute meaningfully to the sophisticated financial negotiations that are the essence of the new partnerships. Planners unquestionably do have a role to play here, but once again it tends to be a rather reactive, circumscribed, and marginal one. Rarely do municipal councils accord much weight to the views of their own planning departments when considering major downtown redevelopment projects – the truly critical calculus is invariably an economic and political one, and planners are generally seen to have little if anything to contribute on either score. Thus, the rise of public/private-sector development partnerships has the distinct potential of driving a second nail into the coffin of Canada's traditional planning departments. Once again, the only way out is for local governments to invigorate their planning departments by marrying them more closely to the city's actual development, expenditure, and strategic planning functions, rather than condemning them to the periphery.

The third major trend is the dramatically increased emphasis that will be placed in future on the *intergovernmental* dimension of urban planning and development. The scope, complexity, and above all the costs of the new urban mega-projects will increasingly be beyond the capacity of any single level of government acting unilaterally. In the past, individual governments *were* able to finance major projects such as Harbourfront (federally) and B.C. Place (provincially), but those initiatives were launched in the heady and bygone days of balanced budgets. Since that time, the financial circumstances of each level of government have deteriorated exponentially. In 1974, for example, the three levels of government had a combined surplus of $2.8 billion. By 1984, this surplus had been transformed into a combined annual deficit of $26.7 billion. Expressed as a percentage of GNP, the combined deficits of all levels of government have nearly tripled in only nine years, from 2.4 per cent of GNP in 1975 to 6.3 per cent in 1984.[12] This evidence strongly suggests that the capacity of any single level of government to finance and undertake further major urban redevelopment projects by itself is severely constrained. Instead, in future we can anticipate more and more creative intergovernmental partnerships, whereby governments pool their efforts to maximize the impact and effectiveness of their increasingly scarce resources through centrally planned and co-ordinated interventions.

Perhaps the most dramatic and ambitious recent illustration of the potential of such intergovernmental urban partnerships has been provided by Winnipeg's Core Area Initiative, which was renewed in late 1986 for a second five-year, $100 million term. The Core Area Initiative is a particularly instructive example from the standpoint of Canadian local governments. Through the skilful exploitation of the initial CAI and its sister agreements, the city of Winnipeg was able to parlay a municipal investment of some $54 million into more than three-quarters of a *billion* dollars worth of public- and private-sector investment in the economic, physical, and social rejuvenation of Winnipeg's disadvantaged inner city (Kiernan, 1987). As other financially strained Canadian cities contemplate Winnipeg's success in multiplying its investment by a factor of nearly fourteen times, and in expanding its sphere of policy and program influence drastically, pressure for other, similar intergovernmental agreements is inevitable. Indeed, given the programmatic and political success of the Core Area Initiative, it is somewhat perplexing that other Canadian cities seem disinclined to follow Winnipeg's lead. Mayors and business and community leaders in other urban centres would be well advised to articulate a set of municipal priorities and then enter into serious discussions with senior governments, with a view to negotiating mutually beneficial programmatic and financial partnerships along the general lines of the Core Area Initiative.

Another factor militates in the direction of further intergovernmental urban interventions: an embryonic but discernible renaissance of interest in urban policy and development on the part of the federal government. Following the demise of the Ministry of State for Urban Affairs in the late seventies, federal involvement in urban Canada was dramatically reduced, and confined itself either to isolated mega-projects such as Harbourfront or else to the "normal" but largely unco-ordinated activities of those federal departments that almost inadvertently happen to be spending billions of dollars in Canadian cities. Today, however, there are indications that all this may be about to change as the federal government begins to reconceptualize its approach to regional development in a way that gives greater emphasis to the role of urban areas as key engines of economic development (Kiernan and Artibise, 1988). Buoyed by the success of the Winnipeg Core Area Initiative, federal officials are beginning to view intergovernmental urban partnerships as a new and promising way of reconciling their regional economic development objectives with the need to streamline expenditures by improving the co-ordination and focusing of federal program activity.[13]

This trend toward greater intergovernmental co-operation could represent either a problem or an opportunity for urban planning. Local governments must first adapt to the new intergovernmental reality, consciously restructuring themselves to enhance their capability to negotiate with senior governments. For most cities, this will demand a significant upgrading in their capacity to plan and act strategically – to co-ordinate better horizontally among specialized line departments, and to interact vertically with senior governments in a more coherent and sophisticated way. To the extent that urban planning departments are able (and allowed) to contribute to this new local government capability, they will prosper and become reinvigorated. To the extent that they are not, they are likely to be marginalized even further.

The fourth and last of the new trends is at present less pronounced than the other three, but in some ways it has even greater potential in the long run to affect the way urban planning is done in Canada. We have argued earlier that, for a variety of historical, ideological, and organizational reasons, Canadian urban planning has tended on the whole to be both reactive and narrowly preoccupied with physical and land-use issues. The functional and political success of projects like Winnipeg's Core Area Initiative may just begin to change all that, and to restore the lost nexus between urban planning and the broader concerns about poverty and social justice that sustained the Canadian profession at its inception seventy years ago.

Nearly 40 per cent of the CAI's budget is devoted in one way or another to disparity alleviation, through support for health, education, employment and training, housing, and social service opportunities for the disadvantaged. The surprisingly broadly based public and political support for the CAI[14] suggests that it may in future be not only desirable but actually *possible* to attack urban problems in a comprehensive, multifaceted, and co-ordinated fashion (Kiernan, 1987). This possibility, too, holds both promise and challenge for the Canadian and urban planning system. Should it prove able to accept and to promote this more holistic approach, the planning system might yet fulfil its potential and become the most central and strategically important of all local government functions. If, however, it cannot meet the challenges that this and the other emerging trends will surely pose, Canadian urban planning will be doomed to a perpetual place at the periphery.

We have argued throughout this chapter that many of the limitations of contemporary urban planning in Canada are derivative of its situation within the broader local government system. It follows, therefore, that for the most part the capacity to cure those deficiencies will also be external to the planning system itself. Canadian city governments generally shape their planning departments in their own image; in that sense they get the sort of urban planning they deserve. If the planning system is to transcend its current limitations and meet the challenges a changing environment will surely set for it, it will clearly *not* be able to do so purely on its own. This will require fundamental changes, not only within the professional departments, but, far more importantly, within local government itself. It will require a determination by both local and provincial politicians, and ultimately by their electorates, that the time has come for city governments to become participants in urban policy rather than spectators. Until and unless that determination is made on a widespread and sustained basis, however, the future of the urban planning function in Canadian local government will remain anything but bright.

NOTES

The writer acknowledges with gratitude the exceptional research assistance of Mr. Brent Rosnoski. He is also grateful to those many Canadian planning officials who gave generously of their time for personal and telephone interviews.

1. See FCM Task Force on Municipal Infrastructure, *Municipal Infrastructure in Canada: Physical Condition and Funding Adequacy,* January, 1985.
2. One of the very few practical examples of an exception to this generalization was the work and approach of Norman Krumholtz and his colleagues in the United States. See Krumholtz (1978, 1982).
3. It has also spawned a rich literature, particularly in Ontario, where the appointed Municipal Board has played an especially dominant role in municipal planning. See, for example, L. Feldman and K. Graham, *Bargaining for Cities: Municipalities and Inter-Governmental Relations* (Toronto: Institute for Research on Public Policy, 1979); Ontario Economic Council, *Subject To Approval* (1973); J. Bossons, *Reforming Planning in Ontario: Strengthening the Municipal Role* (Toronto: Ontario Economic Council, 1978); and K. Jaffary and S. Makuch, *Local Decision-Making and Administration* (Royal Commission on Metropolitan Toronto, 1977).
4. See, for example, in the context of Winnipeg, Institute of Urban Studies, *Core Area Report: A Reassessment of Conditions in the Inner City* (1979).
5. Besides the consistent stress here on the virtues of local consultation on planning and development issues, it must also be admitted that this process *can* be overdone and can become instead a recipe for paralysis. This is arguably what has occurred in Montreal, where after literally years of consultation with local interest groups, the chairman of the blue-ribbon committee conducting the consultations could say only "we have, however, refrained from proposing a final and definitive plan for the Old Port . . . nor have we suggested a target date for the completion of the work envisaged." (Old Port of Montreal, *Public Consultation: Final Report* (Ottawa, 1987). Small wonder that the Montreal Vieux Port project has yet to proceed beyond the drawing board!
6. See Forks Renewal Corporation, *Phase 1 Concept and Financial Plan,* Winnipeg, November, 1987.
7. There exists a small but valuable literature by participant/observers of the new, participatory urban planning of the early 1970s. Illustrative are: Graham Fraser, *Fighting Back: Urban Renewal in Trefann Court* (Toronto: Samuel-Stevens, 1972); James Lorimer, *A Citizen's Guide to City Politics* (Toronto: James Lewis and Samuel, 1972); and John Sewell, *Up Against City Hall* (Toronto: James Lewis and Samuel, 1972). For a more recent and perhaps dispassionate perspective on the accomplishments of the citizen participation "revolution" in Toronto, see Lewinberg (1986).
8. Three notable exceptions are Montreal, Quebec City, and Winnipeg, which have each rehabilitated over 5,000 housing units since the demise of the Neighbourhood Improvement Program by creating alternative intergovernmental programs tailored to local needs.
9. This is by no means to imply that heritage conservation has now become

a universally accepted norm. It frequently remains a contentious issue, particularly in the context of large-scale redevelopment. One current example is a major redevelopment project Cadillac Fairview Corporation is undertaking in downtown Victoria. The degree to which existing heritage buildings will be integrated into the project remains a source of great controversy.

10. In fairness to Harbourfront, however, fiscal pressures from its parent (federal) government are requiring an approach that is increasingly driven by the imperatives of the bottom line. This significantly diminishes the extent to which Harbourfront can accommodate public policy objectives where these collide with commercial considerations.

11. For the Royal Commission's terms of reference, consult Office of the Prime Minister, "Terms of Reference Establishing a Royal Commission to Inquire into the Use of Federal Lands in the Toronto Waterfront Area," Ottawa, March 30, 1988.

12. Statistics Canada, National Income and Expenditure Accounts, cited in Department of Finance, *The Fiscal Plan*, February, 1986, pp. 131-32.

13. This is an argument long recognized by academic commentators (Jacobs, 1984; Savoie, 1986) and one that belatedly seems to be gaining currency (albeit gradually) with senior federal officials, particularly in the Department of Regional Industrial Expansion, the now defunct federal department that originally took the lead on the Winnipeg Core Area Initiative project, and with the Economic Council of Canada (see Kiernan and Artibise, 1988).

14. There are two quantitative indices of the pervasiveness of public support for the Core Area Initiative. One was a Gallup-sized survey of 1,000 Winnipeg households taken in 1984, the project's third year. That survey, whose respondents were divided evenly between the suburbs and inner city, revealed an 82 per cent approval rating for the project. (*Public Attitudes and Perceptions Concerning Core Area Redevelopment*, Results Group, Winnipeg, March, 1984, pp. 7, 12.) The second indication came near the end of the project's first phase, in September, 1985. A series of public hearings attracted support from over 150 organizations, ranging in mandate and orientation from the Chamber of Commerce to the Indian-Métis Friendship Centre.

REFERENCES

Altshuler, Alan (1965). *The City Planning Process*. Ithaca, N.Y.: Cornell University Press.

Armstrong, II.A. (1986). "Thomas Adams and the Commission of Conservation," in L.O. Gertler (ed.), *Planning the Canadian Environment*. Montreal: Harvest House.

Baum, H.A. (1980). "The Uncertain Consciousness of Planners and the Professional Enterprise," *Plan Canada*, 20, 1 (March): 39-52.

British Columbia Place Ltd. (1985). *Annual Report*

British Columbia Place Ltd. (1985). *B.C. Place: False Creek Development Phase II: North Park*.

Bryant, R.W. (1972). *Land: Private Property, Public Control*. Montreal: Harvest House.

Central Mortgage and Housing Corporation (1979). *Evaluation of the Neighbourhood Improvement Program* (Main Report).

Commission of Conservation (1912). *Annual Report of the Commission of Conservation.*

Davidoff, P. (1975). "Working Towards Redistributive Justice," *Journal of Planners*, 41: 317-19.

— (1965). "Advocacy and Pluralism in Planning," *Journal of American Institute Planners*, 31: 341-62.

Denhez, M. (1975). *Heritage Fights Back.* Toronto: Fitzhenry and Whiteside.

— (1981). "What Price Heritage?" *Plan Canada*, 21, 1: 5-14.

— (1984). "Planning and Heritage Planning: A Risky Distinction," *Plan Canada*, 23, 4: 134-35.

Edmonton, City of (1985). *Partners in Pride.* City of Edmonton Planning and Building Department.

Erber, E. (ed.) (1970). *Urban Planning in Transition.* New York: Grossman.

Fainstein, N., and S. Fainstein (1971). "City Planning and Political Values," *Urban Affairs Quarterly*, 6 (March): 341-62.

Forester, J. (1982). "Planning in the Face of Power," *Journal of the American Planning Association*, 48: 67-80.

Fraser, G. (1972). *Fighting Back: Urban Renewal in Trefann Court.* Toronto: Samuel-Stevens.

Gerecke, K. (1977). "The History of Canadian City Planning," in J. Lorimer (ed.),*The Second City Book.* Toronto: James Lorimer and Co.

Gertler, L., and R. Crowley (1977). *Changing Canadian Cities: The Next 25 Years.* Toronto: McClelland and Stewart.

Gunton, T.I. (1984). "The Role of the Professional Planner," *Canadian Public Administration*, 27, 3 (Fall): 399-418.

Higgins, D.J. (1977). *Urban Canada: Its Government and Politics.* Toronto: Macmillan.

Hodge, G. (1986). *Planning Canadian Communities.* Toronto: Methuen Publications.

Hodge, G., and G. Spragge (1978). "Planning in the 1930's: Similar Roots, Separate Routes," *Plan Canada*, 18, 3-4 (September-December): 151-53.

Jacobs, J. (1984). *Cities and the Wealth of Nations: Principles of Economic Life.* New York: Random House.

Jamieson, W. (1984). "Conservation as an Approach to Urban Renewal," *Plan Canada*, 24, 2: 44-45.

Kaufman, J. (1979). "The Planner as Interventionist in Public Policy Issues," in R. Burchel and G. Sternlieb (eds.), *Planning Theory in the 1980's.* New Brunswick, N.J.: Rutgers University, Centre for Urban Policy Research.

Kehoe, D., *et al.* (1976). *Public Land Ownership: Frameworks for Evaluation.* Toronto: D.C. Heath.

Kiernan, M.J., and A.F.J. Artibise (1988). *Canadian Regional Development: The Urban Dimension.* Ottawa: Economic Council of Canada.

Kiernan, M.J. (1987). "Innovation, Urban Revitalization, and the Intergovernmental Dimension," *Plan Canada* (March).

— (1986). "New Directions for Canadian Urban Policy: Winnipeg's Core Area Initiative," *Cities*, 3, 4 (November): 313-21.

— (1985). "Co-ordination for the City Core," *Policy Options*, 6, 7 (September): 23-27.

— (1983). "The Politics of Quiescence: the 'Reform' Experience in Winnipeg," in W. Magnusson and A. Sancton (eds.), *City Politics in Canada.* Toronto: University of Toronto Press.

— (1982a). "Ideology and the Precarious Future of the Canadian Planning Profession," *Plan Canada*, 22, 1 (March): 14-22.

— (1982b). "The Fallacy of Planning Law Reform," *Urban Law and Policy*, 5: 173-215.

Klosterman, R. (1978). "Foundations for Normative Planning," *Journal of the American Institute of Planners*, 44: 37-45.

Krumholz, N. (1982). "A Retrospective View of Equity Planning," *Journal of the American Institute of Planners*, 48: 163-78.

— (1975). "The Cleveland Policy Planning Report," *Journal of the American Institute of Planners*, 41, 5: 184-304.

Lewinberg, F. (1986). "Neighbourhood Planning: The Reform Years in Toronto," *Plan Canada*, 26, 2 (April): 40-45.

Lithwick, N.H. (1970). *Urban Canada: Problems and Prospects*. Ottawa: CMHC.

Lyon, D., and L. Newman (1986).*The Neighbourhood Improvement Program, 1973-83: A National Review*. Winnipeg: Institute of Urban Studies.

McAuslan, P. (1984). *The Ideologies of Planning Law*. Oxford: Pergamon Press.

Page, J., and R. Lang (1977). *Canadian Planners in Profile*. Toronto: Faculty of Environmental Studies, York University.

Perks, W., and I. Robinson (1979). *Urban and Regional Planning in a Federal State: the Canadian Experience*. New York: McGraw-Hill.

Plunkett, T.J. (1985). "The Need for Local Parties," *Policy Options*, 6, 7 (September): 26-28.

— and G.M. Betts (1978). *The Management of Canadian Urban Government*. Kingston: Queen's University, Institute for Local Government.

— (1971). *The Financial Structure and Decisionmaking Process of Canadian Municipal Government*. Ottawa: Central Mortgage and Housing Corporation.

Qadeer, M. (1977). "The Scope of Social Planning in Urban Planning," *Plan Canada*, 12, 2 (June): 86-96.

Rodgers, I.M. (1976). *Canadian Law of Planning and Zoning*. Toronto: The Carswell Company Ltd.

Savoie, D.J. (1981). *Regional Economic Development: Canada's Search for Solutions*. Toronto: University of Toronto Press.

Scott, A.J., and S. Roweis (1977). "Urban Planning in Theory and Practice: A Re-Appraisal," *Environment and Planning* B: 1097-1119.

Shannon, K., and D. Cohen (1985). *The Next Canadian Economy*. Montreal: Eden Press.

Simmie, J. (1974). *Citizens in Conflict*. London: Hutchinson.

Spragge, G. (1975). "Canadian Planners' Goals: Deep Roots and Fuzzy Thinking," *Canadian Public Administration*, 18: 216-35.

Thompson, W (1985). "The Interrelationship between Heritage Conservation and City Planning," *Plan Canada*, 25, 1: 10-20.

Vancouver, City of (1986). Annual Review, 1985/86. City of Vancouver Planning Department.

Winnipeg Core Area Initiative (1986). Proposed Canada-Manitoba-Winnipeg Tripartite Agreement 1986-1991.

4   Barbara Wake Carroll

Housing

Introduction

Over 75 per cent of Canadians live in urban centres. Housing policy and housing problems, then, are largely urban phenomena. Housing is one of the more important urban policy areas because it is an essential good, because it absorbs scarce resources at all levels of government, and because its visibility and durability mean that the quality and appearance of the housing stock shape our current and future urban environments.

In 1968 the Task Force on Housing and Urban Development stated that "Every Canadian should be entitled to clean, warm shelter as a matter of basic human right" (1969: 22). Over the period 1969 to 1980, 28 per cent of all houses built in Canada were built with a federal government subsidy and up to 70 per cent of those purchased in any one year had federal government mortgage insurance (CMHC, 1973-88). By 1984 governments were spending nearly $3 billion per year in direct subsidies, plus an estimated $6.5 billion in annual tax expenditures devoted to housing (Carroll, 1989b; Lithwick, 1985). Yet it is clear that there are still housing problems in Canada.

This chapter focuses on trends in housing policy since 1945 with an emphasis on temporal patterns and interprovincial similarities and variations, and their causes. It looks at the conflict among levels of government and other competing interests over the form and level of intervention in the housing market, a conflict that arises from the complexity of the housing market and the nature of housing as both a public and private good. The analysis begins with a discussion of the nature of housing and housing markets and of government intervention in these markets. This is followed by an analysis of Canadian housing policy from 1945 to the present at both the federal and provincial levels. The final section considers the main housing problems currently facing our urban centres and cautiously predicts what further actions might be expected.

Housing Markets and Forms of Intervention

The characteristics of housing important to understanding housing policy are the complexity of housing markets, the durability and immobility of the housing stock, and the mixed public/private nature of housing as a good. Bourne (1981: 14-16) uses the expression "bundle of services" as a way to conceptualize housing as a good. It is an economic good, both as a source of personal investment to individual homeowners and in terms of its importance to the economy. It is a physical good in terms of providing shelter and in its appearance, which makes up a large portion of the urban environment. It is also a "social" good, providing status and satisfaction to individuals – it is a commonplace to describe people in terms of where they live – and establishing the setting within which much of the social interaction among people takes place.

At the same time, the housing market is subject to a number of economic, social, and demographic influences on both the demand and supply sides that are highly interdependent and not well understood (Bourne, 1981: 69-168). The demand for housing is dependent on demographic factors such as the age of the population, the number and size of households, and their ability to purchase or rent housing. Houses are also durable, nonadaptive, and immobile. New additions to the stock of existing housing represent a very small proportion of the total market. The housing stock, therefore, adjusts very slowly to changes in demand or taste.

Most of the housing in Canada is delivered through the private market, which is based on economic demand. This market for housing is a highly segmented series of linked and interdependent sub-markets differentiated by geographic area, by age, by house type, by size, and by type of tenure. Changes in demand within these sub-markets can be met by only incremental additions of new housing. But the number of new housing units provided is affected less by the individual demand for units than by overall economic conditions, especially the level of interest rates and the availability of land.[1] At the same time, not only does it take a considerable period of time to build the units, but housing requires expensive and extensive infrastructure services in the form of transportation systems, schools, sewer and water services, and recreational services. The result is a significant lag between shifts in demand and the ability of the market to respond, and corresponding cyclical swings in availability and price.

Each of the economic, social, and physical characteristics of housing has led to some form of market intervention. Intervention has been justified as part of economic policies designed to create employment, to compensate for economic cycles, and to protect financial investment in the residential mortgage market. Policy initiatives also have been directed, as part of social welfare policies, to meet the needs of those who cannot compete in the private market and those who have special needs the market does not meet. Thus, while most housing demand is met through the private market, some is also provided through the public sector on the basis of social need rather than economic demand. Finally, planning policies and housing standards regulations, which greatly affect the physical location and design of houses, have been used to compensate for spillovers and to ensure minimum health and safety standards.

To some extent, types of policy coincide with the jurisdictional responsibilities of the levels of government in Canada. The federal government has constitutional responsibility for monetary and fiscal policy, and the provinces for property and social welfare, while municipalities have been delegated responsibility for many of the physical aspects of property. As with most policy areas in Canada, however, the actual divisions are not so clear-cut, particularly when we consider that the ultimate outcome of these policies is the single housing unit – your home. For example, policies intended to protect mortgage investment affect the type of physical product produced, and by stipulating mortgage conditions these policies also determine the income level necessary to purchase a house. Similarly, a municipal planning decision, which allows, for example, only the building of single detached houses on large lots, affects the level of investment in and the social make-up of that community, while a decision to regulate housing quality leads to higher levels of market concentration and in some cases prices (Carroll, 1988). Perhaps ironically, while housing forms the major physical and financial component of our urban areas, municipal governments have played only a minor, primarily reactive role in the development and implementation of housing policy.

The policy instruments used are extensive and varied. Land use, building standards, price levels, the family structure of occupants, and, indirectly, the allowable income levels of occupants are all regulated. Examples of this latter type of regulation include those limiting the percentage of income that can be spent to purchase housing and programs that tie development subsidies to the rents charged and the income of the tenants. There have been grants, subsidies, and forgivable and nonforgivable loans at varying levels of market and non-market interest rates; variations in the sales, income, and property tax treatment; and direct involvement by all levels of government, ranging from the owning and building of housing through the provision of a range of services to all sectors of the market.

The various forms of intervention are a response to the demands of the individuals and groups involved in the market, each wanting housing policies to reflect their own preferences (Lithwick, 1985: 33-37). Organized private interest groups such as the Canadian Home Builders Association and the Urban Development Institute tend to concentrate their efforts at the provincial and federal levels (Coleman, 1984) and to advocate policies for tax relief, minimal regulatory intervention, and programs to stimulate new construction under poor market conditions. Social advocacy groups, such as the Canadian Council on Social Development, also concentrate their efforts at the federal level, but press for greater government involvement in the provision of low-income housing. Others, including the Cooperative Housing Foundation of Canada and its seventeen affiliated organizations, are program specific, advocating only one type of program alternative (Carroll, 1989c).

In addition, one-issue groups or movements develop in response to a perceived threat to their environment – rising rents, housing prices, or interest rates, or the building of low-income projects or group homes in their neighbourhood. Individuals, builders, and developers primarily concerned with a single project or planning decision fall into this category. Their goal is to have the particular problem or threat resolved, but they tend not to have an ongoing role in the policy process. Some one-issue groups do evolve into more mature interest groups, however, and thus are able to exert significant and continuing influence. Citizen groups, such as those formed in the late 1960s to oppose development, for example, have had a broader impact in changing national housing policy through their involvement with urban reform movements (Higgins, 1985).

All governments respond to those demands that are important to their political fortunes, but the importance of these types of groups and their impact vary between levels of government. Municipal governments dependent on the property tax are more open to one-issue problems, having to trade off the demands of groups wanting to protect their lifestyle and investment by opposing lower standards of housing or additional growth with those of developers wanting to develop and build. Federal and provincial governments are more open to broader social and economic pressures and the influence of large organized interests. One-issue groups tend to exert more pressure at the federal or provincial level only when the problem affects a large bloc of voters, such as renters or new-home buyers.

While competing social welfare and economic goals can cause conflict within the same government, they can also be a source of intergovernmental conflict (Carroll, 1985). Municipalities' planning processes, and the desire to reduce the external costs imposed on the local tax base, can conflict with the social welfare or economic growth policies of other governments.

Thus, policies intended to meet the underlying problems of the housing market have become complicated as different levels of government have attempted to respond to the demands of competing interests and to resolve the problems caused by intervention at another time or for another purpose. What has evolved is a range of intervention covering virtually every aspect of housing, involving every level of government, and utilizing a bewildering array of policy instruments and programs that change too rapidly to be evaluated (Fallis, 1980).

Policy Trends

Contemporary Canadian housing policy, and sustained involvement by federal and provincial governments, began with the establishment of Canada (then Central) Mortgage and Housing Corporation in 1945 to implement the National Housing Act (NHA) of 1944. Although there had been earlier sporadic and specific senior government initiatives in housing, the provision of housing for the poor and urban planning had been left primarily under municipal control. From its inception CMHC was the dominant force in Canadian housing policy. While its main focus was on private-market housing, in recent years it has also played a leading role in policy development and the provision of subsidies for social programs.[2]

The preamble to the National Housing Act states as its objective "the improvement of housing and living conditions" (NHA, 1953-54, c. 23, s. 1). Although it has not always been clear how this was to be achieved, to the extent that policy goals can be implied by their outcomes there have been three distinct phases of policy since 1945. Each developed in response to different demographic and economic conditions and was driven by differing ideological values, but there are strong similarities in the way they developed and changed in response to external pressures. They also represent a trend in terms of delivery mechanisms and intergovernmental co-operation that fits within the more general changes in the pattern of intergovernmental relations in Canada and is not dissimilar to the pattern of other social welfare policies (Carroll, 1989a; Maslove and Rubashewsky, 1986). In discussing this evolution the emphasis will be on the patterns and trends of the policies rather than on the specifics of particular programs.

The Development Phase: 1945-68

The major focus of this period was reconstruction through the creation of construction jobs and economic growth. At the same time, a large supply of housing was needed quickly to house returning veterans. The response was to foster the growth of a development industry that could build standardized housing on a large scale. The bases of the policies were a faith in the efficiency of the private market and the ability of government planners to direct growth in the best way. The primary emphasis was placed on the provision of single detached owner-occupied housing for middle-income families, under the assumption that low-income problems could be solved through filtering. That is, the middle-income groups moving to the suburbs would vacate smaller, older, cheaper housing, making it available for lower-income groups. The programs were national in scope with little flexibility or responsiveness to regional or provincial needs.

The period also saw the beginning of a pattern in delivery mechanisms. Initially the federal government carried all of the transaction and learning costs of a program by direct delivery and finance. CMHC, for example, built up a staff of planners, architects, and engineers who developed model subdivision and housing plans. This was followed by a gradual withdrawal by passing on the direct financing costs and delivery costs when the provinces or industry had developed delivery mechanisms and had accepted the viability of the program. CMHC maintained approval authority, however, to ensure the quality of planning and to protect its financial investment in the housing stock.

Between 1945 and 1968 the housing stock in Canada almost doubled. To the extent that large-scale home ownership and the building of an industry were the goals, the policies can be considered successful.

But there were consequences – both unintended ones and those that were a product of success. First, there was a demand for more serviced land than was available. Programs for land assembly and sewage treatment were introduced with a funding mechanism that encouraged high capital-cost programs. Second, as standards of what constituted "adequate" rose, the size of houses and lots increased and the costs of servicing and land grew. Well before the inflationary period of the 1970s the suburban single detached house was becoming affordable for a decreasing segment of the population. Finally, as the new housing was primarily in the suburbs, the exodus from the inner city contributed to the deterioration of the urban core. Urban renewal and slum clearance programs were introduced. As money was available to tear down but not to fix, tearing down became the economic alternative. Existing housing was bulldozed away and new city halls, convention centres, hotels, and public housing were built. The results of this program can be seen in downtowns from Halifax to Vancouver – the city halls of Calgary, Toronto, Winnipeg, and Hamilton were all built on urban renewal land.

Urban renewal also displaced primarily low-income people who could not afford to move to the suburbs. One of the first large-scale public housing projects built as an intergovernmental partnership was Regent Park North in Toronto. It became the forerunner for what many people think of when they hear the phrase "public housing" –

a high-density ghetto. But it had the advantage of providing housing and utilizing the increasing capacity of the development industry.

In summary, in response to demographic and economic pressures for single-family homes, and to bolster the economy and develop an industry, the suburbs were created. Inner-city needs were addressed by urban renewal, and the construction of large low-income housing projects. The impact of these policies has been summarized by Albert Rose and James Lorimer:

> . . . [A] consequence of this set of policies was clearly the expansion of vast suburban areas adjacent to every medium-sized and large urban centre. The problems that have ensued, both for the governments and residents of suburban areas and the governments of central cities which did not directly benefit from this encouragement to home ownership, are immeasurable (Rose, 1980: 20-21).

> [T]he corporate city was created out of faith, not out of knowledge of what its consequences and benefits would be. . . . Most of us are now living with the consequences of these policies (Lorimer, 1978: 219).

The Social Reform Phase: 1968-78

A turning point in Canadian housing policy came in 1968 with the coming together of a number of political and demographic factors. The "baby boom" was entering the housing market, creating new pressures resulting from high demand for household formation combined with high expectations. The Trudeau government introduced comprehensive planning, which carried with it the assumption that policy problems could be solved through rational problem-solving. The urban reform movement at the municipal level increased concern about social and environmental issues (Higgins, 1977). Finally, as part of the province-building process, provincial governments became increasingly involved in social programs.

The period between 1968 and 1971 was one of reports. The Task Force on Housing and Urban Development led by Paul Hellyer, the Minister responsible for CMHC, travelled across Canada and graphically underlined the need for housing for low-income people and the extent of the displacement of families through urban renewal. The Lithwick Report (1970) and the Dennis-Fish Report (1971) enumerated the problems caused by the previous policies and outlined both a perspective and a prescription for resolving these problems that were influential in shaping the later programs.

The overall thrust was toward community involvement, intergovernmental co-ordination and flexibility, and neighbourhood revitalization. Except for suspension of the urban renewal program, the existing programs continued to operate. They were augmented, however, by the neighbourhood improvement and residential rehabilitation assistance programs, which were designed to redevelop existing inner-city neighbourhoods rather than to clear them, and by a non-profit and co-operative housing program. These new programs were a direct response to the demand for community input and income integration.

Again, there were consequences that distorted programs and created new problems. The evolution of the Assisted Home Ownership Program (AHOP) and non-profit programs provide examples of how program and policy goals can be displaced and distorted during the implementation stage.

The baby boom generation, having grown up in suburban single-detached houses, entered the housing market expecting the same kind of housing. When the construction industry had difficulty in meeting this sudden increase in demand, prices rose. The frustration that resulted when somewhat inflated expectations shattered against an increasingly rocky reality is illustrated by a 1971 letter to the editor of a major newspaper demanding government action because the writer could not afford to buy a single-detached house. The author of the letter was a twenty-one-year-old recent university graduate just entering the work force. AHOP was introduced to provide assistance to Canadians to buy new homes, provided that the price was below a maximum level that CMHC deemed to be sufficient to produce a "modest" house.

AHOP quickly produced friction between builders who wanted higher prices, consumers who wanted higher quality, and government agencies that wanted quantity at a given price. Developers pressured municipalities to lower subdivision standards and speed up their approval processes. Both supply and price increased while quality tended to decrease. Lots became smaller, assured levels of amenities lower, land prices higher, and new urban housing increasingly took the form of high-rise or row condominium units. The scope of AHOP-type programs was expanded by the provinces, several of which provided additional assistance to people receiving subsidies under the federal program or created similar but independent programs catering to the same market group.

A growing imbalance between supply and demand started to become evident in 1978 as the number of unsold units began to rise (CMHC, 1978-80). This problem was aggravated by stagnant resale housing prices and increasing mortgage rates that led large numbers of owners of AHOP-assisted houses to abandon their homes, returning them to CMHC, which had guaranteed the mortgages (CMHC, 1986d). The federal government became one of the largest owners of housing units in the country.

The decline of the Assisted Home Ownership Program had an

impact on other housing programs as well. CMHC's evaluation of the non-profit program, for example, points out that changes in the program in 1978 were affected by a desire to utilize the inventory of unoccupied projects, to deal with unemployment in the construction sector, and to reduce the pressure on rental markets (CMHC, 1983).

The non-profit and co-operative housing program was intended to overcome the stigma of government-managed public housing ghettos by having income-integrated housing delivered by local community groups who would develop and manage housing for low-income families within their community. Although intended as a form of self-help program, community groups had difficulty organizing. Instead, service groups and churches that had an existing program delivery capability and institutional support and non-profit agencies directly owned by provincial and municipal governments became the primary delivery mechanism. The delivery capacity for the program had increased but the goal of encouraging broadly based community self-help almost disappeared.

The program was also directed initially to the inner city, including the rehabilitation of existing projects. But when rental vacancy rates declined, non-profit groups were encouraged to build new projects. The emphasis shifted again when CMHC began to develop inventories of new housing. An obvious short-term response was to encourage non-profit groups to purchase existing projects from CMHC or the provinces. Many of the new, or almost new, projects were located in suburban areas. Moreover, despite the need to provide housing for low-income families, only a small portion of the housing provided under the non-profit program actually went to this group. CMHC's own evaluation of the program for 1978-1982 was that the

> *programs are ineffectively targeted to those most in need . . . are not a cost-effective way of producing rent-geared-to-income housing units . . . have only a marginal impact on the outstanding need for assistance . . . [but] have made an important contribution to the stock of affordable rental accommodation.* (CMHC, 1983: Executive Summary 8-9; emphasis in original)

In summary, this period emphasized social involvement and rational planning, with a context of economic prosperity in the early years and inflation in the 1970s. The growing assertiveness of the provinces was responded to by increasing their responsibility for program delivery. The creation of the Ministry of State for Urban Affairs (MSUA) was in part an attempt at overall trilevel co-ordination rather than unilateral federal direction (Doerr, 1980; Higgins, 1985). Nevertheless, the variety of influences and complexity of goals in the housing sphere were such that program objectives changed frequently, and unintended consequences of housing policies created significant problems for the future.

The Financial Control Phase: 1978-present

By 1978, inflation and problems of the economy had come to the fore. As urban renters were faced with potentially dramatic rent increases resulting from high interest rates, rent control or rent review had been introduced by every province as part of the anti-inflation program. As a cost-saving measure and in response to provincial pressure, the land, sewage treatment, and neighbourhood improvement programs were terminated and replaced by a block municipal grant. Federal direct loans under AHOP and the non-profit program were also terminated, to be replaced by private lender financing.

The next step was the elimination of the municipal grants and the replacement of AHOP. Under the short-lived Clark government some consideration was also given to abolishing CMHC and privatizing its mortgage insurance arm (CMHC, 1979). Instead, even more of the direct control over housing delivery was passed to the provinces. Although there were two short-term home rehabilitation and rental initiative programs as job creation initiatives, as part of an overall restraint program the federal government began phasing out its responsibility for both the physical planning and the social aspects of housing policy.

By 1986, only five federal housing programs remained in existence, beyond the traditional mortgage insurance function – Residential Rehabilitation, Non-Profit and Co-operative Housing, Rent Supplement, and Rural Native and Urban Native Housing. During 1986 agreements were signed with provincial and territorial governments to turn over to them the delivery of most of these remaining federal housing programs, the scope of which had been reduced significantly. CMHC would continue to provide subsidies and there would be joint planning, but the only major direct activity of the federal government would be mortgage insurance. This marked the virtual withdrawal of the federal government and CMHC from active involvement in the implementation of housing policy, an area it had dominated for forty years.

The Three Phases

Each of the phases was marked by differences in the types of housing programs. First there were suburban homeowner developments with large-scale land assembly and sewage treatment projects to service them, large-scale public housing, and urban renewal and slum clearance. The second phase gave us townhouse and apartment condominiums, neighbourhood improvement and rehabilitation programs, assistance for first-time home-buyers, income integrated non-profit and co-operative housing, rent control, housing for senior citizens, and in the latter years, energy conservation programs. The third phase brought a reduction in programs, reduced government spending, block grants, the passing on of program delivery to provincial and

municipal governments, and the continuation of non-profit and rehabilitation programs. Throughout, new suburban home ownership
building and varying forms of assistance for builders of rental projects
continued on a cyclical but steady scale.

Despite the program differences, housing policy does reflect a
distinct pattern of evolution and response to changes in the environment
(see Table 1). The economic and demographic pressures in the early
years were economic reconstruction, the needs of returning veterans,
and the pent-up demand from the 1930s and 1940s. The goal was the
development of a large-scale housing industry. By 1968 it was necessary
to keep this industry active and to meet the needs, values, and high
expectations of the baby boom generation. This led to home ownership
assistance and rehabilitation programs. Later programs such as rent
control responded to the inflation of the 1970s but continued to cater
to the expectations and demographic demand of the baby boomers.
The financial control phase responded to the desire for government
restraint and reduced spending.

Each also reflected the dominant government values of the time.
In the post-war period there was a belief in large-scale development
and the private market. The sixties and seventies reflected the social
and environmental reform movement, while the eighties have reflected
a concern with cost containment, disentanglement, and privatization.
(It should be noted that neither disentanglement nor privatization
necessarily reduces costs, but they do pass them to other levels of
government or other sectors [Levine, 1980].)

Coupled with these values was the means of imposing them. In
the first two phases there was a co-ordinating group with a blueprint
or vision of what our urban areas should look like. In the late forties
and fifties these were the policy strategists and planners in CMHC
whose dream of the ideal city is eloquently described by Carver
(1975) in *Compassionate Landscape*. In the 1960s it was a group of
urban reformers at MSUA whose goals included wanting to work with
other levels of government rather than imposing policies on them.
The last stage had neither as clear a blueprint nor a coherent
co-ordinating mechanism, and this will be important to our discussion
of present and future policies.[3]

The clearest pattern across the three phases was in the delivery
of programs. Initially the federal government funded and delivered
programs. As programs gained acceptance they would gradually
withdraw, passing the financing costs to the private sector and the
delivery and regulation costs to the provinces, municipalities, and the
private sector.

Policy initiatives have suffered from overreaction. In part this can
be attributed to the fragmentation and lag within the housing market.
But it is also a result of the responsiveness of governments to the

TABLE 1
Phases of Canadian Housing Policy

Stages

Characteristics	Economic Development	Social Development	Financial Restraint
Time	1945-68	1968-78	1978-present
Economic Conditions	reconstruction and prosperity	prosperity and inflation	recession and recovery
Major Demographic Force	pent-up demand and returning veterans	"baby boom"	aging population and single families
Overall Goals	economic development	social reform	financial restraint
Market Philosophy	filtering and infrastructure support, planned urban landscape	intervention, participation, and flexibility	reduced intervention
Housing Goals	industrial development, suburban development, physical planning	community development, income integration, demand support	supply support
Delivery Instruments	direct federal loans and grants	cost-sharing and direct subsidies and loans	private loans, cost-shared subsidies
Inter-governmental	federal leadership	trilevel consultation, "province-building"	provincial leadership
Outcomes	large projects "corporate city"	widespread, uncontrolled subsidies	administrative overlap

pressures of varying interests (including those internal to governments) and a tendency to respond to housing problems in an incremental fashion. Overreaction in housing policies has repeatedly created a need for programs aimed at correcting problems resulting from previous policies. Thus the neighbourhood improvement program was intended to correct the excesses of urban renewal, the non-profit program the excesses of public housing.

The approach to housing for senior citizens exemplifies both the successes and shortcomings of housing policy. The first projects specifically tailored for the needs of the elderly were subsidized for low-income seniors. Such programs proved popular and many housing projects for seniors were built in both small and large urban areas. As it became recognized that many senior citizens did want to live with other seniors, and also wanted and could afford larger units, the priorities shifted to income-integrated projects. But the units built earlier remain, and at least in some areas, such as Toronto, these are experiencing vacancy problems – in a city with an overall vacancy rate in 1988 of 0.2 per cent.

Housing policies, like other policies, have developed and changed to respond to perceived public demand, to changes in the environment, to shifts in government values, and to meet the deficiencies of previous policies. But housing, once built, is there to stay. Its durability and immobility mean that, although one can change the program, the outcomes of previous policies are still evident. It is through the interaction of these patterns that our current urban environment and its problems have developed.

Provincial Variations

To this point the emphasis has been on broad national problems and trends. There are, however, important variations across provinces in housing conditions and programs. Initially, the provinces had little involvement with major housing initiatives, their role being responsive and limited to cost-sharing. In 1964, however, the Ontario Housing Corporation was formed to implement and manage federal-provincial housing projects and to pressure the federal government to give the province greater control over program allocations. It was successful in attracting funding. By 1969 Ontario was absorbing 98 per cent of the federal public housing budget (Rose, 1982: 69). By 1973 every province had a provincial housing agency.[4]

Following the 1970 changes to the NHA, and in part as a result of these changes, the provinces became more active in the delivery of programs. The period 1970-74 was one of high activity as provinces built their organizations and adjusted their legislative structure to fit the federal cost-sharing programs (Rose, 1982: 74). British Columbia went so far as to buy (and subsequently sell) a private development company, Dunhill Development (Sexty, 1982). These agencies gradually took over the delivery of federal-provincial cost-sharing programs. All of these changes took place within an economic and social environment that allowed the federal government to pass over responsibility without concern for cost.

One of the intents of the 1970 changes was that the three levels of government would work together to develop a unified approach responsive to regional needs. After two highly publicized meetings in the early 1970s the process collapsed (L'Heureux, 1985: 202). What developed instead was a competition between provincial and the federal housing agencies. Part of the problem was the federal government's structure: the Ministry of State for Urban Affairs had a co-ordination mandate but no funds or programs, while CMHC had the delivery mechanism and a working relationship with the industry and municipalities.

Although there were variations in allocations, the federal programs were largely nationally based. But housing requirements and conditions vary across the country. The provinces felt best able to define their own needs and priorities.[5]

These differences in provincial priorities and needs have led to differences in their housing programs. Some provinces have developed unique policies: Nova Scotia has a lease-purchase program; Ontario has a number of programs to assist in converting buildings from other uses to rental housing; and British Columbia, Manitoba, and Quebec have housing allowance programs for senior citizens. In other instances provinces have created their own alternative versions of federal programs. The Ontario Home Ownership Made Easy (HOME) and the Ontario Home Assistance Program (OHAP) were addressed to the same needs as the federal AHOP and rehabilitation programs, for example, but were intended to overcome the national requirements of the federal programs and thus better meet provincial needs.[6] Such programs sometimes outlast their federal counterparts. CMHC discontinued its support for community resource groups, for instance, but Quebec has maintained a major program in this area. Still other provincial programs expand and supplement those of the federal government. Examples include funding for mobile homes in Alberta and expanded rehabilitation programs in several of the Prairie and Maritime provinces.

Overall, provincial programs have come to exceed federal programs in the amount of direct subsidies (CMHC, 1985: 7), but at the same time "provinces are paying a lower share of the subsidy for current activity than they do for past subsidy obligations. This portrays the shift away from cost-shared programs to unilateral federal subsidies" (Task Force on Program Review, 1985: 27). The desire to disentangle the multitude of programs, reduce federal involvement, and equalize the subsidy share led to the most recent shift in policy, the 1986 agreements discussed in the previous section. The outcome is that all but the Urban Native program are to be delivered by the provinces, but the cost-sharing of subsidies is to be split 75 per cent federal and 25 per cent provincial in all provinces but Ontario and Quebec, where the distribution is 60/40.

Over time, provincial policies may begin to diverge even more from those they have inherited, but provincial governments also face spending restraints. Some provinces may rely largely on federal program assistance, possibly with stricter guidelines, or they may attempt to pass more responsibility to the municipal level.

In Ontario, for example, the basic programs have remained with minor variations in their structure. A few small innovative programs such as "convert-to-rent" have been set up but the bulk of funding and attention has gone to those programs inherited from the federal government. The emphasis on income integration and small, community-based projects, however, has been lost as control of the program has passed to a number of powerful interest groups and development interests. In addition, virtually all responsibility for housing has been passed to municipalities and for-fee development consultants (Carroll, 1989c).

Urban Variations

There are also variations between urban centres, primarily between large and small urban centres in their housing requirements, their ability to meet these requirements, and their ability to influence the type of assistance available. Large metropolitan centres such as Toronto, Vancouver, Winnipeg, and Montreal have the ability to define their own needs and the tax base to implement programs. Smaller centres have neither the financial nor the political capability to undertake major social programs or to withstand development pressure. The major centres, which benefited earlier from urban renewal and public housing, have also been able to use programs such as the non-profit and neighbourhood improvement programs, which require a local delivery capacity. Smaller urban centres are more dependent on externally initiated programs such as public housing for senior citizens. This variation can be seen in the extent of involvement in the municipal non-profit program. In Ontario, reflecting its greater degree of urbanization, there were sixty-nine municipal non-profit corporations in July of 1986 (a number that had grown to 119 by July, 1988); Prince Edward Island, Newfoundland, and the Territories had none; Saskatchewan had dissolved those that did exist. In other provinces they have tended to be active only in the larger centres, such as Halifax, Saint John, Edmonton, and Calgary.

There are also broad differences in housing conditions among urban centres. Large cities have higher housing costs and a relatively larger rental stock. At the same time, they act as a magnet for single individuals who require short-term, low-cost housing. Smaller centres, on the other hand, have a relatively greater proportion of senior citizens and families who require affordable housing in markets where rental accommodation is less common and home ownership the norm. Thus, although affordability may be a problem in all areas, as the type of household, tenure, and housing available varies, the type of mismatch between supply and demand also varies.

Finally, larger centres, because of their visibility and greater organizational capacity, are better able to influence housing policy. Toronto was the development base for many of the program changes of the 1970s (Filion, 1986). What all urban areas have in common, albeit to varying degrees, is a reliance on the property tax base and a political system that makes them the level of government at which private interests are more influential. Urban governments are, therefore, least able to withstand private pressures for development, least able to underwrite the social costs of housing, and least able to withstand local resistance to the building of subsidized housing in particular locations – the familiar NIMBY (Not in My Backyard) syndrome.

Current Problems

In forty years Canadian housing policy has returned almost to its original point. Federal activity has been reduced to the role of mortgage insurer and the broader responsibility for housing policy is left to the provincial and municipal governments. This raises the questions of what problems are these governments facing and how will they cope with problems, the solutions to which have eluded us in the past.

The major housing problems facing our urban areas are the changing demographic composition of our population, the physical problems of obsolescence and urban sprawl, and the social issues of affordability and expectations.

Not only is the Canadian population aging, but household size is declining as families have fewer children and more single-parent families are formed. This has major implications for the effective use of the existing housing stock and for the type of new housing that will be needed (Burns and Grebler, 1986). At the same time, a high proportion of the Canadian housing stock – rental and homeowner, publicly and privately owned – is now more than twenty years old and in need of upgrading and rehabilitating. Similarly, municipal infrastructure and urban renewal projects also require replacement or upgrading. The preoccupation of government policy, responding to economic demands and public pressure for housing, has been with new housing. Increasingly, the problems of the "new" stock of the 1950s, 1960s, and 1970s must be considered. These problems have been responded to, to a limited degree, by expansion of rehabilitation programs (CMHC, 1986c) and by recognizing the impact on the construction industry (CMHC, 1987), but a major rethinking of how urban centres are to cope with rebuilding their infrastructure and upgrading and altering their housing stock is also needed.

Closely tied to the question of new versus existing housing stock is the issue of affordability and expectation. It is a truism to state that Canadians are well housed, but despite the efforts of governments over the last forty years one million Canadian households still do not have the earning capacity to provide themselves with this essential good (CMHC, 1986: 11). Affordability is tied to the question of expectations. The idea that only 25-30 per cent of income should be spent on shelter has become institutionalized in our society. While this may be realistic for families with dependent children at the lower income levels, it becomes less so as income rises or family dependency is reduced. It may be that this ratio has fostered an unrealistic expectation as to the price of shelter, particularly in the rental sector where market rents have fallen below the economic costs of providing accommodation. The entire philosophy behind the definition of affordability needs to be reconsidered.

Nevertheless, many people still require some form of assistance. The existing programs have been financing an average of 20,000 units a year, primarily new construction. But only a portion of these units are targeted to low-income groups (CMHC, 1987: 36-37). In the face of changing demand, obsolescence, and the number of families in need, the emphasis on new housing is both expensive and inefficient (Lewis and Rice, 1985). It is the responsibility of government to assist in the provision of housing for those in need. This does not mean that governments must do so directly, nor does it imply "the subsidization of the consumption of housing as a luxury" (Laver, 1986: 188). A wide range of policy instruments are available, all of which lie within the jurisdiction of the federal and provincial governments. Passing the responsibility for initiation and location of assisted housing projects to municipalities leaves it in the hands of the level of government least able to withstand the private pressures against social intervention.

Finally, there is the question of housing patterns and expectations. The continued building of low-density suburban developments on the urban fringes, while meeting the aspirations of an affluent middle class, has high social costs. The services for these developments are paid for out of the property tax, which is in itself regressive, and the provision of servicing for low-density developments represents a redistribution of income across income levels and between owners of new and old homes. Moreover, there is the question of who will live in these houses as family size declines and the age of households increases. But the most important effect is the continued consumption of recreational and agricultural land for residential purposes to satisfy the short-term development needs of municipalities and the high expectations of a few at the long-term expense of society as a whole. Once the land is taken up for housing it is difficult, if not impossible, to return it to its original use.

Conclusion

Housing exemplifies the " 'tragedy of the commons' in which behavior that is perfectly rational for the individual, or the group, becomes extremely dysfunctional for the society as a whole" (Peters, 1984: 22). The competing interests within the housing market all make legitimate claims. But self-interest pressures tend to lead to reactive and visible, rather than viable, solutions.

The short-term interests of municipalities and the development industry and the private interests of a large sector of the public are met by the provision of new housing. As Laver (1986: 180) has pointed out, however, "[p]ractical housing policy is much more about the management of an existing stock than it is about anything else." Greater concern with the management of the existing stock could do more in a cost-effective way to alleviate the problems. These areas should be of concern to both federal and provincial governments, which share the costs of housing programs and the jurisdictional responsibility for housing policy. If reasonable trade-offs between short-term demands and longer-term societal benefits can be achieved at all, they are more likely to be achieved at the federal and provincial levels, which have longer political mandates and a broader range of policy instruments from which to choose.

In 1946 and 1969 there was a consensus on the problem to be dealt with and the general direction for action. Both consensuses lasted for twenty years before reactive pressures caused distortions sufficiently visible to spark a major overhaul of the policies and the development of a new set of programs to attempt to rectify these distortions. Each time this was achieved by imposing on existing institutions a co-ordinating mechanism with a defined perception of the future.

The initiatives that began in 1969 are now twenty years old. The distortions and drift they have created have been addressed by financial controls and disentanglement. It is too early to tell whether disentanglement has resolved or further aggravated the existing problems. But there is no consensus on the direction for further action and the federal mechanism, which in the past was able to ensure some degree of equity and co-ordination, is now primarily concerned with cost containment, not housing policy.

This lack of central co-ordination could open up opportunities for innovation. The nature of the policy process and the use of national programs that assumed a uniformity of housing problems have caused some of the difficulties we currently face. Disentanglement could lead to further fragmentation, with provincial governments passing greater costs and responsibility on to municipalities. This appears to be the most likely outcome. To date, disentanglement has been primarily a means for senior (and to some extent, municipal) governments to evade their responsibility for our housing problems. The older programs in use have simply been replicated at a lower level of government with all of the program and policy flaws intact. But provincial and larger urban governments may also begin to respond to these problems with co-ordinated, small-scale initiatives that allow for experimentation. This would be desirable, since errors in housing policy form a part of the urban environment for decades.

NOTES

I would like to acknowledge the helpful comments made by Professors Tom Lewis and John Weaver of McMaster University. A shorter version of this chapter has appeared in *Urban History Review* (Carroll, 1989a).

1. One of the factors affecting land availability is the role of land speculators. Their importance has been the subject of considerable debate within the housing field. Unfortunately, the debate has no ready resolution. For a discussion of the varying viewpoints, see Bourne, 1981: 111.
2. For a review of housing policy prior to 1945, see Hulshanski (1986) and Wade (1986). For a detailed outline of both federal and provincial housing programs from 1945, see Sayegh (1987), Cogan and Darke (1982), CMHC (1985), and the (Nielsen) Task Force on Program Review (1985). Social housing programs include all subsidy programs designed to provide assistance to those whose housing needs are not met within the private market.
3. The Matthews Report (CMHC, 1979), which questioned the role of CMHC and the federal government in the housing market and recommended the partial privatization of the corporation, may come closest to articulating a dominant policy goal for this period.
4. Nova Scotia created a Department of Housing while the other provinces created Crown corporations. I would like to thank the provincial and territorial housing agencies that provided the information for this section.
5. CMHC (1985) provides a comparison of provincial housing conditions across Canada. For a summary of program activity by province, see CHS, 1988, Tables 59-60, 64-65, RRAP Evaluation (CMHC, 1986a: 27). These also provide breakdowns of housing program activity by size of urban centre.
6. One such "provincial need" is the governments' desire for re-election. In the fall of 1986 the government of Saskatchewan announced a generous low-interest loan program for home improvement almost simultaneously with the start of the provincial election campaigns. This program was reported to have provided assistance to large numbers of homeowners who wish to install swimming pools (*Globe and Mail*, September 4, 1986).

REFERENCES

Bourne, Larry S. (1981). *The Geography of Housing*. London: Edward Arnold.
Burns, Leland S., and Leo Grebler (1986). *The Future of Housing Markets*. New York: Plenum Press.
Canada Mortgage and Housing Corporation (1973-1988). *Canadian Housing Statistics*. Ottawa: CMHC.

— (1969). *Report of the Task Force on Housing and Urban Development*. Ottawa: Queen's Printer.

— (1979). *Report on Canada Mortgage and Housing Corporation*. Report of the Task Force on Canada Mortgage and Housing Corporation. Ottawa: CMHC.

— (1983). *Section 56.1 Non-Profit and Cooperative Housing Program Evaluation*. Ottawa: CMHC.

— (1985). *Consultation Paper on Housing*. Ottawa: CMHC.

— (1986a). *Residential Rehabilitation Assistance Program Evaluation*. Ottawa: CMHC.

— (1986b). *A National Direction for Housing Solutions*. Ottawa: CMHC.

— (1986c). "Housing Issues in the 1980's and 1990's," a paper prepared for the 43rd National Conference of the Canadian Home Builders, Edmonton, Alberta. Ottawa: CMHC (mimeo).

— (1986d). *National Housing Act Mortgage Loan Insurance: A background document of options for the future*. Ottawa: CMHC.

— (1987). *Human Settlements in Canada: Trends and Policies, 1981-1986*. Ottawa: CMHC.

Carroll, Barbara W. (1985). *The Allocation of a National Housing Budget*. Toronto: IPAC.

— (1988). "Market Concentration in a Geographically Segmented Market," *Canadian Public Policy*, 14, 2: 295-306.

— (1989a). "Postwar Trends in Canadian Housing Policy," *Urban History Review*, 18, 1: 64-74.

— (1989b). "Administrative Devolution and Accountability: The Case of the Non-profit Housing Program," *Canadian Public Administration*, 32, 3: 345-66.

— (1989c). "The Housing We Prefer: A Self-Interest Analysis of Low Income Housing Alternative," paper presented to the Fourth Annual Conference on the Future of the Welfare State, October 24-27, Toronto, Ontario.

Carver, Humphrey (1975). *Compassionate Landscape*. Toronto: University of Toronto Press.

Cogan, S., and D. Darke (1982). *Canadian Social Housing Managed by Provincial and Territorial Housing Corporations*. Report to the B.C. Housing Management Commission with the support of the Canada Mortgage and Housing Corporation. Ottawa: CMHC.

Coleman, William (1984). "The Political Organization of Business Interests in the Canadian Construction Industry," Berlin: International Institute of Management Discussion Paper IIM/LMP 84-11.

Dennis, Michael, and S. Fish (1972). *Programs in Search of A Policy*. Toronto: Hakkert.

Doerr, Audrey (1980). "Public Administration: Federalism and Intergovernmental Relations," *Canadian Public Administration*, 25, 4: 564-79.

Fallis, George (1980). *Housing Programs and Income Distribution in Ontario*. Toronto: Ontario Economic Council.

Filion, Pierre (1986). "The Neighbourhood Improvement Program in Montreal and Toronto: Differences of Attitude Towards Neighbourhood Interventions," paper given at the Canadian Political Science Association Annual Conference, Winnipeg, Manitoba.

Higgins, Donald J. (1977). *Urban Canada*. Toronto: Gage.

— (1986). *Local and Urban Politics in Canada*. Toronto: Gage.

Hulshanski, J. David (1986). "The 1935 Dominion Housing Act: Setting the Stage for a Permanent Federal Presence in Canada's Housing Sector," *Urban History Review*, 15, 1: 19-39.

Laver, Michael (1986). *Social Choice and Public Policy*. Oxford: Basil Blackwell.

L'Heureux, M. (1985). "Municipalities and the Division of Powers," in Richard Simeon (ed.), *Intergovernmental Relations*. Volume 63, Collected Research Studies, Royal Commission on the Economic Union and Development Prospects for Canada. Toronto: University of Toronto Press.

Levine, Charles (ed.) (1980). *Managing Fiscal Stress*. Chatham, N.J.: Chatham House Press.

Lewis, Thomas J., and James J. Rice (1985). "Finding the Right Formula: Social Housing for Low Income Families," *Perspectives*, 8, 5: 42-45.

Lithwick, N. Harvey (1970). *Urban Canada: Problems and Prospects*. A report prepared for the Honourable R.K. Andras, Minister Responsible for Housing, Government of Canada. Ottawa: CMHC.

— (1985). "The Decline and Fall of the Housing Market," in Allan M. Maslove (ed.), *How Ottawa Spends 1985: Sharing the Pie*. Toronto: Methuen.

Lorimer, James (1978). *The Developers*. Toronto: James Lorimer and Co.

Maslove, A.M., and B. Rubashewsky (1986). "Cooperation and Confrontation: The Challenges of Fiscal Federalism," in Michael J. Prince (ed.), *How Ottawa Spends 1986-87: Tracking the Tories*. Toronto: Methuen.

Miron, John (1988). *Housing in Postwar Canada: Demographic Change, Household Formation, and Housing Demand*. Kingston: McGill-Queen's University Press.

Peters, B. Guy (1985). *The Politics of Bureaucracy*. New York: Dorsey.

Rose, Albert (1982). *Canadian Housing Policy 1945-1980*. Toronto: Butterworths.

Sayegh, Kamal S. (1987). *Housing: A Canadian Perspective*. Ottawa: Academy Book.

Sexty, Robert (1982). *Housing Corporation of British Columbia*. Toronto: IPAC.

Spurr, Peter (1975). "The Land Problems Problem," a report prepared for Central Mortgage and Housing Corporation. Ottawa: CMHC (mimeo).

Task Force on Program Review (1985). *Service to the Public: Housing*. A Study Team Report of the Task Force on Program Review. Ottawa: Department of Supply and Services.

Wade, Jill (1986). "The Wartime Housing Limited: Canadian Housing Policy at the Crossroads," *Urban History Review*, 15, 1: 41-51.

5 Harry M. Kitchen

Transportation

Introduction

Although transportation services (municipal transit and municipal roads) represent one of the traditionally local government services, responsibility for delivery and funding is not easily separated among local, provincial, and federal governments. The nature of most transportation services (that is, the benefits from transportation services in one locality or for a particular service spill over onto residents of other localities or users of other services) requires the co-ordinated involvement of all levels of government.

In the provision of roads and highways, provincial governments are primarily responsible for intercity road systems, roads in unorganized territories, and major arterial roads running through organized territories (Siegel, 1980). This leaves local roads the sole responsibility of municipalities. However, construction and maintenance costs are subsidized by provincial governments. This is especially true in Atlantic Canada, where a greater proportion of combined local and provincial transportation services is placed in the hands of provincial governments (Kitchen, 1984: 86-92). Federal involvement consists of expenditures and subsidies designed to control, regulate, and provide facilities for international and interprovincial travel.

Municipal transit systems (buses, subways, etc.) exist in most cities and towns (villages, rural areas, and some small towns do not have municipal transit systems); however, the arrangements for providing and funding transit services vary. Some municipalities operate their own transit systems, while other communities contract out the provision of this service, either to the private sector or to a neighbouring municipality. Funding of municipal transit operations is shared by both the province and the municipality. Provincial government responsibility in the transit field revolves around intercity rail, air, and bus commuter systems and ferry services. As well, the federal government provides capital assistance to the provinces for improvements to the urban transit infrastructure (transit projects, railway relocation and grade separation projects).

Given these two components of urban transportation services, this chapter will separate the following discussion into three parts. The first part will be devoted to urban transit systems; the second will concentrate on municipal road services; the third part will integrate both services. While attention will be directed to the historical evolution, interprovincial differences and similarities, and general characteristics of each of the services, most of the analysis will concentrate on the advantages of establishing correct pricing policies. After all, the price paid for a service will determine the quantity demanded and revenues generated from users, and hence, resources devoted to it by local and provincial governments. Since local government officials are continuously making policy decisions involving trade-offs, incorrect prices in one sector may lead to an incorrect level of resources being devoted to that sector and, consequently, an inefficient level of resources in other sectors.

Municipal Transit Services

Historical Evolution

Transit systems began in Canada as early as the 1850s with the introduction of horse-drawn buses. By 1890, these omnibuses had been replaced, in many communities, by electric streetcars. In fact, the first electric streetcar began operation in Windsor, Ontario, in 1886. Despite the problems associated with the financing of electric companies, forty-six cities across Canada (at least one in every province except Prince Edward Island) operated with electric streetcars throughout the 1890s (CUTA, 1984: 2). At the same time, local real estate developers, businessmen, and vocal groups of citizens were exerting pressure on local transit systems to expand in specific ways and geographical areas so as to satisfy the desires of those applying the pressure. To gain greater control over municipal planning and development activities and to prevent haphazard and socially undesirable expansion, local councils at the turn of the century began to assume greater responsibility for the provision of municipal transit services (Kitchen, 1986: 2; Hatcher, 1975: 8-79).

The combination of reduced travel time brought about by the use of electric streetcars and the tremendous growth in ridership at the time of World War One created an environment for the development and expansion of a more complex and integrated municipal transit system (CUTA, 1985). However, following the war, the buoyancy of the Canadian economy and the concomitant increase in disposable incomes led to a substantial increase in the demand for private automobiles. Since the auto served as an effective substitute for public transit, many local transit systems faced a decrease in their ridership and consequent losses in revenue. These mounting losses led to reduced services. The depression of the thirties, continued declines in ridership, and ever-increasing losses threatened to destroy the Canadian transit industry. To save it, many local governments took over the operation of a number of private systems even though they had little or no money for maintaining service levels. Ultimately the industry survived, but only after increased ridership and the booming economy of World War Two; for example, in Halifax, the city's population doubled from 1940 to 1945 while annual transit ridership increased from 9 million to 31 million over the same period (CUTA, 1984: 3).

Once again, the end of the war brought increased affluence, greater dependence on the private auto, and, consequently, reduced demand for public transit. Throughout the fifties and early sixties, transit operators responded to declining use and increasing costs by raising fares, reducing service, and, in some instances, simply giving up.

By the late sixties and early seventies, however, increasing urban congestion, rising gasoline and auto maintenance costs, and the general concern about the real benefits of a large urban highway network (recall the controversy over the Spadina expressway in Toronto) led to increased use of public transit systems. Throughout this period, transit operators, for the most part, were able to turn a profit. However, by the early seventies, rapidly escalating costs and a desire by local citizens and officials (both provincial and local) to provide specific services that were more costly on a per-ride basis (services for the disabled or servicing the less heavily populated urban sections of each municipality, for example) created a necessity for provincial subsidies of one form or another. In fact, Ontario was the first province to announce formally an urban transit support policy (1971), with Nova Scotia being the last (1978). In 1978, the federal government became involved for the first time (through the Urban Transportation Assistance Program) in the provision of financial support for urban transit systems (CUTA, 1986, 1987a).

Some General Characteristics of Urban Transit

Although there is some variation in the level and type of service, almost all municipalities with a transit system provide a fixed-route service with the occasional community involved in dial-a-bus. Service for the disabled, regional commuter service, and, in one community, a service for the employees of a Crown corporation constitute additional features. Special transportation needs are also met through the use of express buses, reserved bus lanes, downtown shuttle operations, and the like.

While the mode of transit is at the discretion of each municipality, over 80 per cent of all municipal transit vehicles are motor buses. Heavy rail vehicles account for an additional 11 per cent, trolley coaches 5 per cent, light rail vehicles 3 per cent, and commuter rail vehicles 1 per cent. With the exception of the largest cities (Vancouver, Calgary, Edmonton, Hamilton, Toronto, Montreal) where more than one type of transit vehicle is employed, municipalities only use motorized vehicles (CUTA, 1985: 10).

The administrative structure responsible for providing urban transit shows some variation, with municipal departments being the most common. Next in frequency is provision through a commission (either separately or in combination with other utilities), and, finally, there are some privately contracted services, almost all of which are located in Ontario and British Columbia. Commission-run operations tend to be more prominent in Atlantic Canada and Quebec while municipal departments dominate the administrative structure in the Prairie provinces. In addition to privately contracted services in Ontario, there are a number of commission and municipal department operations. British Columbia has a number of commission-run operations and privately contracted systems (Kitchen, 1986: 66-85).

Financing of Municipal Transit

Municipal transit systems everywhere are financed by fares and by provincial and local government subsidies. In addition, some systems generate funds from charter/rental services, advertising, and miscellaneous income. Table 1 records the percentage of operating costs covered by operating revenues for each of the provinces and by population group for Canada in 1984 and 1985 (the latest year for which data are available). This percentage ranged from a high of 63 per cent in Ontario in each year to a low of 35 per cent in British Columbia in 1984. As well, cities of more than 250,000 people recovered, on average, 54 per cent or more of their operating costs from operating revenues while municipalities of less than 50,000 recovered less than half. Overall, operating revenues covered 53 and 55 per cent of all operating costs in 1984 and 1985, respectively. Almost all of the remaining operating costs are funded by provincial subsidies and local revenues (subsidizing from general funds).

Table 2 lists the provincial operating and capital subsidies in 1986. Seven of the ten provinces provided some form of direct operating assistance, ranging from per capita grants to a set percentage of operating costs or operating deficits. Capital subsidies are generally set at a fixed percentage of provincially approved capital expenditures. The provinces of Newfoundland and New Brunswick do not have a specific subsidy policy for transit; however, unconditional grants to municipalities are provided, parts of which may be allocated to urban transit. The federal government does not offer operating subsidies for urban transit. The bulk of federal assistance has taken the form of capital subsidies for specific projects.

TABLE 1
The Percentage of Operating Costs Covered by Fares

Province*	By Province 1984	1985
Newfoundland	42%	40%
Nova Scotia	62	58
New Brunswick	55	52
Quebec	45	47
Ontario	63	63
Manitoba	50	49
Saskatchewan	55	55
Alberta	51	53
British Columbia	35	48
By Population Group		
500,001 +	54%	56%
250-500,000	54	55
100-250,000	51	53
50-100,000	52	51
Under 50,000	41	45
Weighted Average	53%	55%

*Prince Edward Island does not have an urban transit system.
SOURCE: *1985 and 1986 Urban Transit Facts in Canada* (Toronto: Canadian Urban Transit Association, 1985 and 1986).

Although provincial governments provide relatively large subsidies to offset part of the operating deficits, the provinces do not have total control over the size of these deficits, nor do they contribute to the establishment of fare policies. Controls of this type are not deemed necessary because local governments share in financing the deficit and, hence, there is an incentive to ensure that the service is being provided in a cost-efficient manner. In fact, municipal councils are responsible for approving local transit budgets regardless of the administrative structure responsible for providing this service. Such

TABLE 2
Provincial Subsidies for Regular Urban Transit Services, 1986

Province	Operating Subsidies	Capital Subsidies
Newfoundland*	None	None
Prince Edward Island**	None	None
Nova Scotia	$4.60 per capita.	50% of capital expenditures.
New Brunswick*	None	None
Quebec	40% of revenue generated by regular urban transit services. In addition, a special operating grant offsets the cost of monthly passes.	75% of approved capital capital exp. with the exception of rapid transit facilities, which are 100% funded by the province.
Ontario	The subsidy is a percentage of operating cost and depends on the size of the municipality. It is 13.75% of operating costs in cities of more than 1 million; 17.5% in cities of 200,000 to 1 million; 20% in cities of 150,000 to 200,000; 22.5% in cities of 100,000 to 150,000; 25% in cities and towns from 0 to 100,000.	75% of approved capital expenditures.
Manitoba	Conditional grant of 50% of provincially approved net audited operating deficit. In lieu, Winnipeg receives an unconditional block grant.	50% of capital expenditures.
Saskatchewan	$4.00 per capita plus incentive grants for largest cities and $3.00 per capita for other towns and cities.	60% of approved capital expenditures.
Alberta	$8.00 per capita.	75% of approved capital expenditures.
British Columbia	Subsidy is a percentage of operating deficit, ranging from 66.7 to 75%.	All vehicles are owned by BC Transit. The cost of leasing is included in the annual transit operating cost.

* The provinces of Newfoundland and New Brunswick do not have a specific subsidy policy for transit, but unconditional grants to municipalities are provided, parts of which may be allocated to urban transit.
** There are no urban transit systems in Prince Edward Island.
SOURCES: Taken from *1986 Urban Transit Facts in Canada* (Toronto: Canadian Urban Transit Association, 1987); *Government Funding Policies For Urban Transit in Canada, 1986* (Toronto: Canadian Urban Transit Association, 1987).

approval appears to give municipal councils effective control over the financial and operational sides of the transit system. As well, most municipalities and/or provinces require transit systems to submit audited financial statements and, in some instances, an annual report.

While direct provincial controls over operating budgets do not exist, provincial authorities do exert considerable control over capital expenditures. By and large, these capital subsidies, which are designed to assist municipalities in the acquisition, upgrading, and maintenance of transit vehicles and facilities, are not available unless provincial approval has been granted in advance of incurring expenditures.

Fare Policy

Concern over the size of operating deficits has generated numerous discussions on the level of fares to be charged to transit users. Needless to say, local officials consider a number of social, economic, and political factors in setting fares. These include consideration of the availability of and access to substitute forms of transportation, the ability of local residents to pay for transit services, the attitudes of local politicians toward the acceptable level of fares, and the portion of operating cost to be recovered from fares. While pinpointing precise determinants of fare structures and absolute rates is impossible, the tendency, in almost all communities, is to set different fares for different groups of riders. In fact, in Ontario, only two of fifty-six municipalities surveyed set identical fares for all riders (MTC, 1985). Where variation exists, the highest fare is set for adults, with lower fares for senior citizens, students, and children and discounts often available for quantity purchases or monthly passes.

Average fares charged by transit systems display some variation according to the size of the municipality and the administrative organization responsible for its provision. Average fares tend to be higher in larger communities when compared with smaller centres (CUTA, 1987a). This is predictable because provinces generally fund a smaller percentage of the deficit in larger communities. As well, there is some evidence indicating that fares are lower in privately contracted systems when compared with commission or municipal department operations (Kitchen, 1986).

Evaluation

An evaluation of municipal transit policy may cover a number of areas; however, any evaluation ultimately turns to an analysis of financial issues, that is, decisions to expand or to alter existing routes and decisions to alter fares have serious implications for, or depend on, the generation of additional funds (from fares or subsidies) or the incurring of additional costs.

The subsidization of transit services can be justified on allocative (economic) efficiency grounds as long as the subsidy makes society, in total, better off than it would be in the absence of the subsidy. Allocative efficiency exists when the social cost (this includes the cost of operating the transit system plus road maintenance, pollution, and congestion costs) of providing the last unit of service equals the price that individuals are willing to pay for this last unit. Two groups of individuals benefit – direct users, from being able to use the service, and non-users, such as automobile riders, because it reduces the number of automobiles on the road and, hence, imposes lower congestion and pollution costs. The per unit price paid by transit users ought to be equal to the direct cost of providing the last unit of service; on the other hand, the subsidy rate ought to be equal to the value of the reduced pollution and congestion costs, etc., arising from the last unit of the service.

In other words, given that transit services generate benefits for both users and non-users and given the impossibility of getting the non-users to pay voluntarily for these benefits, a case can be made for subsidizing public transit in order to secure the optimum level (Frankena, 1979). The current subsidization policy (part from the province and part from the municipality), however, is unlikely to be allocatively efficient. Subsidies, for instance, are paid to cover operating deficits, and as long as operating revenues and costs differ from social benefits and social costs (the true measure of society's benefits and costs), as they are almost certain to do, then resources are not being used in the most allocatively efficient manner (Bird, 1976). Clearly, the issue is not one of whether a subsidy should be provided, but rather, of the correct rate of subsidy to employ. Historically, subsidy rates have not been set with the intention of generating allocatively efficient levels of transit services. Instead, subsidies have been provided to ease the financial burden on local transit users and local governments.

As was suggested earlier, the general fare structure tends to be similar across municipalities, although the absolute rates differ. The current fare structure creates some economic problems in terms of both what it does and what it does not do. On the one hand, failure to charge higher prices in peak hours in order to reduce the demand at this time and to encourage usage during off-peak hours has often been noted. This emphasis on the same fare structure regardless of the time of day may generate an overexpansion and greater capacity than can be justified on efficiency grounds. On the other hand, higher peak-load fares can lead to greater use of private autos, a result that for other socio-economic reasons may be undesirable. Perhaps what is needed is some experimentation to find an optimal policy mix, which may lead to a more allocatively efficient level of local transit (public and private) services.

Given that the additional cost of carrying a rider tends to vary with distance travelled, the failure to use zone charges, as is frequently the case in most municipalities, to cover the added cost makes little economic sense. Furthermore, lower rates for senior citizens and students, vis-à-vis other riders, may be difficult to justify, especially at times when transit systems are overused (peak-hours). Subsidies supplied on the basis of age or status and completely unrelated to income are difficult to support on efficiency or equity grounds.

This evaluation has been conducted on the assumption that both subsidies and fares ought to be set to generate maximum gains for society. Unfortunately, political pressures from special-interest groups, including local and/or provincial politicians, have led to the creation of subsidy and fare policies designed to maximize the politicians' chances of re-election rather than the maximization of society's gains. For example, policy decisions that have been politically popular but allocatively inefficient consist of (i) providing transit subsidies on the basis of income distributional rather than allocative efficiency grounds; (ii) not imposing zone charges (in fact, political pressures led to the removal of zone charges in Metro Toronto a few years ago); and (iii) setting differentials in fares charged to individuals that are not related to income. In each of these instances, it can be argued that the political process has interfered with, if not prevented, the achievement of economically efficient transit policies.

Finally, while the variation in the administrative structure responsible for providing urban transit services is more wide-ranging than for any other municipal service (this is especially true in the province of Ontario), there is no evidence suggesting that the decision-making process involved in the determination of fares and investment levels differs under the various organizational types. However, lower average fares under privately contracted vis-à-vis other organizational structures seem to be attributed to relatively lower operating costs under private systems (for a discussion of why organizational cost differentials exist under alternative organizational structures, see Kitchen, 1988).

Municipal Roads

Historical Evolution

As with the provision of most government services, the provision and funding of roads began at the municipal level. Indeed, the claim in the late 1800s was that most roads were only for the benefit of local residents, so that local residents should pay for their construction and maintenance. In the early 1900s provincial governments provided limited and sporadic assistance to municipalities, primarily in the form of technical aids, regulation, loans, and small grants in selected instances. As well, the provinces' major direct responsibility in road provision was concentrated in the area of a few developmental roads financed by a variety of expedient measures, including tolls (Bryan, 1972).

Early in the twentieth century, the municipal road function was primarily controlled by the province, that is, the province essentially dictated what municipalities could do and what taxes could be used to finance road expenditures. While the taxes designated for road expenditures varied across the country, they were usually of the poll type, completely unrelated to the taxpayer's road use or his/her personal income; for example, in British Columbia an annual tax of up to $2 could be imposed on every male resident except for those in the service or over sixty years of age. In Prince Edward Island, the comparable road tax (imposed by the province for local use) consisted of an annual tax on resident males under sixty ($.75) and a horse tax ($.25) and dog tax (either $1 or $3, depending on the circumstances) levied on their owners (Bryan, 1972).

The first provincial charge levied against the automobile was the motor vehicle registration fee (Table 3 lists the year in which each of the provinces enacted this legislation). Initially these funds were not earmarked for road expenditures; however, the sudden increase in the use of automobiles after World War One generated a demand for a more extensive and improved road system. In attempting to meet these demands by collecting revenues from users, most provinces earmarked registration fee revenues for road purposes. The insufficiency of this revenue source throughout the twenties led to the imposition of provincial gasoline taxes (listed in Table 3), which, in seven of the ten provinces, were likewise earmarked for road construction and maintenance. When combined with the earlier vehicle registration fee, these two charges were defended on the grounds that users ought to be paying for some of the road construction and maintenance costs; however, no serious attempt was made to define the relative proportion that ought to be paid by users versus non-users.

While earmarking of funds for road expenditures had been useful at one time, inadequate yields soon terminated (in the thirties) this policy. At roughly the same time, local governments began to experience increasing demands for an improved and more extensive municipal/provincial road and highway network. This led to increased provincial funding through the use of expanded conditional grants. Today, every provincial government offers some form of grant support to local governments for constructing and maintaining local roads and bridges.

Financing of Municipal Roads

Construction and maintenance expenditures are now financed from provincial grants and locally generated revenues (in a few isolated

TABLE 3
Beginning of Provincial Vehicle Registration Fees and
Gasoline Taxes

Province	Vehicle Registration Fee	Gasoline Tax (cents per gal.)
Newfoundland	1906	1930 (5)
Prince Edward Island	1913	1924 (2)
Nova Scotia	1907	1925 (3)
New Brunswick	1905	1926 (3)
Quebec	1906	1924 (2)
Ontario	1903	1925 (3)
Manitoba	1908	1924 (3)
Saskatchewan	1906	1928 (3)
Alberta	1906	1927 (3)
British Columbia	1904	1923 (3)

SOURCE: Nancy Bryan, *More Taxes and More Traffic* (Toronto: Canadian Tax Foundation, 1972).

instances, toll charges are used to raise revenues on provincial roads and/or bridges). Depending on the province and the type of expenditure to be subsidized, the rate of subsidy may range from full funding for all bridge construction, for example, to partial funding (usually 50 per cent is the minimum) for all road and bridge maintenance and repair costs (for an example of this type of provincial policy, see MTC 1985). Indeed, concern over the extent to which the provincial subsidies have been exerting an increasing claim on provincial revenues over the past decade had led to an expansion in the use of provincial controls designed (i) to prevent unnecessary road and bridge expenditures and (ii) to establish a uniform policy for all municipalities within each province.

While these controls differ slightly from province to province, they are basically designed to ensure that provincial grants are given only to those municipalities where a need for improving the road system has been demonstrated and/or where the local revenue base is deemed to be inadequate as a means of supporting required expenditures (needs and resource deficiencies are established by provincial authorities).

Since local governments do not earmark specific revenues for road expenditures, local funds come out of general revenues. As such, expenditures on roads come at the expense of forgoing expenditures on other municipal services or lowering taxes or charges on local residents.

Evaluation

Because of the use of local and provincial resources, an evaluation of current road policies must revolve around the funding of municipal road expenditures. Therefore, two issues must be addressed. First, can one justify the use of provincial government subsidies to finance a portion of local government's maintenance and construction costs? Second, is there a rationale for funding local road expenditures from general revenues or could a more efficient pricing scheme be instituted?

One can argue that subsidies from a senior level of government are justified to secure an optimal level of service as long as the benefits from the existence of local roads accrue to non-users (through spillovers or externalities) as well as users. While acceptance of this rationale is relatively easy, determining the correct rate of subsidy is much more difficult. Nevertheless, if local governments are to provide proper levels of road service, it is important that they attempt to estimate the size of the externalities that the subsidy ought to capture.

Addressing the second question is equally difficult. Clearly, without any road-pricing policy that levies a charge or price each time the road is used, users have an incentive to demand more than if a price were imposed for each use. A comprehensive system of road-pricing charges in which the users are charged for the marginal social costs* for each trip – this would represent the allocatively efficient level of the service – is unlikely to be implemented in any province in the near future. Yet, there are at least two reasons why one ought to be familiar with these issues. First, understanding the optimal pricing policy will illustrate the consequences of not having such a policy (for a more detailed discussion of pricing policies, see Frankena, 1982). Second, information on the importance of setting prices in order to avoid wastage may eventually put pressure on governments to look at some means of imposing more accurate charges for road services. At the moment, the only charges directly incurred by the users consist of their vehicle operating costs and travel time. No direct charges exist for road maintenance expenditures caused by users or for pollution and congestion costs imposed on others. One study, although somewhat dated, estimated that road maintenance costs ranged from 0.2 to 0.6 cents per vehicle mile for Ontario users in 1968 (Haritos, 1973). Similarly, it was estimated that air pollution

---

* Marginal social cost consists of the travel time and vehicle operating cost of the individual making the trip, plus the extra wear and tear on the road, plus the extra congestion and pollution costs imposed on others.

costs amounted to 0.2 cents per vehicle mile (Dewees, 1974) and that congestion costs ranged from a high of 38 cents per vehicle mile during morning rush hour to a low of 1.4 cents per mile at midday (Dewees, 1978). Failure to include road maintenance, pollution, and congestion costs in charges imposed directly on road users is inefficient because it leads to a demand for road services that is larger than would exist if the users had to cover these costs directly.

Recognizing the impossibility of charging road users precisely the marginal social cost for each vehicle mile, various methods have been suggested as ways of approximating the ideal charge. For example, it has been suggested that a case might be made on efficiency grounds for imposing higher automobile registration fees and fuel taxes on users in larger urban areas, primarily because congestion and pollution are more serious problems in these communities. Furthermore, a tax based on total vehicle mileage and actual or estimated emissions per vehicle mile for each type of vehicle may cover some or all pollution costs. Finally, road maintenance costs may be covered by a tax that is a combination of vehicle weight and vehicle mileage (Frankena, 1982).

Despite the efficiency gains that could accrue to society from a more allocatively efficient subsidy and pricing policy, it remains a fact that most road subsidy and pricing policies have been set in the political arena. As such, these decisions have not been made with the intent of generating the greatest gains for society. Instead, road expenditures tend to be highly visible. Subsidies, then, have been used to support road projects in certain geographical areas or for specific projects with the prime objective of maximizing the possibility of the government being re-elected. The use of toll charges or prices for road users has been equally opposed by politicians who see these options as weakening their popularity and, hence, their chances of being re-elected.

In spite of the fact that governments have not followed efficient pricing and subsidy policies in providing road services, it is essential that the case continue to be made for more efficient policies. After all, in a time of dwindling resources, greater gains for society will come from providing all government services in a more allocatively efficient manner.

Integration of Transit and Road Services

Any discussion of transit policies can be integrated with a discussion of road policies or vice versa. Deliberations over establishing the level of fares for transit riders, for example, must consider not only the impact on ridership levels but also the extent to which these fares will cause commuters to substitute greater use of the public transit system for less dependence on private autos.

While the earlier arguments in favour of setting prices to cover the marginal social costs in one sector (transit or roads, for example) are premised on the basis that efficiency exists in the other sector, the reality of the situation is that efficient prices do not exist in either sector. For example, if road services used by motorists are underpriced because the motorist is not required to cover the costs associated with wear and tear on roads, congestion, and pollution, then it can be demonstrated that transit services ought to be similarly underpriced to secure an efficient level of service. This is referred to as the second best argument (see Boadway and Wildasin, 1984, for an amplification of this point). Furthermore, if local officials have decided, for whatever reason, that one form of transportation service is to be preferred, then they may wish to subsidize this service to encourage its use and, hence, discourage the use of the alternative(s). An example of this, especially in larger urban areas, exists in the subsidization of transit services. The intent here is to encourage commuters to use public transit rather than private automobiles, particularly during rush hour. Whether or not this policy is successful depends on the extent to which users are willing to switch from one mode of transportation to another when the differential in the relative price of the alternative is increased (that is, when local governments make it relatively cheaper to use public transit vis-à-vis private autos).

Some evidence suggests that the price elasticity of demand for public transit is very low. One study on transit ridership in Montreal (Gaudry, 1978) indicated that the elasticity of demand was -.22 for adults and -.52 for children. In other words, a 100 per cent drop in transit fares (that is, complete removal) would generate an increase in ridership of only 22 per cent for adults and 52 per cent for children. At the same time, it has been suggested that the cross-elasticity of demand for automobile use with respect to transit fares is similarly low. In fact, it has been estimated (Frankena, 1979) to lie between -.15 and -.5. This suggests that if transit fares are reduced by 100 per cent (completely eliminated), automobile use will decline (because of the increased use of public transit) by between 15 and 50 per cent. If these figures roughly approximate reality, lower transit fares will cause very few people to switch to public transit and away from automobiles. Apparently, the modal choice is dependent on factors other than price.

Furthermore, these lower fares generate lower revenues for transit authorities, thus necessitating higher subsidies and/or reduced expenditures. In fact, it has been argued that the primary effect of subsidizing public transit is to increase the total amount of travel; that is, if subsidized public transit takes some autos off the roads, this will reduce the travel time for the remaining road users. Since travel time is an important cost, additional motorists will use the roads leading to an increase in total travel demand (Dewees and Waverman, 1977).

Although no solid evidence exists, it is generally felt that the size of the external benefits created by the existence of a transit system are substantially smaller than the size of the subsidy provided. At the same time, as was noted in the previous section, a strong case can be made for increasing the charges imposed on the consumers of road services. In fact, if the users were required to pay a higher percentage of the direct costs, one would expect that a more allocatively efficient level of each service would be supplied.

In addition, to accept the claims frequently made by politicians that transit fares and road user charges ought to be restrained so as to absorb a small percentage of users' income is an inappropriate policy option for local governments. For example, such a policy provides a subsidy to every user regardless of the user's ability to pay. As well, local governments do not have access to the appropriate revenue sources used for redistributing income, such as the personal income tax, and hence ought not be involved in income redistributional issues (Kitchen, 1984; Kitchen and McMillan, 1985).

Summary

While most municipal governments in Canada provide and maintain local roads, only the urban areas are involved in the provision of transit services. Provision and funding of transportation services are divided between provincial and local governments, although the extent to which each of these levels contributes depends on the province in which the municipality is located and the population and/or revenue base of the municipality itself.

Although municipalities have frequently complained about the inadequacy of provincial assistance in the funding of local transportation services, the fact remains that municipalities are creatures of the province and, as such, the province essentially dictates the size of provincial subsidies, leaving local governments to fund the remainder of their costs from direct charges and/or general revenues (Kitchen and McMillan, 1985). Securing a more optimal level of transportation services requires direct users to pay a price per unit that is more closely related to the marginal cost per unit of the services used. At the moment, the evidence suggests that price is considerably less than marginal cost. If the pricing structure were altered to generate a more efficient level of service, local users would be more aware of the cost and, therefore, better able to judge the merits of continuing with the existing level of services, as opposed to upgrading or reducing that service.

Emphasizing the importance of establishing subsidy and pricing policies so as to achieve greater gains for society must not be treated in a vacuous fashion. Unfortunately, most of these policies have been set to achieve political objectives (satisfying a certain constituency or maximizing the possibility of being re-elected, for example). Thus, transportation policies have not really been concerned with allocative efficiency. What is needed from policy-makers is a greater willingness to set subsidy and pricing policies designed to generate greater gains for society as a whole, that is, to set policies based on the criterion of improving allocative efficiency.

NOTE

The author would like to thank Torben Drewes, Vaughan Lyon, and Rick Loreto for helpful comments on an earlier draft of the chapter. Any remaining errors or omissions, however, are the responsibility of the author.

REFERENCES

Abouchar, Alan (1985). "Pricing Highways," mimeograph, Department of Economics, University of Toronto.

Bird, Richard (1976). *Charging for Public Services: A New Look At An Old Idea*. Toronto: Canadian Tax Foundation.

Boadway, R.W., and D.E. Wildasin (1984). *Public Sector Economics*, Second edition. Boston: Little Brown and Company.

Bryan, Ingrid (1982). *Economic Policies in Canada*. Toronto: Butterworths.

Bryan, Nancy (1972). *More Taxes and More Traffic*. Toronto: Canadian Tax Foundation.

CUTA (1984). *Government Funding Policies For Urban Transit in Canada, 1983-84*. Toronto: Canadian Urban Transit Association.

CUTA (1985). *1984 Urban Transit Facts in Canada*. Toronto: Canadian Urban Transit Association.

CUTA (1986). *1985 Urban Transit Facts in Canada*. Toronto: Canadian Urban Transit Association.

CUTA (1987a). *Government Funding Policies for Urban Transit in Canada, 1986*. Toronto: Canadian Urban Transit Association.

CUTA (1987b). *1986 Urban Transit Facts in Canada*. Toronto: Canadian Urban Transit Association.

Dewees, D.N. (1974). *Economics and Public Policy: The Automobile Pollution Case*. Cambridge, Mass.: MIT Press.

— (1978). "Simulations of Traffic Congestion in Toronto," *Transportation Research*, 12: 53-61.

— , and L. Waverman (1977). "Energy Conservation: Policies for the Transport Sector," *Canadian Public Policy*, III: 171-86.

— , E. Hauer, and F. Saccomano (1979). *Urban Road User Subsidies: A Review of Theory and Measurement*. Transportation Paper No. 4, University of Toronto/York University Joint Program in Transportation.

Frankena, M.W. (1979). *Urban Transportation Economics*. Toronto: Butterworths.

— (1982). *Urban Transportation Financing: Theory and Policy in Ontario*. Toronto: Ontario Economic Council.

Gaudry, M. (1978). "A Study of Aggregate Bi-Modal Urban Travel Supply, Demand and Network Behaviour Using Simultaneous Equations With

Autoregressive Residuals." Centre de Recherche sur les Transports, Université de Montréal.

Glazebrook, G.P. de T. (1938). *A History of Transportation in Canada.* Toronto: Ryerson Press.

Haritos, Zis (1973). *Rational Road Pricing Policies in Ontario.* Ottawa: Canadian Transport Commission, mimeo.

Hatcher, Colin (1975). *Stampede City Streetcars.* Montreal: Railfare Enterprises Ltd.

Kitchen, Harry (1984). *Local Government Finance in Canada.* Toronto: Canadian Tax Foundation.

— (1986). "Local Government Enterprise in Canada," Discussion Paper No. 300, Economic Council of Canada, Ottawa.

— (1988). "Private Vs. Public Provision of Municipal Transit Services in Ontario: A Cost Comparison," Trent University, Department of Economics, Working Paper 88-07, September.

—, and Melville McMillan (1985). "Local Government and Canadian Federalism," in *Intergovernmental Relations*, Richard Simeon, Research Coordinator. Vol. 63 of the Royal Commission on the Economic Union and Development Prospects for Canada. Toronto: University of Toronto Press.

Mohring, H. (1972). "Optimization and Scale Economies in Urban Bus Transportation," *American Economic Review*, 62: 571-604.

MTC (1985). *Subsidies or Grants Available Under Municipal Roads Programs.* Toronto: Ministry of Transportation and Communications.

MTC (1987). *Ontario Urban Transit Fact Book, 1986.* Toronto: Ministry of Transportation and Communications.

Palmer, John P. (1988). *An Economic Analysis of Canada's Ground Transportation Sector.* Vancouver: The Fraser Institute.

Siegel, David (1980). "Provincial-Municipal Relations in Canada: An Overview," *Canadian Public Administration*, 23 (Summer).

6

Trevor Price

The Environment

Introduction

Concentrated human settlement has always inherently had to deal with the problem of disposal of wastes. Wastes posed a danger to health and were an affront to amenity and urban aesthetics. Until relatively modern times the problem of waste disposal was held within tolerable limits by virtue of the fact that wastes were almost entirely organic and were biodegradable in soil or water. Burning was also a reasonably effective way of disposing of wastes. Industrialization and the major changes in the composition of wastes from organic materials such as textiles and plant and animal wastes to glass, plastics, metals, and synthetic chemicals and paper has made the problem of waste disposal a much more difficult task (Roebuck, 1974).

This chapter restricts itself to the involvement of local government in the removal and treatment of wastes, including industrial wastes, household refuse, and sewage, and to the municipal responsibility for a clean and uncontaminated water supply. It will deal with the problems of establishing a healthy environment and discuss the efforts made by the local, provincial, and federal levels of government in establishing policies that try to ensure that wastes are disposed of efficiently and with due regard for future impacts on the ecosystem.[1] The chapter begins with a discussion of the dimensions of the contemporary environmental problem and relates various aspects of the problem to the constitutional responsibilities of the federal and provincial levels of government. The jurisdictional limitations are related to basic strategies for dealing with environmental problems.

Concern about the environment and health impacts, real or perceived, has given rise to a particularly activist orientation to the political process at the local level. This activism and the growing sensitivity of public opinion to environmental issues have led governments to treat these issues quite seriously and to develop quickly new regulatory systems that are only now being considered and implemented. The whole field of environmental policy is evolving rapidly and it is somewhat difficult to outline with complete precision policies that are constantly being revised (D'Amore, 1983).

Constitutional Responsibilities and Jurisdiction over the Environment

The environment includes air, water, land, and all organisms that live on or in these milieux. There is a complete physical continuity among all these elements and jurisdictional boundaries, therefore, are not easy to define. Pollution of air, land, and water is not easily contained, so that transboundary effects can only be dealt with by intergovernmental co-operation. This has, in fact, been well recognized in the development of environmental legislation and administration.

Notwithstanding the need for co-operation, the growth and development of the Canadian constitution has resulted in judicial interpretations that have shaped the mandates of the provincial and federal governments. The responsibilities delegated by the provinces to their municipalities also vary quite considerably from province to province, depending on local resources, the degree of urbanization, and the extent of powers delegated to municipal governments.

The British North America Act (1867) assigned an extensive list of responsibilities that have environmental implications to both levels of government. Environmental policy as such was not conceived of at that time. Judicial interpretation of the allocated powers makes it clear which areas may be legislated on by federal and provincial governments.[2]

The major federal powers derive from jurisdiction over navigation, fisheries, works of national or interprovincial nature, trade, and the implementation of treaties. It can also be argued that the federal government has the duty to take a leadership role in matters of national urgency under the general powers of "peace, order, and good government." The federal government has given policy leadership in such areas as housing, health, welfare, and education, matters not strictly speaking within its jurisdiction.

Those powers that form the basis of provincial responsibility constitute a much more substantial corpus of authority for initiating environmental policy. The provincial list includes: public lands, municipal institutions, local works and undertakings, property and civil rights, punishment of provincial offences, matters of a local or private nature, agriculture, exploration for development and conservation and management of non-renewable natural resources in the province, and development, conservation, and management of sites and facilities in the province for the generation and production of electrical energy (Girling, 1983).

During the heyday of federal involvement in urban initiatives, a philosophy of comprehensive planning and a close network of consultations among three levels of government seemed to be envisaged. J.W. MacNeill's constitutional study prepared for the government of Canada advocated such an approach. The problem of "pollution havens" and sources of technology from outside the country were matters that could only be addressed by the federal government.

> Action by the federal government is usually the most effective way of applying strategies aimed at the primary sources of pollution. Often it is the only way. Many potential air and water pollutants can be eliminated during the design and manufacture of various products, or during the refining of fuels. (MacNeill, 1971)

In the development of environmental policy since 1972 the federal government has not taken a strong lead in direct regulation, except for certain polluting products such as automobiles. The major responsibility for environmental regulation and the creation of agencies to control pollution has rested with the provinces.

The main focus of federal activity would appear to have been research and advice to the provinces. The Task Force on Program Review felt that the relationships between federal and provincial departments were effective and mutually beneficial but did not urge a more active role, only a continuation of more effective liaison (Task Force on Program Review, 1985). The strong role originally envisaged for the Environmental Protection Agency in the United States, with its ability to monitor pollution levels and enforce standards, is not one the federal government of Canada has eagerly sought (Congressional Quarterly, 1982). The role of the present federal government is mirrored in a statement made by the Pearse Commission on Federal Water Policy.

> Under any interpretation of Canada's constitution the provinces have wide jurisdiction over water. We believe that federal policy should respect this broad provincial authority, intervening only when an issue of federal or national interest is at stake. Our conclusions will therefore disappoint those who argue that the pervasiveness, acuteness or cost of solving water management

problems in Canada would justify federal intervention. (Environment Canada, 1987)

All the political parties participating in the federal election in the fall of 1988 sought to present the appearance of taking a strong stand on environmental issues. The Environmental Protection Act of 1988 was presented as a major achievement by the government, consolidating a good deal of previous federal environmental legislation and updating and improving laws having to do with federal jurisdictions.

After the September, 1988, PCB fire at St. Basile le Grand on the outskirts of Montreal, the federal government gave the impression of moving to eliminate the PCB menace. In terms of program delivery and financial contribution, however, the refusal of the federal government to participate as an equal partner with the provinces and municipalities in an infrastructure renewal program proposed by the Federation of Canadian Municipalities is a more telling indication of federal priorities.

The real brunt of dealing with water pollution and hazardous wastes lies with the provinces and municipalities. Federal help has been restricted to such programs as a grant to Halifax to help clean up the heavily polluted Halifax harbour. This came under the guise of regional development rather than any kind of national program to improve municipal facilities.

The Emergence of Environmental Policy

Environmentalists advocate the establishment of policies that conform to the concept of assessing the ecological impact of all human activity. The integrity of the biosphere, according to this philosophy, is fundamentally important because human welfare is ultimately guaranteed only by not drastically upsetting the balance of the earth's life support systems – air, land, and water. This total ecosystem approach was central to the planning of national parks and wilderness areas but has not been a guiding principle of urban development, industrial growth, or agricultural and forestry practices. Early environmental legislation in the 1960s and 1970s assumed that the establishment of standards for pollution discharges and air emissions and monitoring agencies to oversee them would be sufficient to arrest environmental deterioration.

The initial concept of environmental management was for total elimination of contaminants by eradicating the polluting activity, intercepting the pollutants, or modifying the activity so that it did not produce pollutants (MacNeill, 1971). It is now a standard procedure to precede any major resource or public works project with an environmental impact assessment. Nonetheless, strong economic pressures can still overcome serious environmental objections; for example, the dams on the Souris River in southwestern Saskatchewan, which will eliminate prime wetlands (a major staging area for waterfowl), have been given federal approval after strong lobbying by agricultural interests and the province of Saskatchewan. Despite a broad range of legislation emanating from both federal and provincial levels and the creation of agencies to monitor and research the problems of pollution, much more remains to be done before we can say that "stress" on environment has been brought within tolerable limits.

A thorough study of environmental regulation in Ontario (Peat, Marwick, 1984) came to the following conclusions:

> The [Ministry of Environment] has enjoyed a large degree of voluntary compliance with its environmental objectives by a variety of sources in Ontario. There are also indications that Ministry efforts and programs are contributing to improvements in ambient quality conditions as well as to protect against further deterioration.

While giving these positive reassurances, the report also went on to assert that the system was lacking in complete effectiveness.

> Individuals, firms and even government agencies generally seek to minimize costs and will follow least-cost courses of action. Consequently when confronted with abatement requirements, a polluter weighs the cost implications of the alternatives: to comply or not to comply.

After approximately fifteen years of operation of environment ministries, our current condition is as follows.

1. Politicians and public opinion in Canada are concerned about environmental problems and appear to support strong measures to control pollution (D'Amore, 1983).
2. Many indicators of the pollution situation have improved (Statistics Canada, 1986).
3. Other indicators show that municipalities and provinces are barely holding their own in controlling toxic wastes, acid rain, sewage treatment, and solid waste disposal (International Joint Commission, 1986).
4. The problem does not lie in the lack of scientific knowledge but more in the political will to apply resources or to make basic changes in the way we manufacture and consume products and dispose of wastes (Caldwell, 1984).

We are now quite aware that pollution imposes significant costs to our health and in destruction of natural resources, loss of recreational potential, and a deteriorating quality of life. What is also evident is that the political horizon is fairly short and it is difficult to adjust our political, economic, and social systems to an ecosystem perspective unless there is an overwhelmingly powerful and popular ideology to support it. While there is something called an environmental movement, which has manifested its political presence directly in some countries as the Green Party, it is far from being a dominant presence in the political spectrum of most Western countries, where the problems of economic growth and technological innovation dominate the political agenda (D'Amore, 1983; Boggs, 1986).

Solid Waste Disposal and Collection

In the early stages of urbanization the need for an organized system of garbage collection and removal was not great. Before 1920 most garbage was organic and could be disposed of by burning or by biodegradation in pits, backyards, and small dump sites. Scavengers picking up refuse were employed by Toronto and other city public health boards in the late nineteenth century. As the twentieth century progressed a higher percentage of garbage consisted of glass, metal, and, more recently, plastics. The amount of paper and plastic packaging has grown and the organic proportion is less. The collection and removal of garbage has become a gigantic industry operated by municipalities or by privately owned solid waste disposal companies contracted to do the work for municipalities and industries (Crooks, 1983).

Until the 1960s, the disposal of solid waste in all parts of Canada was mostly in open dump sites, which were often water courses, depressions in the land, gravel pits, and quarries. Since paper was a major component a primitive incineration was used either at the dump sites or in low-temperature incinerators in apartments and institutions. This proved unsatisfactory because: (1) leaching from the dump site carried contaminants to ground water, rivers, and lakes, because no prior hydro-geological studies had been done to ensure leachate could not escape; (2) odours and smoke from dumps and incinerators were disagreeable and possibly toxic to residents living near the sites; (3) flies and rodents lived on the garbage and were potential sources of infectious diseases.

The unsatisfactory nature of dumps, the increasing quantities of residential and industrial garbage, and the large amounts of plastics and toxic residues in garbage meant that other solutions to the problem of solid waste disposal had to be found. The solutions now being used, or under consideration, are: (1) landfill sites; (2) incineration; (3) recycling and resource recovery.

Landfill Sites

Provinces have made it mandatory for large communities to dispose of their solid wastes in landfill sites specially engineered to accommodate garbage on top of a suitable bed of clay, which is impermeable and will not allow leachate to escape into surrounding waters or aquifers and thus into the surrounding land and waters.

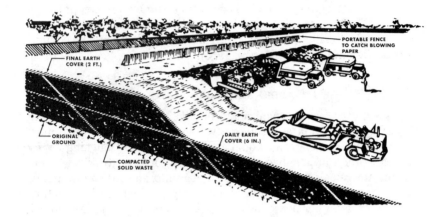

As the diagram shows, the garbage is spread evenly by bulldozers and covered with a layer of soil to seal it off from flies and rats. Toxic wastes are not to be buried in such sites but disposed of in special facilities (see below). Although regulations forbid the dumping of toxic waste in landfill sites, much material is overlooked, particularly within household refuse. Once the landfill reaches a height of twice the depth of the original excavation the site can be closed and the land reclaimed. Because methane is being generated and the garbage continues to decompose and hence cause sinking of the land, landfill sites are not suitable for use as building sites. The most likely use is recreational and many such sites have been planned for future parks (Simpson-Lewis *et al.*, 1983).

Landfill sites are not easily acquired because they must be large and must meet stringent geological requirements of a proper base, adequate soil cover, and lack of drainage out of the site by reason of slope and drainage. Landfills are preferably located in remote rural areas where there are few people to object to odours, noise, and traffic.

Since it is more economical to have one large site than many small sites, this function is usually regional in scope; and where a regional authority is in charge a unified decision might be more easily made on locating a landfill operation. Many metropolitan areas have to dispose of their garbage outside the boundaries of the main population centre and this has produced fierce conflicts with rural and suburban residents who have strenuously resisted the transportation of urban garbage to their "backyards." The "not in my backyard" (NIMBY) syndrome has applied to all kinds of waste disposal facilities, including landfill sites.

In addition to the opposition to landfill sites for environmental and aesthetic reasons there has been opposition to landfill sites occupying prime farm land, which has already been diminished significantly by other urban uses.[3]

The ever-increasing quantities of garbage have resulted in a shorter life for landfill sites even though compacting and shredding measures have been used to reduce the bulk and hasten decomposition. The imminent exhaustion of the capacity of landfill sites across North America is triggering a new crisis in this sector because of a lack of politically acceptable new sites.

It is not an exaggeration to state that in many parts of Canada there is now a landfill site crisis. Many existing sites are reaching capacity and opponents of new sites are using the consultation and assessment provisions of environmental legislation to stall or prevent the development of new sites. Desperate strategies are being conceived, such as the transporting of garbage hundreds of miles to remote northern sites (*Globe and Mail*, August 28, 1989). Some U.S. cities now charge garbage fees by the bag or container as an incentive to reduce refuse. This policy, however, could backfire by causing home-owners to resort to burning and illegal dumping, thus exacerbating rather than reducing pollution.

Many landfills have also not been managed in such a way as to inspire the confidence of neighbours to these sites. Bad odours, contaminants leaking out of the sites, a constant flow of heavy trucks, spillage of garbage on rural roads, wind-blown trash from the sites, hordes of sea gulls are all complaints that have created strenuous resistance to new sites and extension of old sites (Bureau of Municipal Research, 1974: Simpson-Lewis *et al.*, 1983). Careful planning, efficient operation, and close consultation with representatives of the community in which the site is located are all measures advocated to reduce opposition. In addition, the promise of future benefits in terms of a well-planned development that could appreciate property values may be calculated to turn hostility into acceptance of a landfill site.

Even if alternatives such as incineration and recycling come into greater vogue, landfill sites will still be needed for the incinerator ash and materials that cannot be recycled or burned.

Incineration

Incineration as a disposal method for solid waste and toxic waste is a technology being widely considered, although it is not currently used to any great extent in Canada (Kidd, 1984).

The opposition to landfill sites and the impending exhaustion of the capacity of major sites all across the country have forced municipalities seriously to consider alternative means of solid waste disposal. There is also the complex problem of how to get rid of toxic organic chemicals such as PCBs, which are very stable and non-biodegradable and which cannot be safely deposited in landfill sites without the risk of possible future contamination of ground water and soil. For such substances as PCBs, high-temperature incineration in some kind of centralized or mobile facility seems to be the only method of destruction (Ontario Ministry of Environment, 1974). The only facility of this kind in Canada in 1989 was at Swan Hills, Alberta. Large amounts of toxic wastes, including PCBs, are currently shipped out of Canada for disposal.

Since the early 1970s the SWARU (Solid Waste Reduction Unit) plant at Hamilton, Ontario, has been incinerating garbage. The process first shreds the garbage and magnetically removes metals. The remainder – organic waste, paper, and glass – is shredded and incinerated. Heat is used to produce steam, which is used to power the plant and could be marketed for heat to neighbouring buildings (Bureau of Municipal Research, 1974). The Hamilton incinerator is one of a few installations of its kind in Canada, but it has been criticized for its deficiencies in recycling and for harmful emissions to the atmosphere (Kidd, 1984).

There is considerable concern in some areas of Canada that U.S. cities, unable to find further landfill sites, will turn to incineration on a huge scale as a means of solid waste disposal. The largest incinerator in the world has been constructed in Detroit, Michigan, at a cost of $560 million. This plant will recover metals and glass and burn the remaining garbage to produce power from steam. The cost of incineration is very high, especially if it is burned at high temperatures and if the proper pollution control equipment is installed and effectively maintained. The Detroit incinerator is being opposed by environmental groups in Michigan and the city of Windsor and by the government of Ontario because it is not using the best available technology. Detroit officials, in rebuttal, point out that to date Canadian incinerators do not meet existing U.S. air-quality standards (Michigan Department of Natural Resources, 1986; Vander Doelen, 1986).

The Detroit incinerator will use electrostatic precipitators, which will only remove heavy particles. Critics suggest that pollutants in the form of gases and fine particles will not be removed and will escape through the stack. Possible emissions include sulphur dioxide, PCBs, dioxins, and heavy metals. To lessen the possibility of the emissions it is advocated that there be added a "bag-house" to trap small particles and scrubbers to remove gases, especially sulphur dioxide. The health threat and the economic threat to Canada are likely to come from polluted air, which impacts on rainfall onto the Great Lakes and increases toxics in the water; a further addition of sulphur dioxides, responsible for acid rain; and a direct addition to the air pollution in the border area of southwestern Ontario.

At the present time garbage incineration is not regarded as a major cause of air pollution compared with industrial, automobile, and residential sources. Incineration might become a major means of disposing of solid wastes if the present plans of many Canadian and U.S. cities come to fruition. Since plastics are not a recoverable resource with current technology, incineration might pose a significant addition to air pollution. Incineration, as well, can produce a substance called dioxin, regarded as the most toxic substance known and for which there is no minimum safe limit. In theory, exposure to even a single molecule of dioxin could trigger cancer in human cells (Mellon *et al.*, 1986).

At present there is very limited experience in monitoring incinerators and limited investigation of how dioxins find their way into the ecosystem or of their eventual impacts on human health. There is sufficient concern about the toxicity of dioxin to realize that it should be treated with considerable caution and all possible measures should be taken to guard against inadvertent production and release into the environment.[4]

Recycling and Resource Recovery

During the early 1970s the first burst of public interest in environment occurred and the publication of the Club of Rome's sensational warning of dwindling global resources in their report, *Limits to Growth*, caused considerable concern (Meadows *et al.*, 1972). Added to this was a huge increase in energy costs from the management of oil and gas supplies by the OPEC cartel. These events stimulated considerable efforts by volunteers on a local basis to develop recycling of paper, metals, and glass. Such efforts met with some temporary success but failed after a period because of a lack of available markets for the resulting products. Low prices for scrap metal and waste paper inhibited the growth of a recycling industry. The enthusiasm of volunteers, who did much of the sorting and handling, declined. Machinery for sorting and separating the components of garbage into recoverable components was also not very successful at that time.

What these early experiments did reveal was the necessity of separating the various components of solid waste at the point of collection. The concept is based on separating general household waste from glass, metals, and paper. These latter items are put into separate compartments of a large plastic container and the rest of the refuse is dealt with in the usual way.

Early efforts were amateurish, underfunded, and on a small scale. For resource recovery to have any chance of success a sustained pilot project had to be mounted by a provincial government, so that major technical, economic, and social problems could be understood and dealt with. Since 1978 the Ontario government has operated such a pilot plant at Downsview. The experimental plant has explored "the conditions under which waste can be mechanically separated into its components, what can be recovered and how mechanical means can best be used for the recovery of raw materials from municipal solid waste" (Ontario Ministry of Environment, 1984-85). The recovery process obtains the following raw materials from solid waste:

- refuse-derived fuel;
- ferrous metals;
- compost;
- corrugated cardboard;
- a glass-rich fraction.

Recovery of fuel, metals, cardboard, and compost was relatively successful. The expense and difficulty of extracting glass convinced the managers of the project that glass was better extracted at the source. Other lessons from the experimental plant include learning how to cope with different components in the flow of waste and how to procure dependable long-term markets for the resources recovered.

In addition to its own plant the Ontario government has now developed a full-scale subsidy program for municipal recycling efforts. A privately owned recycling operation – Total Recycling Systems in Kitchener – is the largest of its kind in North America. The operation started in 1976 and has grown steadily since then. In 1984, 30,000 plastic boxes were bought and supplied free to homeowners for the disposal of such recyclables as paper, glass, and cans. The voluntary co-operation of the householder was necessary and a participation rate of approximately 80 per cent was reported.

During the late 1980s the garbage crisis was highlighted by some widely publicized incidents bringing the subject to world attention: a garbage scow from New York roamed the world to find a place to dump its cargo; toxic wastes were dumped in the Third World, endangering the health of inhabitants; a PCB fire on a storage site at St. Basile le Grand in Quebec caused a mass evacuation. And, in February of 1990, a massive fire at Hagersville in southern Ontario raged out of control for weeks on end at Canada's largest tire dump, consuming millions of tires, spewing toxic fumes, and causing untold damage to the local environment.

In Canada all provincial governments now appear to be looking at a program in reduction, re-use, recycling, and recovery. In Ontario this program subsidizes municipal operations to introduce new methods of recovering and recycling wastes. In 1987, $25 million was spent on the program and seventy-two municipalities had participated. Recyclable material represented only 3 per cent of the waste generated, but there is a long-term objective of getting this up to 15 per cent, and if composting is brought in even higher proportions might be recovered. Such technical breakthroughs as biodegradable plastic and more re-use of products, especially by industry, could further minimize the waste problem.

In the final analysis it may be that the otherwise irreducible remnant of garbage may have to be reduced by incineration under very controlled, safe methods and a residue of ash placed in some kind of landfill site. These methods will be costly and this municipal function will continue to be a burden until an efficient resource recovery system is fully operational.

Municipalities and Water Pollution

A supply of abundant, cheap, and pure water is a resource that many Canadians have taken for granted. Canada has much of the world's supply of fresh water but its cheapness and abundance can no longer be taken for granted. Lakes, rivers, and underground water supplies have been contaminated by acid rain, sewage, run-off from farms and urban areas, industrial spills, leakage from dumps, and deposits from long-range aerial transport of toxic substances (International Joint Commission, 1986).

Municipalities are responsible for carrying away waste water through sewers and treating the wastes. Supplies of water are distributed to consumers and treated water is rid of silt, bacteria, and some contaminants (Maclaren, 1986). In the nineteenth century cities started to build sewers to carry wastes away. Sewage treatment was not undertaken on any major scale until about twenty-five years ago. Water supply systems were also begun in the late nineteenth century, and water purification to eliminate sources of bacterial infection began in the 1920s.

The first pumped water supply in Canada was provided by a privately operated company in Toronto, which was taken over by the municipality in 1873. Water supply systems, mainly run by municipalities, became standard practice and were accelerated as much by the need for fire protection as by a demand for an accessible water supply. The filtration of water to eliminate turbidity and the addition of chlorine greatly improved the quality of the water and eliminated such diseases as typhoid, cholera, tuberculosis, and infant mortality from dysentery. The treatment of water supply averted the need for treatment of sanitary wastes, which continued to be dumped into the same waters from which drinking water was pumped.

Since Canada has so many broad rivers, large lakes, and ocean bays it was far cheaper to allow sewage to be diluted in water and broken down by natural processes than by treating it. Eventually the volume of sewage in rivers and lakes became large enough to severely deplete available oxygen supplies and kill much of the aquatic life in lakes such as Erie. In addition, there was an outcry against the offence to aesthetic sensibilities from shoreline residents. Also, dangerously high bacterial levels made using water for recreation hazardous to health. By the late 1950s and early 1960s governments at last decided to act on a problem that was at a crisis level in such communities as Ottawa, Winnipeg, and Toronto.

The major emphasis has been on sewage treatment by those cities situated on inland lakes and rivers. Cities on the Prairies and on the Great Lakes were the first to clean up. Urban areas on the St. Lawrence River watershed or near the oceans have been much slower to treat their sanitary wastes (see Table 1). In the early 1980s Quebec began a large program to catch up and spent hundreds of millions of dollars, much of it for Montreal and its environs (Maclaren, 1986; Environment Canada, 1988). Quebec's record was the worst in Canada, as can be seen from the figures in Table 1. The Atlantic provinces have lacked the revenues to mount major programs, though in 1988 a major program was announced to clean up Halifax harbour with federal/provincial/municipal cost-sharing.

TABLE 1
Wastewater Systems:
Extent of Service in Each Province or Territory

Province or Territory	Total Population Surveyed	Percentage Served by Sewers	Percentage Served by Sewage Treatment
Newfoundland	497,018	60.0	12.8
Prince Edward Island	57,587	100.0	94.4
Nova Scotia	536,604	83.3	21.4
New Brunswick	409,900	91.8	60.7
Quebec	6,685,434	81.9	6.2
Ontario	7,641,607	86.1	83.5
Manitoba	839,158	94.9	94.7
Saskatchewan	611,072	99.0	99.0
Alberta	1,852,714	99.3	99.3
British Columbia	2,175,754	77.5	77.5
Yukon Territory	21,888	88.0	86.2
Northwest Territories	43,953	91.6	52.5
TOTAL	**21,372,690**	**85.3**	**57.3**

NOTE: Data are provided by provincial governments on an irregular basis. Although data were compiled in January, 1985, they do not represent sewage services at the time but rather the extent of services at the date of last provincial report.

SOURCE: Adapted from Environment Canada, Environmental Protection Service, *National Inventory of Municipal Waterworks and Wastewater Systems in Canada 1981* (Ottawa: Supply and Services Canada, 1982). Data updated to January, 1985.

While some provinces struggle to catch up and to install primary treatment for sanitary wastes, there are even larger and more complex problems looming. Sewage treatment plants have been built to accomplish primary treatment and phosphorous removal. They were also built to accommodate the urban growth of the 1960s and early 1970s. Today there is a triple challenge to face.

1. Many existing sewage treatment plants are operating at close to capacity and need a substantial expansion.
2. The treatment process needs to be upgraded to test for and remove toxic contaminants from various sources.
3. Many of the sewer systems are old and are combined storm and sanitary sewers. They are in need of renovation and improvement. (*Windsor Star*, February 14, 1987)

From 1986 through 1988, leading up to the federal election of November, 1988, a concentrated effort was made by the Federation of Canadian Municipalities, supported by the provinces, to obtain a commitment from the federal government to participate in a long-term investment in the renewal of municipal infrastructure. The case was made not only on the basis of future needs and the serious deterioration of the existing facilities but also as a means of spurring economic activity in Canada's depressed regions. The answer given by the federal government was that the federal budget deficit would not allow for new spending commitments on projects that, constitutionally, belong to the provincial-municipal sector. Tom McMillan, the federal Environment Minister, went further and stated that Canadian water is cheap and undervalued and that a more efficient use of water and revenue for needed improvements could come from surcharges on the water rates (Federation of Canadian Municipalities, 1987).

As Figure 2 shows, the major expansion of sewers and sewage treatment plants in the 1960s and 1970s was greatly assisted by federal contributions toward the cost. The Central Mortgage and Housing Corporation, under an amendment to the National Housing Act, was able to make "a loan to any province, municipality or municipal sewage corporation for the purpose of assisting in the construction or expansion of a sewage treatment project." CMHC made low-interest loans for part of the cost of construction and allowed for forgiveness of 25 per cent of the principal and 25 per cent of the interest for prompt repayment. This program, known as the Municipal Infrastructure Program, ended in 1978. Other programs continued funding after 1978, but all these programs were terminated in 1984 and have not been resumed (Maclaren, 1986). The backlog of work that has accumulated since 1984 is not only related to sewers and sewage treatment plants; large sums are also required to repair aging water mains, water pumping plants, roads, bridges, and sidewalks.

During the federal election of 1988 both the Liberal and New

Figure 2
Average Annual Levels of Federal Funding for Municipal Infrastructure in Current Dollars

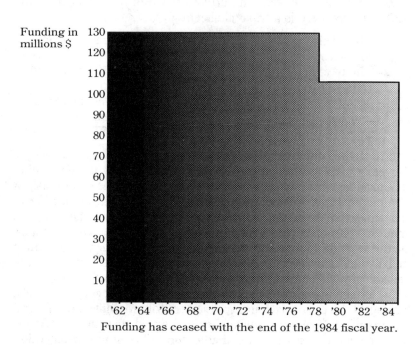

Funding has ceased with the end of the 1984 fiscal year.

Included are the following programs:

Municipal Infrastructure Program (1961-1978): $ 2 billion
Neighbourhood Improvement Program (1974-1977): $ 199.5 million
Municipal Incentive Grant Program (1975-1978): $ 128 million
Community Services Contribution Program (1979-1980): $ 400 million
Urban Transportation Assistance Program (1978-1984): $ 230 million

SOURCE: Federation of Canadian Municipalities, Technical Committee, *Canada's Urban Infrastructure*, Appendix E: Finan and Knight, "Federal Support for Municipal Infrastructure in Canada," June, 1984.

Democratic parties pledged a $5 billion federal contribution on a program to renew municipal infrastructures. In this they were moving back to the older tradition of federal leadership in city renewal, started by Diefenbaker and continued through the Pearson and Trudeau years. Both parties argued that the job-creating potential of such large-scale works would help create revenues and cut unemployment costs across the country without seriously increasing the federal budget deficit.

Toxic Waste Disposal

A serious problem has become the focus of considerable attention during the last ten years – the escape into the environment of highly toxic substances, many of which are known carcinogens. The range and sources of these toxics are many, and it is beyond the scope of this chapter to cover all of them. The sources include aerial transmission from industrial stacks, direct leaks into water bodies and ground water from industries, urban run-off, pesticides and herbicides from agriculture, the dumping of liquid wastes into municipal sewer systems, and leachate from landfill sites.

Studies of the Great Lakes Basin as an integrated ecosystem reveal a growing chemical broth in the water, the sediments, and the living creatures and plants within it. Already the government of Ontario issues warnings to fishermen in its annual fishing guide not to eat more than certain maximum amounts of fish from specified regions of the Great Lakes. Similar warnings are issued for many lakes and rivers all across Canada. The International Joint Commission, in its *Third Biennial Report on the Great Lakes Water Quality Agreement of 1978* (1986) stated that:

> many more toxic chemicals and low ambient concentrations of chemical mixtures threaten the health of the ecosystem to an extent and in ways that were not realized in 1978, and many are not adequately addressed by monitoring and control programs. . . . many toxic chemicals bioaccumulate in predator species and can, in combination or singly, affect the health, diversity and resilience of biological communities and have possible long term implications for humans.

The problem of toxic wastes at the municipal level are related to two past practices: (1) inadequate control over substances, mainly of industrial origin, placed in landfill sites or old municipal dumps – some of this toxic material is undoubtedly leaching out; (2) dumping into municipal sewer systems of toxic liquids, which are flowing through to the outflow because of inadequate sewage treatment or inadequate detection of the substances dumped and of their sources. The conclusion reached by scientific investigators that toxic substances are reaching lakes, rivers, and ground water in increasing quantities and that these substances are carcinogenic and gene mutating, even in very minute quantities, has led to a major revision in pollution control legislation.

Programs in many provinces are now under way. Ontario has planned an ambitious program, the Municipal-Industrial Strategy for Abatement (MISA), because it faces the most critical problems. The MISA initiative was announced by the Ontario government in June,

1986. Municipalities and industry are to be given major responsibility for the following:

1. Identify and measure all discharges (toxic and otherwise) to build up a comprehensive data base on contaminant discharge.
2. Through *best available technology* (BAT) effluent limits will be set for each industrial and municipal sector.
3. In addition to BAT, effluent limits will be set to protect existing water quality.
4. Monitoring and regulating under the Environmental Protection Act will ensure adherence to the standards by each discharger.

Ontario municipalities fear that a potential upgrading of their treatment plants and the monitoring of discharges into their sewer systems will prove to be very costly. They would like to ensure that industries are made to treat effluents before they are discharged into the sewers. If substantial costs are involved they also want provincial and, possibly, federal participation (Ontario Ministry of Environment, 1987). The Ontario government is making no commitment on these questions until they see the results of a major sewer use control study. There seems to be no doubt that this higher level of monitoring and abatement procedures will add to the already huge cost facing municipalities and provinces in the task of preserving and improving water quality standards.

The widespread dumping of toxic wastes in unsatisfactory sites under municipal and/or private control has been recognized as a potential source of danger and provincial governments have been seeking a solution to this problem for the last ten years. Sensational eco-catastrophes such as the Love Canal dump in New York state, a serious PCB spill on the Trans Canada highway, and the PCB fire at St. Basile le Grand reinforce the NIMBY syndrome. Such disasters make the local populace resist any kind of disposal or storage site for toxic wastes in their vicinity (Economic Council of Canada, 1985).

The Ontario Waste Management Corporation was established in July, 1981. The task of the corporation was to construct and manage a hazardous waste disposal system. To do this it has engaged in a lengthy and elaborate consultative process to select a central site for its main plant and to inform the public about the procedure for site selection and the risk factors.

By 1989 Canada had only one toxic waste disposal site, at Swan Hills north of Edmonton. Neither the main industrial provinces, Ontario and Quebec, nor major generators of toxic wastes had an operating system. Ontario is still going through the process of developing its main toxic waste disposal site southeast of Hamilton. Quebec faces the embarrassment of shipping PCBs to Britain for disposal only to have them returned to a wrathful reception by Quebec residents.

It now appears that this unwelcome publicity will compel the federal and provincial governments to spend the huge sums needed to build state-of-the-art high-temperature incinerators and chemical precipitators on safe landfill sites as a permanent solution. One fact is evident – no other province or country is freely willing to receive another's toxic wastes.

Conclusions

Local governments have always had a primary interest in basic environmental services such as removal of wastes, sanitation, the provision of clean water, and the elimination of such nuisances as offensive odours, noise, gases, etc. The problems became more massive and complex in the post-1945 surge of urban development and, beginning in the 1960s, provinces moved to increase financial support, regulation, monitoring, and in some instances, direct operation of sewage and water installations. A much higher level of treatment of wastes is called for because of much larger volumes of waste products and the presence of toxic contaminants now present in the air and water.

Although the rate of spending on municipal facilities has been high and a substantial share of the burden has fallen on the property tax, much remains to be done (see chapter by D. Siegel in this volume). The withdrawal of federal participation in 1984 from financing municipal infrastructure and the steadfast refusal of the government in Ottawa to be more than a co-ordinator of national efforts leave provinces and municipalities with a heavy joint responsibility for the existing system, plus costly new programs such as MISA and toxic waste disposal.

The problems of incineration and toxic waste disposal are now in their embryonic stages and long-term assessments of the problems associated with these programs are just beginning. Recycling and greater control over production systems to assure a minimal impact on the environment are not an integral part of the planning of the economic system. In the short period since the publication of the Brundtland Report (World Commission on Environment and Development, 1987), all countries have been sensitized to the view that preservation of the environment is vital to the protection of the world's productive capacity. The developing world is not as willing as it once was to provide pollution havens for industry or to accept the industrialized countries' toxic wastes.

A combination of greater alertness to environmental threats and the NIMBY syndrome imply that many pollution problems must be solved where they happen. They cannot be shunted off "down the river." Federal, provincial, and international regulations will try to establish standards, but much of the action on delivery of pollution controls will be at the local level. This will be all the sharper because community activism has undergone a vigorous growth where people feel their health and amenities are threatened. Citizens' groups and their representatives may become major participants in the struggle to reduce stress on the environment and to bring about conditions where there is not a continuous and worrying decline in environmental quality.

NOTES

1. The term "environment" can mean a variety of things. A more appropriate term with a more specific meaning is "ecosystem," which is "short for ecological system. It refers to living and non-living elements functioning as a unit in nature. An ecosystem can be large or small. Whatever its size it includes all the plants, animals and microorganisms within the system, together with the physical environment with which the organisms interact. . . . Because of the interactions among the different parts of an ecosystem significant changes to one part will affect the other parts" (Environment Canada, 1986: 2).
2. British North America Act 1867, 30 and 31 Victoria, c 3, S. 51, 92, 92A, 95 as amended.
3. Between 1976 and 1981 approximately 100,000 hectares of rural land were converted to urban use. About 50 per cent of this converted land was in the top five categories of agricultural classification. This represents a significant loss and the Lands Directorate of Environment Canada is monitoring the loss and pointing out the implications for policy purposes.
4. The Regulation of Toxic and Oxidant Air Pollution in North America (p. 35). The last inventory data indicate that incineration contributes approximately 3 per cent of the total emissions of volatile organic compounds in the U.S. and approximately 1.5 per cent of these emissions in Canada. The section goes on to say that incineration is an important source of dioxins and a number of toxic heavy metals.

REFERENCES

Boggs, Carl (1986). "The Greens," *Our generation*, 10, 1: 1-61.

Bureau of Municipal Research (1974). *The Politics of Waste Management.* Toronto.

Caldwell, Lynton K. (1984). "Science will not save the biosphere but politics might," Guest lecture for Foundation for Environmental Conservation, Washington.

Congressional Quarterly (1982). *Environmental Issues: Prospects and Problems.* Washington, D.C.: Editorial Research Reports.

— (1981). *Environment and Health.* Washington, D.C.: Editorial Research Reports.

Crooks, Harold (1983). *Dirty Business: The Inside Story of the New Garbage Agglomerates.* Toronto: James Lorimer.

D'Amore, L. J., and Associates (1983). "Study of Trends in Canadian Environmental and Water Issues Concerning Ontario and the Great Lakes Region," Inland Waters Directorate, Environment Canada.

Economic Council of Canada (1985). *Managing the Legacy*. Ottawa: Proceedings of a Colloquium on the Environment.

Environment Canada (1983). *Stress on Land*. Ottawa.

— (1986). *Canada's Environment: An Overview*. Ottawa.

— (1987). *Currents of Change*. Inquiry on Federal Water Policy, Final Report. Ottawa.

— (1988). Wastewater Update. Correspondence with Environment Canada, November.

Federation of Canadian Municipalities (1987). *Work, Work, Work, Municipal Economic Development Program*. Ottawa.

Flett, Jillian (1986). *Recycling and Municipal Waste Management: A Proposal for Legislative and Policy Reform*. Edmonton: Environmental Law Centre.

Girling, James A. (1983). "Land as the subject of Environmental Law," *Stress on Land*. Ottawa: Environment Canada.

International Joint Commission (1986). *Third Biennial Report on the Great Lakes Water Quality Agreement of 1978 to the Governments of the United States and Canada and the States and Provinces of the Great Lakes Basin*. Windsor, Ont.

Kidd, Joanna (1984). *A Burning Question: Emissions from Municipal Refuse Incinerators*. Toronto: Pollution Probe.

— and Kai Milliard (1984). *Up the Stack: Air Emissions from Municipal Refuse Incinerators*. Toronto: Pollution Probe.

Maclaren, J.W. (1986). *Municipal Waterworks and Wastewater Systems*. Research Paper #3, Inquiry into Federal Water Policy. Ottawa: Environment Canada.

MacNeill, J.W. (1971). *Environmental Management; Constitutional Study Prepared for the Government of Canada*. Ottawa: Information Canada.

Meadows, Donella, *et al.* (1972). *The Limits to Growth: A Report for the Club of Rome's Project on the Predicament of Mankind*.

Mellon, Margaret, *et al.* (1986). *The Regulation of Toxic and Oxidant Air Pollution in North America*. A joint project of the Canadian Environmental Law Research Foundation, Toronto, and the Environmental Law Institute, Washington, D.C.

Michigan Department of Natural Resources, Air Quality Division (1984). Staff Activity Report, Permit to Install No. 468-83, 16 October.

Ontario Ministry of Environment (1974). *Origin and Management of PCB Wastes*. Toronto.

— (1984-85) "Recycling of Domestic Waste Switches to High Gear" and "Six Years of Operation Answer Many Questions," *Legacy*, 13, 1 (Winter).

— (1986). *Municipal-Industrial Strategy for Abatement (MISA): A Policy and Program Statement of the Government of Ontario on Controlling Municipal and Industrial Discharges into Surface Waters*. Toronto.

— (1987). *The Public of the MISA White Paper and the Government's Response to it*. Toronto.

Peat, Marwick and Partners in association with W.S. Sims (1983). *Economic Incentive Policy Instruments to Implement Pollution Control Objectives in Ontario*. Report to Ontario Ministry of Environment, Toronto.

Roebuck, Janet (1974). *The Shaping of Urban Society: A History of City Functions*. New York: Charles Scribner's Sons.

Simpson-Lewis, Wendy, *et al. Stress on Land in Canada*. Ottawa: Environment Canada, Lands Directorate.

Statistics Canada (1986). *Human Activity and the Environment: A Statistical Compendium*. Ottawa.

Task Force on Program Review (1985). *Improved Program Delivery: Programs of the Ministry of the Environment*. A Study Team Report to the Task Force.

Vander Doelen, Chris (1986). "Error may allow Detroit plant to shower us with toxins," *Windsor Star*, March 7.

World Commission on Environment and Development (1987). Gro Harlen Brundtland, Chairman. *Our Common Future*. Oxford: Oxford University Press.

7   Peter Woolstencroft

Education

Introduction

Every person in Canada is affected in some manner by education. In 1983 over 6 million students – one Canadian in four – were enrolled in primary, secondary, or post-secondary programs; there were over 338,000 full-time teachers; and, of course, all Canadians contributed to the financing of education through taxes paid to school boards or municipalities and to provincial and national governments. Education spending for the 1986-87 school year was estimated to have exceeded $34 billion; two-thirds of this amount were spent on elementary and secondary education (Canadian Tax Foundation, 1988: 5.4). Education, however, is more than a big economic enterprise: questions about what ought to happen in education are at base political.

Conflicts about educational goals serve as a barometer of fundamental divisions about the organization of society; of the values that are appropriately fostered by social institutions; and, at root, of the legitimate role of the state, especially as it pertains to the rights of parents to be directly responsible for children's education.

Education can be approached from three different (albeit interrelated) perspectives. The first focuses on questions relating to the development of the individual. How are the individual's capacities for learning interpreted? Does the system mould the individual to perceived ends? Or do the individual's capacities, interests, and inclinations structure what teachers and schools offer as education? The second perspective concerns the social goals used to justify the state's extensive commitment to education and the elaborate infrastructure of schools, colleges, and universities. Is the system designed to create, say, an academic elite, in which graduates master the demands of an exacting curriculum of traditional academic subjects, such as English, foreign languages, and mathematics? Or is the goal to generate a technologically proficient work force able to compete in the international marketplace? Or is the function of the education system to provide opportunities to those children and young adults burdened by disadvantages and constraints based on family and class? The third perspective focuses on education's role in transmitting, manifestly and latently, important social values. Educational institutions are one of the main socializing agencies of society, integrating those of diverse backgrounds (whether they be ethnic, religious, or economic) into a socially compatible and harmonious whole. The system of education also serves as a conserving institution, transmitting social values from one generation to the next. Among other things, this approach asks if the system of education serves to legitimize the ongoing social order, particularly the inequalities of the capitalist economy, by creating an acquiescent labour force (Bowles and Gintis, 1976).

In recent times, Canadians have increasingly questioned education, a result of three factors: greater social diversity, expanded expectations about what should be done in the name of education, and enhanced awareness of educational alternatives.

The intensification of debate about education occurs in a society in which education traditionally has received low political attention. For the most part, education has been left to the quiet work of experts, administrators, and professionals, rather than being subject to much popular discussion, let alone heightened public debate and direction. On occasion educational policies, such as the Manitoba Schools Question, Regulation 17 in Ontario, and the question of the use of either English or French as the language of instruction in Quebec, have given rise to some of the most divisive issues in Canadian politics. That contentious issues have involved minority groups' education rights, especially pertaining to language, suggests that Canadians have attributed different purposes to their systems of education operating within a culturally pluralistic society. Generally, however, the tendency has been to separate educational decision-making from conflicts over values.

Along with health care and income maintenance and security, state involvement in education is one of the pillars of the welfare state. It also represents the first extension of the state into what were ostensibly private, that is, family or religious matters. That extension, which, except in Manitoba and Quebec, occurred more or less without rancorous debate, was primarily motivated by desires to establish social order and economic growth (Prentice, 1977; Henley and Pampalis, 1982; Gidney and Millar, 1985). It has been only latterly that education as a state responsibility has been justified as a means of encouraging individual self-development and growth (Manzer, 1985). The extent of the state's involvement in education reached its zenith in the 1970s, when education spending was surpassed by health-care spending (Chandler and Chandler, 1979: 216-37). Nonetheless, education in Canada, compared to other industrial systems, generally commands high expenditure levels relative to the Gross National Product or all public spending (Statistics Canada, 1983).

A study conducted by the Canadian Education Association (1984) indicated that Canadians perceive education to be very important for personal success, and that they have higher confidence in education than in governments, the judicial system, labour unions, big business, or churches. The Gallup Poll (1986) reported that two-thirds of Canadians favoured increased government spending for education (elementary, secondary, and post-secondary) and about one-fifth were opposed.

Studies of public opinion in Ontario regarding education show that there is great support for a level of education spending that keeps up with or is greater than inflation. In one study, only 15 per cent wanted education spending to be less than the inflation rate (Livingston et al., 1983). In four surveys conducted from 1978 to 1982, respondents were asked to indicate which public policy area should have first or second claim on tax money: public education was either second or third, with health care and medical care ranked first (Livingston, 1982).

Other surveys of public opinion indicate that Canadians have serious reservations about various aspects of school systems and the quality of education. The Gallup Poll (1983) reported that the proportion of Canadians who thought that children were being better educated than they were was equal to the proportion (41 per cent) who thought things were worse (13 per cent said education was the same). In 1948, by comparison, 74 per cent thought education was better and 12 per cent said education was worse. George E. Flower (1984) reported that 43.8 per cent of respondents thought education had improved and 36.3 per cent thought that education had worsened. A Gallup Poll report (1984) indicated that 40 per cent of respondents believed the quality of teaching had gone down while 17 per cent said it had gone up; in 1964, the comparable proportions were 16 per cent and 48 per cent. Flower's study indicated that more people thought standards and teachers' interest in students had worsened rather than improved. In Ontario, in response to a question about the quality of education in the high schools in the past ten years, 37 per cent of respondents indicated that they felt quality had deteriorated, 28 per cent saw improvement, and 17 per cent saw no change (Livingston et al., 1984: 5). Similar generally negative evaluations of the schools have been reported in the media (Radwanski, 1987: 28).

Changes in the public's estimation of education may mean that Canadians are more sophisticated and discriminating in their estimations of education; or perhaps they are less predisposed to accept at face value the authority and expertise of the school; or, indeed, the quality of education may have deteriorated in the last thirty years or so. Whatever the explanation, it seems clear that Canadians, on the whole, have considerably less confidence about what is happening in the schools than was the case a generation ago, but they nonetheless give education, as an area of public policy, a great deal of support and are willing to see increased levels of public spending.

This essay has two parts. First, it discusses the pattern of educational governance in Canada. Second, three issues – the structure of educational opportunity, multiculturalism, and the fragmentation of the public school system – are analysed.

The Nature of Educational Governance in Canada

The state is the major vehicle for the delivery of education programs and the attainment of individual and social goals. As Frank Mackinnon (1960: 4) argued:

> To the schools the state gives no power of their own; and the teaching profession is kind of a low-drawer civil service, trained, licensed, hired, inspected, and directed by the state. No other activity, institution, or profession is in this extraordinary position; education in North America is now the most completely socialized activity in North America.

The structure of Canadian educational governance has five salient features that, in sum, distinguish it from any other system and contribute to how educational issues are addressed and programs are implemented.

The most important characteristic of the structure of Canadian educational governance is the predominant role given to the provinces and the minor role assigned to the national government. Canada's system stands out from all other political systems, except Switzerland, in the degree to which the national government is not involved, directly or indirectly, with the making or implementing of educational policies. In Canada, the relatively few groups, such as the Canadian Education Association and the Canadian School Trustees' Association, that perceive education as a national concern have not been very successful in establishing education as a national issue. For the most part, groups interested in educational policy organize along provincial lines, think about educational policy in provincial terms, and operate within the system of provincialized educational systems, all without much apparent public dissatisfaction.

Provincialization of education means that Canadians do not share in similar educational experiences, whether curriculum, programs, teachers' qualifications, standards, or extent of funding. Unlike other federations, however, the fact that provinces are important in establishing educational policies has not resulted in a lower societal commitment to educational spending (Cameron and Hofferbert, 1974).

Provincialization of education is the result of the Constitution Act (1982), which, in Section 93, gives the provinces responsibility for education. That provision is an integral part of the Confederation agreement, reflecting the compromise between the English and French peoples to create a federation that would avoid political conflict by giving each group jurisdictional control over potentially divisive matters.

The specific provisions of Section 93 created the second feature of educational governance, namely publicly funded denominational schools, the existence of which distinguishes Canada from many systems, most notably the American, and contributes greatly to the diversity of Canadian education. Section 93 was designed to protect the educational privileges of religious and cultural minorities that existed at the time of Confederation or were subsequently enacted by provincial legislatures. The national government was given the responsibility to ensure that those privileges were not violated, but subsequent political events, especially the Manitoba Schools Question, indicated that Ottawa had neither the legal capacity nor the political will to ensure that provinces adhered to the educational rights guaranteed in the British North America Act. The status of denominational schools in some provinces has been an enduring political controversy. This was perhaps most notably evident in Ontario, where the issue of public funding for Roman Catholic schools had been one of the major differences between the Progressive Conservative Party and the two other major parties, the Liberal and the New Democratic parties, until 1984 when Premier William Davis, in a startling reversal, supported funding for Roman Catholic schools beyond grade 10.

As a result of denominational schools existent within the Canadian provinces when they entered Confederation and political accommodations since that time, seven types of publicly supported denominational schools have evolved (Blair, 1981).

1. Alberta and Saskatchewan: separate school system (Catholic) parallels the public system; each is publicly funded and governed by the Ministry of Education.

2. Newfoundland and Labrador: as part of the Terms of Union of Newfoundland and Labrador with Canada in 1949, there are four kinds of denominational schools: Catholic; Pentecostal; Seventh Day Adventist; and, since 1968, schools formed out of a combined Anglican, United Church, Presbyterian, and Salvation Army base, under the jurisdiction of Integrated School Boards (Rowe, 1976: 159-64).

3. British Columbia: one public system, with no funding for religious schools; since 1977 independent schools, which may have a religious orientation, may be partially funded.

4. Ontario: public schools and separate schools (most of which are Roman Catholic but some are Protestant); Roman Catholic schools were publicly funded up to grade 10 until 1985, when full funding was introduced.

5. Quebec: "dual confessional" system; Catholic and Protestant schools operate independently, under the authority of the Ministry of Education.

6. Manitoba (Gregor and Wilson, 1984), Nova Scotia, and New Brunswick: public system, but administrative arrangements allow Catholic schools to operate in various places (Blair, 1986).

7. Prince Edward Island: public system, no religious schools with public funds.

The third characteristic of educational governance pertains to the language of instruction. The bilingual character of Canada has led governments to be concerned with ensuring that students are taught in their "mother" tongue and have the opportunity to study the other national language. Since 1981, New Brunswick has constitutionally guaranteed English- and French-speaking students the right to be taught in their own language by establishing minority-language school boards. Quebec's schools, divided along denominational lines, are essentially also linguistically divided, although some Catholic schools provide instruction in English. Other provinces – the exceptions being Alberta and Newfoundland and Labrador – legislatively provide for instruction in the minority language where numbers warrant.

The fourth element in the pattern of educational governance is the existence of locally elected school boards. Only two countries in the world – Canada and the United States – have locally elected representatives ("trustees") who play at least some role in determining educational policies and providing citizens some measure of direct control, which is not available in other policy areas, though provincial authorities determine the bulk of educational policy, standards, and curriculum. Trustees are elected in most provinces, except for Nova Scotia and Newfoundland and Labrador, and, until recently, New Brunswick. Generally, trustees are elected on a non-partisan basis, although partisan elections for school boards have occurred in the larger cities, particularly Toronto, Vancouver, and Winnipeg (Humphreys, 1986).

How monies are raised for educational funding constitutes the fifth variation in the governance of education (Lawton, 1987). Elementary and secondary education has two main sources of funds: provincial grants, which come from general provincial tax revenues, and real property taxes, raised at the municipal level. Provinces vary in the ratio of educational costs covered by provincial grants and property taxes. In Prince Edward Island and New Brunswick only provincial revenues are used for elementary and secondary education. In other provinces – Newfoundland, Quebec, Nova Scotia – the bulk (that is, over 80 per cent) of educational expenses is paid out of provincial revenues. In Alberta, Saskatchewan, Manitoba, and Ontario, education funding is shared between the provincial government and the municipalities. British Columbia's system is similar on the surface to the four provinces to its east, but in practice (at least since 1981) the provincial government has had responsibility for educational funding inasmuch as it has imposed severe restrictions on the ability of local school boards to impose property taxes (Allen, 1986).

The upshot of these five features of educational governance is that the ten provincial education systems are extraordinarily complex and diversified. Canadians are often said to live in a highly provincialized political system; it probably is the case that more diversity occurs in education policies and governance than in any other policy field. For example, high school graduation requirements (including the number of years of elementary and secondary education necessary for graduation) vary considerably from province to province. Programmatically, provinces vary enormously, as is evidenced by what is available for exceptional children (Stewin and McCann, 1987). There are nineteen teacher organizations in Canada (including the Territories), plus the Canadian Teachers' Federation, which is a federation of teacher organizations, except for the single largest organization, the Central des Enseignements de Québec (McCreath, 1986: 26). Ontario's teachers are organized on the basis of denominational affiliation, language, and gender. As well, as Table 1 indicates, there are considerable variations in per student education expenditures by province and in the proportion of provincial and municipal budgets given to education.

No doubt the differences between the provinces are due to many factors. One of the most important is the economic resources available to provincial governments. Spending per student is lower in poorer provinces (Newfoundland and Labrador, Prince Edward Island, Nova Scotia, New Brunswick) and higher in more affluent provinces. Differences in spending among the provinces decreased from 1960 to 1976 but increased from that year until the early 1980s, as a result of more buoyant economic conditions in the western provinces (Brown, 1983: 14-15). Provinces vary in the proportions of provincial and municipal monies assigned to education. And education spending is irregularly related to the proportion of the population in the elementary and secondary school ages. This suggests that factors other than economic conditions and demography account for differences in education spending. These are likely to be found in the political culture, especially to the degree that education is seen to be either a "common good" or a means of providing for individual social mobility. The institutionalization of interest groups concerned with the extent

Table 1
Education Expenditures by Province, 1982

Province	School Board Expenditures Per Student	Education Expenditures as Proportion of Provincial and Municipal Taxes	Elementary and Secondary Students as Proportion of Total Population (1981)
Newfoundland and Labrador	$2,435	24.5	25.6
Prince Edward Island	2,440	21.7	21.4
Nova Scotia	2,671	23.1	21.9
New Brunswick	2,487	25.4	21.4
Quebec	4,357	25.2	17.1
Ontario	3,233	26.0	20.9
Manitoba	3,084	20.7	19.5
Saskatchewan	3,075	20.7	20.9
Alberta	3,300	17.9	19.8
British Columbia	3,502	21.1	18.3
Canada	3,438	23.6	

SOURCE: Statistics Canada, *Financial Statistics of Education, 1983-4* (Ottawa, August, 1987), Chart 8; Statistics Canada, *Advance Statistics of Education, 1987-88* (Ottawa, September, 1987), Table 12; Statistics Canada, *Elementary and Secondary School Enrolment, 1981-82*, Catalogue 81-220, Table 5.

of the state's commitment to education is also a significant factor. Such groups generally are partial to more rather than less spending, and to the degree that they are successful there will be increases in the proportion of governmental resources apportioned to education (Wilkinson, 1986).

Controversies in Education

The Canadian education systems have become the crucible for an extraordinary kaleidoscope of social issues, many far removed from traditional educational matters, ranging from language instruction through racism, holocaust studies, driver training, and hungry school children, to education about sex and AIDS (Stewin and McCann, 1987). Underlying these issues, however, is one fundamental question: to what extent do the Canadian education systems address and meet the goal of equal educational opportunity? That question in turn raises the issue of what policies will meet the goal of equal educational opportunity.

Equal Educational Opportunity

John Porter, at the close of his classic study of Canadian society, *The Vertical Mosaic* (1965: 557), argued that Canada "has a long way to go to become in any sense a thorough-going democracy." One reason for this was the failure to develop education systems in which class barriers to individual achievement were removed. Porter's interpretation points to one of the crucial functions of education in modern societies, namely, that of providing students equality of educational opportunity (Porter, 1979). Since families vary in their capacities or willingness to advance their children's education, it is necessary for the state to intervene in such a way as to offer each child the opportunity to attend school with minimal family costs. Otherwise, it is argued, the bright child born into a poor family unable or unwilling to pay for education is denied the opportunities that a similar child born into a well-to-do family (or a poor family committed to devoting its resources to education) would have.

Another argument for education based on the principle of equality of opportunity is that an advanced industrialized society requires a technologically proficient, specialized, and adaptable work force capable of meeting the labour, research, and management needs of an economy operating in a competitive international market in which capital and technology are highly mobile. Education, then, is seen as an engine of economic growth, fuelled by the provision of equal educational opportunities that lead to long-term and well-paid remuneration (Radwanski, 1987: 11-20).

James Coleman (1969: 13) has argued that the concept of equal educational opportunity contains four elements: (1) providing a "free" education up to a given level, which constitutes the principal entry point to the labour force; (2) providing a "common" curriculum for all children, regardless of background; (3) providing that children from diverse backgrounds attend the same school; and (4) providing equality within a given locality, since local taxes provide the source of support for schools. Application of these elements to the Canadian education systems illustrates that equal educational opportunity faces some important barriers. First, the existence of denominational schools results in different educative processes for children. Canadian students, as well, experience different curricular emphases and orientations from province to province (Hodgetts, 1968). A third difficulty arises from the use of property taxes to finance education.

Three important issues are raised when education is funded by monies raised though property taxes. First, education is not a public service related to the maintenance, development, or servicing of property. Yet, in those provinces in which the property tax is a significant revenue source for education, it represents the major component of municipal taxes. Second, to the extent that a province relies on local municipalities to provide funds for education the potential for inequalities exists because two communities with comparable school-age populations may differ greatly in their capacities to raise funds for comparable education programs. Such variations have led provincial governments to implement equalization programs that reduce the differences in the fiscal resources available to school boards. Stephen Lawton has argued that the greater willingness of Canadian governments compared to American states to develop equalization programs is evidence of greater societal commitment to the value of equality (Lawton, 1979). The third issue pertains to the right of public and denominational school boards to have access to commercial and industrial property taxes. Prior to 1989 separate school boards in Ontario were not able to impose such taxes, which meant that public boards had a wider tax base and lower taxes. This situation has been alleviated by amendments to the Education Act and related statutes.

In general, two approaches have been taken by provincial governments to address the question of equal educational opportunities. The first is for the provincial government to assume responsibility for educational expenditures in an attempt to alleviate differences between richer and poorer municipalities. The record has been inconsistent, however, with some provinces – most notably Ontario – experiencing a decline in the proportion of elementary and secondary education costs borne by the province (Ontario, 1985).

The second policy approach has been to create consolidated school districts. The premise of this approach is that larger, better-equipped schools are able to offer more courses, programs, faculty, and facilities – and, thus, more educational opportunities – than do their much smaller predecessors. Such consolidation has a price. The smaller school offered students a close-knit community and participation opportunities that are not readily available in the large and much more anonymous schools found in consolidated districts (Smitheram, 1982). The development of large secondary schools, with enrolments of well over 2,000 students, first in urban, then rural areas, meant that pressure developed to have programs that met students' diverse educational needs. Accordingly, students were streamed into academic or vocational programs on the basis of academic standing and aptitude tests. The policy of streaming has been a considerable part of the contention that education has reproduced the patterns of social stratification because those who enter academic programs tend to come from higher reaches of the social strata whereas those who enter vocational programs tend to come from lower rungs of the social hierarchy (Mifflin and Mifflin, 1982: 211-12; Radwanski, 1987).

The systematic effects of school consolidation on students' attainment levels are largely untested. One recent study in British Columbia of the correlates of student achievement found that resources (e.g., teacher qualifications, pupil/teacher ratios, and operating expenditures) are negatively correlated with mathematics scores and suggested that attitudes toward instruction at the level of school district accounts for much of the difference in districts' achievement scores (Coleman, 1986).

Considerable evidence suggests that educational opportunities are very much structured by the socio-economic characteristics of students and their families. Examination of census data from 1941 to 1961 by Ronald Manzer indicated considerable variations in the proportions of young people living at home and attending school. For example, in 1941 almost 60 per cent of children of professionals attended school compared to about 15 per cent for those coming from families in which the head worked in logging, fishing, trapping, and hunting. Despite some improvement between 1941 and 1951, and greater access to education in all occupational classes from 1941 to 1961, by 1961 the difference between those two groups had barely narrowed (to about 40 percentage points) and among all occupational classes "disparities . . . in access to education remained unchanged" and "the pattern of class inequalities in access to education in 1961 was not essentially different from that in 1941" (Manzer, 1974: 190).

More recent evidence suggests there has been some weakening over time of the relationship between social origin and educational attainment, especially at the elementary and secondary levels, although social class still makes a major contribution to differences in attainment (Guppy et al., 1984). Retention rates in the elementary and secondary school systems in 1980-81 indicate considerable variation from province to province in the ratio of enrolment in grade 12 (grade 11 in Quebec and Newfoundland and Labrador) to enrolment in grade 2, with the lowest retention rate being Nova Scotia (60.3), the highest being Quebec (84.9), and the national rate being 75.5 (Brown, 1983: 16).[1]

Radwanski (1987: 67-74) reported that one-third of Ontario students entering high school did not graduate and presented evidence that there were considerable differences between social classes in terms of continuing through the school system. The solution proposed by Radwanski (p. 163) is to replace streaming "by provision of a single and undifferentiated high-quality educational stream for all students." This single-track system of education will also contain highly specified and common educational goals and province-wide departmental examinations at both elementary and secondary levels of the system.

The irony is that both the practice of streaming and the Radwanski proposals flow out of a desire to bring about equal educational opportunities for each and every student in the system. Since students do not have equal learning abilities or academic interests, it is necessary to develop programs that address the varying needs of students. Arguments for the single-track system make the valid point that the various streams lead to differential educational outcomes and economic opportunities. Yet the single-track system creates enormous pedagogical problems for teachers who must try to meet the needs and interests of heterogeneous classes of students. And are the academic aspirations and interests of all students served by a program that does not distinguish between students' varying academic capabilities, interests, and aspirations?

The point is that identification of the problem of equal educational opportunities does not point to any necessary policy route. This is so, as has been argued by Amy Gutmann, because the principle of equal educational opportunity contains three different interpretations of desirable policies: maximization of students' life chances; equalization of least and most advantaged children's life chances; and allocation of resources according to children's abilities and motivations (Gutmann, 1988).

Each interpretation leads to problematic policy effects. For example, maximization means the adoption of programs directed to improving life chances of children without specifying spending limits. Education is not the only concern of society, yet maximization requires the full utilization of societal resources – and the denial of other social goods – that no society would likely support.

Policies designed to equalize life chances between children pose similar problems. For example, are we required to allocate enormous resources to those children from the poorest families to provide them with opportunities equal to those enjoyed by children of the richest families? Is it necessary to move dollars away from the bulk of children to favour those who have physiological or psychological learning disadvantages in an attempt to raise the latter to the level of the former? Affirmative answers to such questions require an enormous shifting of resources (with an accompanying denial of the other interpretations of the principle of equal educational opportunity). Both maximization and equalization will necessitate intervention in family affairs so that familial differences responsible for differences in educational attainments are systematically addressed. Such policy commitments would require the state to abrogate the idea of family autonomy far beyond the limits tolerated by any liberal-democratic society (Gutmann, 1988).

The third interpretation of the principle of equal opportunity – in which the state commits educational resources to children commensurate with their abilities and motivations – is the dominant policy route. The commitment is problematic inasmuch as apportionment of educational resources on the basis of merit results in providing "the least educational resources and attention to those children who have relatively few natural abilities and little inclination to learn and the most to those children who have relatively many natural abilities and high motivation" (Gutmann, 1988: 113). This results in programs that reproduce the educative capacities of students, negating other interpretations of the principle of equal educational opportunity.

Ministers of education, teachers, administrators, and, indeed, society at large support the idea of equal educational opportunity. The well-documented studies of the relationship between social class and educational attainment make the point that the Canadian education systems have not made remarkable progress in attenuating the impact of class origins on students' educational attainments. To achieve that laudable goal would not only require a much greater single-mindedness of purpose than hitherto has been the case in Canada, but also a much greater commitment to education in financial terms. There is little to suggest that such purpose and commitment will be forthcoming.

Even so, the goal of equal educational opportunity is problematic, given the increasing commitment by Canadian governments to policies designed to meet the needs and demands arising from the multicultural character of Canadian society and increasing pressure to diversify the institutional structure of the Canadian education systems.

Multiculturalism and Education

Canada's population has changed enormously since the end of World War Two. In 1951, the proportion of the Canadian population that was non-French and non-British was 21.3 per cent, with many living in western Canada. By the 1980s, primarily as the result of changes in immigration laws and regulations that brought about "ethnic-blind" procedures, the proportion had increased to over one-third, with most recent immigrants located within the larger urban areas.

These demographic changes led national politicians to become increasingly cognizant of the importance of "non-charter" groups and to develop political responses and public policies that addressed the needs and wants of such groups. Foremost among these was the statement on multiculturalism produced in 1971 by the national government, in good measure because of the concern expressed in many quarters that the Royal Commission on Bilingualism and Bi-culturalism had not adequately addressed multiculturalism (Wardhaugh, 1983: 199-200). Subsequent initiatives – the most recent being enunciated in 1987 by then Secretary of State and Minister Responsible for Multiculturalism David Crombie and legislatively outlined in the Canadian Multiculturalism Act – committed Ottawa to promoting "the full and equitable participation of individuals and communities of all origins in the continuing evolution and shaping of all aspects of Canadian society and assist them in the elimination of any barriers to such participation."

Not surprisingly, the increasing commitment by Ottawa to multi-culturalism legitimated the interests of groups seeking educational programs that would address their specific needs and aspirations. Pressure was put on provinces to develop appropriate policies and programs because multiculturalism involved so many matters falling within provincial jurisdiction. Such initiatives were contentious in some quarters because they were seen as contradicting the bilingual and bicultural character of Canadian society. This view, for example, led Francophone teacher organizations to be hostile to the concept of multiculturalism, and the Canadian Teachers' Federation in the 1980s had heated debates on the question of recognizing Canada as a multicultural society (McCreath, 1986: 26-27, 30-31; Mallea, 1977). Others perceived that multiculturalism means that the dominant culture and its institutions are being transformed by responding to the preferences and demands of what are labelled minority groups.

The record to date indicates considerable diversity in what has happened in the Canadian education systems. As a result of the federal government's initiatives in multiculturalism in the 1970s Ontario, Manitoba, Quebec, Saskatchewan, and Alberta adopted policies directed toward the delivery of multicultural educational programs (Burnet, 1979: 49). Some provinces are oriented to distinctiveness and separation. In Alberta – perhaps the most notable example – provincial legislation allows schools to have classes to be conducted in languages other than English or French (Lupul, 1977). Other provinces – Ontario, for example – have developed multiculturalism programs in education that are more assimilationist in character (Kach and DeFaveri, 1987; Wardhaugh, 1983: 207-08). The stress in Ontario has been on what are called "heritage languages" in which school boards offer training in various languages outside the regular classroom and normal school hours (Mallea, 1984: 86-89; Berryman, 1986).

Multiculturalism has come to mean the acceptance of the view that all peoples – whether native, "charter group," or new arrivals – comprise the sociological reality of Canada. Canada's education systems, in being called on to develop programs that address that reality, have seen one important assumption of education challenged, namely, that it should serve as a means of assimilating minority groups into the dominant group's culture, whether it be French or English (Mazurek and Kach, 1983: 48-50).

Canadian communities, as they absorb increasingly heterogeneous populations, have had to ask questions about the purposes and goals of basic social institutions. Education is no exception. Are society's goals served by the development of educational programs that highlight differences among students through heritage language programs, ethnic studies, and so forth? Or should the system's purpose be to integrate all students into an undifferentiated social whole?

The import of these questions can be seen in how the public school system addresses its students' diverse religious backgrounds. Schools in many provinces have allowed (or required) religious exercises with a Christian (or Judeo-Christian) character (Stamp, 1986), leading many to see the school as a Judeo-Christian institution. Ontario had the most stringent requirements in that opening religious exercises included "the reading of the Scriptures or other suitable readings and the repeating of the Lord's Prayer or other suitable prayers" (Ontario, 1980: 155-56). No exemption was allowed, though many school boards apparently did not adhere to the statutory requirements (Shapiro, 1985: 64). In 1989 the Ontario Court of Appeal ruled that Ontario's practices regarding religious exercises and classes were unconstitutional inasmuch as they violated the provision in the Charter of Rights and Freedoms protecting freedom of religion.

The Waterloo County Board of Education is responsible for schools in the Regional Municipality of Waterloo in Ontario (comprised of three cities, Kitchener, Cambridge, and Waterloo, and four townships, with a population in 1987 of over 300,000 that included large groupings of British and non-British peoples). The political relations between majorities and minorities were highlighted by a number of issues during the 1980s. One was raised by Jewish students who complained that teaching of *The Merchant of Venice* in grade 10 was causing anti-Semitic incidents. After heated debate, the Board's response was to eliminate the play from the secondary school curriculum rather than, as many preferred, to have the play taught at a higher grade.

During the debate it became apparent that many parts of the community were dissatisfied with the overall approach of the Board to the question of how minority groups fared within the school system.[2] This led to the development of a policy on race and ethnocultural relations (Waterloo County Board of Education, 1988). The debate on this policy exemplifies the political tensions intrinsic to the process of developing multicultural education programs and policies and echoes the controversies that have arisen on these issues in the United States, the United Kingdom, and Australia, three societies that also have absorbed immigrants in great numbers from varying ethnic, linguistic, and religious backgrounds (Lynch, 1987).

The most contentious issue before the Waterloo County Board of Education was that of religion. Some wanted the elimination of all religious exercises, arguing that the public school system ought to be a secular institution. Others wanted the Board to recognize religious pluralism in prayers and readings, arguing that all religions should be treated on an equal basis. Many of these people argued that education was inherently value-laden and that it was specious to pretend that the schools were, or could be, value-free or objective institutions. Still others argued for the status quo, claiming that the public school system was essentially a Judeo-Christian institution reflecting society's dominant religious grouping. The Board, in opting to maintain the status quo, angered many who sought to have the education system reflect its students' diverse religious backgrounds. Other groups were upset that the Board, because of its unwillingness to appoint a full-time race relations officer and to establish a race relations committee composed, in part, of members from the community, along with its decision to have curriculum guidelines that encourage rather than require proactive revisions, had not taken the lead on the questions of multicultural education and racism.

Another dimension of the demand for inclusion of multicultural groups in educational programs is found in the case of language education. Many immigrants have come to Canada from war-torn countries with little preparation to function successfully in a highly technological economy. The federal government's Canadian Multiculturalism Act, Section 3 (1) (c), declares that government policy is to promote "full and equitable participation of individuals and communities of all origins in the continuing evolution and shaping of all aspects of Canadian society and assist them in the elimination of any barrier to such participation." Language competency in either of the two official languages is one such barrier. The Canadian School Trustees' Association (1988) estimated that about 55 per cent of the 188,000 children who immigrated to Canada with their families from 1980 to 1987 had no facility in either English or French. In addition, there are Canadian-born children who speak a language other than English or French.

Immigration is a joint federal and provincial responsibility, with Ottawa being the superior jurisdiction in the event of conflict. The costs of providing education (as well as many other social services) fall on provincial and municipal governments and, in the case of the latter, put additional burdens on local taxpayers. Some have called on the federal government to assume (some) responsibility for financing programs designed to address the educational needs of recent immigrant groups (Canadian School Trustees' Association, 1988). Yet to do so would be a remarkable transformation of the Canadian political system given the constitutional status of the provinces' responsibility for education. Certainly, moves by the federal government to provide conditional funding for English as a second language would meet opposition from the government of Quebec, if not other provinces, on the grounds that such funding would lead in time to expansion, not contraction, of the federal government's involvement in education.

Increased interest in multicultural education has prompted an enormous outflowing of rhetoric about the purported effects of multicultural education programs. Bullivant (1981: 236) documents three "quite dubious claims" that commonly are put forward to justify such programs: that children's educational achievements improve by learning about cultural and ethnic origins; that equality of opportunity will be improved by learning about cultures, traditions, and so forth; and that such learning will reduce prejudice and discrimination. One problem is that there is little evidence to support these assertions. Moreover, to justify multicultural education as a way of establishing and enhancing tolerance is to overlook the fact that cultural groups may be intolerant. Multicultural education policies may allow the propagation of certain attitudes, such as female subordination or ethnic hostility, which run counter to the goal of tolerance (Kach and DeFaveri, 1987: 233-34; DeFaveri, 1986).

Bullivant (1981: 241) has argued that the dominant emphasis of multicultural education on lifestyles, rather than life chances, is a means by which dominant social groups are able to perpetuate themselves while purporting to improve the lot of children from ethnic communities. The pluralist dilemma, put simply, is that recognition of cultural differences undercuts social integration and detracts from developing policies that focus on economic barriers restricting individual social mobility.

Kas Mazurek (1987) has criticized multicultural education programs on the grounds that their promise of equality of opportunity is a myth since the Canadian education systems have failed to recognize that cognitive abilities are related to ethnicity and cultural consciousness. Insufficient attention, therefore, has been given to curriculum development that acknowledges individual learning needs and cultural differences. In an earlier statement Mazurek (1983: 28) argued that "the cognitive strategies and facilities which the basic subjects in our schools require are possessed in different degrees by different ethnic groups." Accordingly, the strengthening of ethnic consciousness and differentiation increases differences in mental abilities.

Parsonson (1986: 42), after reviewing literature in support of the proposition that cultural groups have varying cognitive styles (that is, level of psychological differentiation), achievement motivations, and perceptions of control, argued that such differences must be understood but cautioned against the formation of homogeneous classes. Marjoriebanks documented that students' level of attainment is related to family environment, which includes ethnicity and class, and noted that for parents from non-dominant cultures "one of the most urgent requirements is the establishment of further programmes for the teaching of English" (1980: 137).

For many ethnic groups, especially those that fear assimilation into the dominant culture, language is perceived as the means of ensuring cultural survival. Many ethnic groups have defined multicultural education programs in terms of language training, though the difficulties encountered in producing a fully ethnicized curriculum have resulted in "merely adding a linguistic component to existing school programs" (Mazurek, 1981: 32). Even so, the pattern of language retention over generations is such that one "can hardly fail to conclude that all languages other than English or French in Canada are seriously endangered species" (Wardhaugh, 1983: 196).

Multiculturalism and education contain an enduring tension. On the one hand, there is pressure to assimilate as quickly as possible because mobility and economic success demand integration into the dominant culture. Those who do not do well academically are conceived as suffering from some cultural deprivation that the schools are expected to address. On the other hand, there is a desire to preserve and recognize cultural differences, both for their own sake, as part of a pluralistic social order, and for the sake of the educational attainments of children whose ethnic backgrounds and socialization processes result in differences, as opposed to deficits, in learning. Diversity and opportunity seem to collide; the contradiction may be compounded by demands for extension of state funding to "independent schools."

Fragmentation of the Public School System

Institutional diversity is a leading feature of the Canadian education systems. Nonetheless, the extensive control of education by the state means that parents have little say about the education their children receive outside whatever denominational schools are in a particular province. There is, then, a form of monopoly, one defined by geography: your child receives the quality and kind of education that the school in your neighbourhood offers. Those who do not want their children to attend the publicly funded neighbourhood school must pay for the education of their choice.

It is always difficult to pinpoint the time and place of the origins of a movement. One thing, however, is reasonably clear: over time there has been more and more dissatisfaction with the state-centred education systems. Some provinces – British Columbia, Quebec, and Alberta – have legislation providing for public funding for what have become labelled "independent" schools (Wilson and Lazerson, 1982; Bezeau, 1979; Downey, 1986). The extension of funding of Roman Catholic secondary schools in Ontario in the 1980s precipitated an inquiry into the relationships between the provincial government and independent schools, with special emphasis on funding (Shapiro, 1985).

Three arguments were identified as justifying the extension of public funds to such schools. One was that parents who send children to alternative schools bear "double taxation" inasmuch as they pay both education taxes and tuition bills. This argument was rejected by the Commission on the grounds that an education tax is not equivalent to a tuition bill; rather, it is a levy intended to pay for a common good as identified by society, and as such it does not contain a right of opting out (Shapiro, 1985: 48).

The second argument is that parents should not only "be able to choose school environments that affirm and extend their own values but they also have a prior right to select the kind of education they believe to be appropriate for their child(ren)" (Shapiro, 1985: 46). The Shapiro Commission recognized some validity in this claim as choice is of considerable value in a democratic society. However, parental choice is not a prior right "but one whose claims must be measured against the competing claims of other social policies and goals" (Shapiro, 1985: 48).

The argument that caught the greatest support of the Commission pertained to the claim that one religious group in Ontario (the Roman Catholic) was provided with an educational option that other groups, especially religiously defined ones, were denied, namely, public funding of denominational schools. The Commission, while acknowledging the constitutional context of public funding of Roman Catholic schools, found that situation to be discriminatory and made a number of detailed recommendations to allow for limited public funding to independent schools, whether defined in religious or non-religious terms (Shapiro, 1985: 37-51).

Weighed against these arguments were three claims in support of the status quo. One makes the point that public funds, under severe constraint, should not be expected to bear the strain that would result from the extension of funding to independent schools. The second argument is that increased fragmentation of the education systems will result in the formation of more homogeneous schools, which will erode the function assigned to education of providing common acculturation experiences and establishing social cohesion and tolerance. Third, public funding of independent schools will result in different types of schools: the public system, as it is commonly understood in Canada (except in Newfoundland and Labrador), and a multiplicity of independent schools receiving public funds.

The existence of so many different types of schools challenges the concept of equality of educational opportunity because the independent school, which almost by definition can provide the specialized and focused education deemed to be in a student's interests, is not obligated to take all who appear before its door. The public school, by contrast, must enrol all applicants, for whom, on an individual basis, it has much greater difficulty providing the precisely defined and well-focused education that may be desirable. On the other hand, the public school has the capacity to override deficiencies that students bring with them arising from their familial, class, and ethnic backgrounds. The capacity of the public system to provide educational opportunities will be diminished to the extent that academically strong students exit the public system to attend independent schools. The risk, then, in the public funding of independent schools is that society's capacity to offer its members (in the aggregate) equal educational opportunities will be weakened though certain individuals might obtain advantages otherwise not available (Shapiro, 1985: 49-51). It is worth noting that in the debate on the question of public funding of independent schools little is said about the effects of different ways of structuring education systems on students' academic achievements; the focus is on the school in society rather than on the individual in the school.

Recent developments in the United States have been in the direction of greater parental choice in education. Various states in the 1980s have moved toward open-enrolment schools. Minnesota, for example, allows children to be enrolled in any publicly financed school that will accept them. The Republican Party in the United States committed itself during the 1988 presidential campaign to provide vouchers that will allow parents to pay tuition at the schools of their choice with public monies. In the United Kingdom, the Conservative government's Education Reform Act reflects similar thinking. It provides for greater parental choice in education and breaks down the essential monopoly traditionally held by British schools. There is no necessary relationship between what happens elsewhere and Canadian developments. Canadians, however, have had a history of institutional diversity; moreover, it is hard, from the perspective of equity, to justify the practice of providing public funds to some denominational schools but not to others.

The argument for greater parental direction over education can also be connected with arguments about the social and economic conditions of a liberal-democratic political system. Robert Dahl has argued that a necessary condition for a competitive political system is a pluralistic social order. He claims that the existence of a decentralized economy (whether capitalist or socialist), which creates pluralistic conditions, does not allow for other sources of diversity (Dahl, 1971: 57-61). Another argument is that the expansion of the effective range of parental influence on the provision of education strengthens the conditions necessary for competitive politics (Woolstencroft, 1983). Contrary to the Shapiro Commission, in which choice is conceptualized as part of an array of democratic values, choice is important in establishing the social conditions supportive of political competition. If we move beyond system-level arguments to the level of individuals, there have been many laments about the demonstrably low level of citizens' political involvement. Liberal-democratic societies have not been noted for providing many opportunities for citizens' direction over public policy; the emphasis, rather, has been on voting and elections. Choice in education is a means for allowing citizens to assume greater control over an important aspect of life and, in so doing, encourages citizens to assume greater control and responsibility for their affairs.

Robert Lane (1983), in tracing the relationships between markets and education, argues that market-induced attributes of curiosity and creativity correct the routinization and monotony of so many schools. John E. Chubb (1988), reporting the results of a national study of American high schools, argues that one significant variable distinguishing high-performance and low-performance schools is the character of school organization, that is, the goals of the school, the nature of its administrative leadership, and the degree of teacher autonomy. Factors such as teachers' qualifications, salaries, teaching philosophies, and class sizes, which are commonly put forward as determinants of academic attainment, have little connection with students' performances. In general, the factors correlated with school organization were parental involvement and school autonomy, suggesting that the school's larger environment affects students' academic performances. Market-based educational systems – such as magnet schools that specialize in particular subject areas, open-enrolment schools, and voucher funding – provide "students and their parents more choice among schools and more reason to become cooperatively involved in them" (Chubb, 1988: 49).

Perhaps increasing parental choice and direction in education – the analogues of a market economy – will bring the energy and commitment that distinguishes between education that elevates and that which enervates.

Conclusion

Diversity has long been a hallmark of the Canadian education systems. Demands for more diversity are likely to increase rather than decrease, and among the responses to those demands undoubtedly will be concern for the principle of equal educational opportunity. Canadian education systems can validly point to some long-term improvement in the pattern of educational attainments, but it is difficult to be sanguine about the prospects. On the other hand, there has been no evidence that parental involvement results in lower academic attainments; to the contrary, as the study by John E. Chubb and Terry M. Moe (1989) demonstrates, parental involvement can lead to higher achievement.

That suggests the direction in which Canada's education systems should evolve, but that development should not be without control by the state, which has an obligation to ensure that minimal standards are met and that what is taught is not antithetical to the basic values of a liberal-democratic polity.

No doubt there will be much said about those values and their connection to education and schools. The debates will be long, perhaps fierce, and certainly open-ended, for every generation will have to address the question of what the next generation should be taught. The debates will also remind us of the essential political nature of education and how important it is to have parents, cultural groups, administrators, students, elected officials, and teachers directly involved in the processes of defining and implementing educational goals (Townsend, 1988).

NOTES

1. Such estimates suffer from a number of measurement problems. None-theless, alternate ways of estimating retention rates produced remarkably similar estimates (between 31 and 33 per cent) of the high school dropout rate in Ontario (Radwanski, 1987: 68-70).
2. The passive and limited approach of the Board was evident in its 1976 statement of its aims and objectives, which referred to new Canadians as bringing "a new cosmopolitan flavour and new skills" to the county; the single pertinent objective was "to disregard colour, creed, culture, race and sex as factors either to limit or to favour a student's pursuit of any particular opportunity."

REFERENCES

Allen, Robert C. (1986). "Investment and Education in British Columbia," in Robert C. Allen and Gideon Rosenbluth (eds.), *Restraining the Economy: Social Credit Economic Policies for B.C. in the Eighties.* Vancouver: B.C. Economic Policy Institute.

Berryman, Jack (1986). "Implementation of Ontario's Heritage Languages Programs: A Case Study of the Extended School Day Model" (Ed.D. dissertation, University of Toronto).

Bezeau, Lawrence M. (1979). "The Public Finance of Private Education in the Province of Quebec," *Canadian Journal of Education*, 4, 2: 23-42.

Blair, Andrew G. (1981). *The Policy and Practice of Religious Education in Publicly-Funded Elementary and Secondary Schools in Canada and Elsewhere.* Toronto: Ontario Ministry of Education.

Bowles, S.D., and H. Gintis (1976). *Schooling in Capitalist America.* New York: Basic Books.

Brown, Wilfred J. (1983). "The Educational Toll of the 'Great Recession,'" in Barry D. Anderson *et al.*, *The Costs of Controlling the Costs of Education in Canada.* Toronto: Ontario Institute for Studies in Education.

Bullivant, Brian M. (1981). *The Pluralist Dilemma in Education: Six Case Studies.* Sydney: George Allen & Unwin.

Burnet, Jean (1979). "Myths and Multiculturalism," *Canadian Journal of Education*, 4, 4: 43-58.

Cameron, David R., and Richard I. Hofferbert (1974). "The Impact of Federalism on Education Finance: A Comparative Analysis," *European Journal of Political Research*, XXX, 2: 225-58.

Canadian School Trustees' Association (1988). *The Impact on Local School Boards of Immigration and Settlement in Canada.* Ottawa.

Chandler, William M., and Marsha A. Chandler (1979). *Public Policy and Provincial Politics.* Toronto: McGraw-Hill Ryerson.

Chubb, John E. (1988). "Why the Current Wave of School Reform Will Fail," *The Public Interest*, Number 90 (Winter): 28-49.

Chubb, John E., and Terry M. Moe (1989). *What Price Democracy? Politics, Markets and American Schools.* Washington, D.C.: The Brookings Institution.

Coleman, James (1969). "The Concept of Equality of Educational Opportunity," in Harvard Educational Review, *Equal Educational Opportunity.* Cambridge, Mass.: Harvard University Press.

Coleman, Peter (1986). "School Districts and Student Achievement in British Columbia: A Preliminary Analysis," *Canadian Journal of Education*, 11, 4: 509-21.

DeFaveri, I. (1986). "Multiculturalism and Education," in Nick Kach *et al.*, *Essays in Canadian Education*. Calgary: Detselig Enterprises.

Downey, L.W. (1986). "The Aid-To-Independent Schools Movement in British Columbia," in Nancy Sheehan *et al.*, *Schools in the West: Essays in Canadian Educational History*. Calgary: Detselig Enterprises.

Flower, George E. (1984). *Speaking Out: the 1984 CEA Poll of Canadian Opinion on Education*. Toronto: Canadian Education Association.

Gidney, R.D., and W.P.J. Millar (1985). "From Voluntarism to State Schooling: The Creation of the Public School System in Ontario," *Canadian Historical Review*, LXVI, 4: 443-71.

Guppy, Neil, *et al.* (1984). "Changing Patterns of Educational Inequality," *Canadian Journal of Sociology*, 9, 3: 319-31.

Gutmann, Amy (1988). "Distributing Public Education in a Democracy," in Amy Gutmann (ed.), *Democracy and the Welfare State*. Princeton: Princeton University Press.

Henley, Richard and Pampalis (1982). "The Campaign for Compulsory Education in Manitoba," *Canadian Journal of Education*, 7, 1: 59-73.

Hodgetts, A.B. (1968). *What Culture? What Heritage?* Toronto: Ontario Institute for Studies in Education.

Humphries, Edward H., *et al.* (1986). *Alternate Approaches to School Board Representation*, Volume 1. Toronto: Ontario Ministry of Education.

Kach, Nick, and Ivan DeFaveri (1977). "What Every Teacher Should Know About Multiculturalism," in Leonard L. Stewin and Stewart J.H. McCann (eds.), *Contemporary Educational Issues: The Canadian Mosaic*. Toronto: Copp Clark.

Lane, Robert E. (1983). "Political Education in a Market Society," *Micropolitics*, 3, 1: 39-65.

Lawson, Robert F., and Ratna Ghosh (1986). "Canada," *Education and Urban Society*, 18, 4: 449-61.

Lawton, Stephen B. (1979). "Political Values in Educational Finance in Canada and the United States," *Journal of Educational Finance*, 5 (Summer): 1-8.

— (1987). *The Price of Quality: The Public Finance of Elementary and Secondary Education in Canada*. Toronto: Canadian Education Association.

Livingston, D.W. (1985). *Social Class and Schooling*. Toronto: Garmond Press.

Livingston, D.W., *et al.* (1984). *Public Attitudes Toward Education in Ontario*. Toronto: Ontario Institute for Studies in Education.

Lupul, Manoly (1977). "Multiculturalism and Canadian National Identity: The Alberta Experience," in Alf Chaiton and Neil McDonald (eds.), *Canadian Schools and Canadian Identity*. Toronto: Gage.

Lynch, James (1987). "Multicultural Education in Britain; Retrospect and Prospect," in Keith A. Mcleod (ed.), *Multicultural Education: A Partnership*. Toronto: Canadian Council for Multicultural and Intercultural Education.

Mackinnon, Frank (1960). *The Politics of Education*. Toronto: University of Toronto Press.

Mallea, J.R. (1977). "Multiculturalism within a Bilingual Framework: A note on the Québécois Response," *Multiculturalism*, 1, 2: 3-5.

— (1984). "Cultural Diversity in Canadian Education: A Review of Contemporary Developments," in Ronald J. Samuda *et al.* (eds.), *Multiculturalism in Canada: Social and Educational Perspectives.* Toronto: Allyn and Bacon, Inc.

Manzer, Ronald (1974). *Canada: A Socio-Political Report.* Toronto: McGraw-Hill Ryerson.

— (1985). *Public Policies and Political Development in Canada.* Toronto: University of Toronto Press.

Marjoriebanks, Kevin (1980). *Ethnic Families and Children's Achievements.* Sydney: George Allen & Unwin.

Mazurek, Kas (1981). "The Price of Ethnicity," *Education Canada*, 21, 4: 30-33.

— (1983). "Multiculturalism and Schools: A Critical Analysis," in Peter S. Li and B. Singh Bolaria (eds.), *Racial Minorities in Multicultural Canada.* Toronto: Garmond Press.

— (1987). "Multiculturalism, Education, and the Ideology of the Meritocracy," in Terry Wotherspoon (ed.), *The Political Economy of Canadian Schooling.* Toronto: Methuen.

Mazurek, Kas, and Nick Kach (1983). "Culture and Power: Educational Ideologies in Multicultural Canada," *New Education*, 5, 2: 47-59.

McCreath, Peter (1986). "The Multicultural Policies of Teacher Organizations in Canada," in Ronald J. Samuda and Shiu L. Kong (eds.), *Multicultural Education: Programmes and Methods.* Kingston: Intercultural Social Sciences, Inc.

Mifflen, Frank J., and Sydney C. Mifflen (1982). *The Sociology of Education: Canada and Beyond.* Calgary: Detselig Enterprises.

Ontario. *Revised Regulations of Ontario 1980*, Regulation 262, Sections 28 and 29, III, 155-56.

Organization for Economic Cooperation and Development (1976). *Review of National Policies for Education: Canada.* Paris: OECD.

Parsonson, K. (1986). "Review of the Effects of Learning Styles on Achievement," in Samuda and Kong (eds.), *Multicultural Education: Programmes and Methods.*

Porter, John (1965). *The Vertical Mosaic.* Toronto: University of Toronto Press.

— (1979). "Education, Equality, and the Just Society," in John Porter, *The Measure of Canadian Society.* Toronto: Gage.

Prentice, Alison (1977). *The School Promoters: Education and Social Class in Mid-Nineteenth Century Upper Canada.* Toronto: McClelland and Stewart.

Radwanski, George (1987). *Ontario Study of the Relevance of Education, and the Issue of Dropouts.* Toronto: Ontario Ministry of Education.

Rowe, Frederick W. (1976). *Education and Culture in Newfoundland.* Toronto: McGraw-Hill Ryerson.

Shapiro, Bernard J. (1985). *The Report of the Commission on Private Schools in Ontario.* Toronto: The Commission on Private Schools in Ontario.

Smitheram, Verner (1982). "Development and Debate over School Consolidation," in Verner Smitheram *et al.* (eds.), *The Garden Transformed: Prince Edward Island, 1945-80.* Charlottetown: Ragweed Press.

Stamp, Robert M. (1986). *Religious Exercises in Elementary and Secondary Schools.* Toronto: Ontario Ministry of Education.

Townsend, Richard G. (1988). *They Politick for Schools.* Toronto: Ontario Institute for Studies in Education, Occasional Papers Number 25.

Wardhaugh, Ronald (1983). *Language & Nationhood: The Canadian Experience*. Vancouver: New Star Books.

Wilkinson, B.W. (1986). "Elementary and Secondary Education Policy in Canada: A Survey," *Canadian Public Policy*, XII, 4: 535-72.

Wilson, Donald J. (1981). "Religion and Education: the Other Side of Pluralism," in Donald J. Wilson (ed.), *Canadian Education in the 1980s*. Calgary: Detselig Enterprises.

Wilson, Donald J., and Marvin Lazerson (1982). "Historical and Constitutional Perspectives on Family Choice in Schooling: The Canadian Case," in Michael E. Manley-Casimir (ed.), *Family Choice in Schooling*. Lexington, Mass.: D.C. Heath and Company.

Woolstencroft, Peter (1983). "Politics and Education: Issues of Public Policy and Political Philosophy," paper presented to the Annual Meeting of the Canadian Political Science Association, Vancouver, British Columbia.

8   Brian Wharf

Social Services

This chapter has three objectives: first, to describe the social services provided in the past and at the present time by municipal governments; second, to consider whether the present responsibilities are appropriate; and third, to outline directions for the future.

Before addressing these objectives it is necessary to indicate how the term "social services" will be used. The most usual understanding of the term is social assistance, or welfare or relief. However, social services are defined here to include income security, the personal social services, and social planning. Each of these are defined and described below.

Income Security Programs

Income security programs are defined in an inventory prepared by Health and Welfare Canada (1987: 1) as "any federal, provincial or municipal program having as its main objective the provision of direct financial benefits to individuals and families in Canada." The inventory specifies four different types of income security programs and the distinction between these programs is important for the discussion in this chapter. Family allowances and old age pensions are examples of demogrant programs that pay benefits to or on behalf of citizens in a defined age range regardless of their financial situation. Demogrant programs are planned by and delivered directly to beneficiaries by the federal government. Social insurance programs such as the Canada

Pension Plan and Unemployment Insurance are again the responsibility of the federal government, while Workers' Compensation programs are an example of this category of program at the provincial level. The third type, income-tested programs, includes the Child Tax Credit and the Guaranteed Income Supplement for the elderly. Both of these examples are federal programs but a number of provincially administered income supplementation programs for families and the elderly have been developed. A breakdown of the programs provided by the federal government is contained in Figure 1.

Figure 1
Income Security Programs in Canada,
Benefit Expenditures by Program,
1985-86
($ millions)

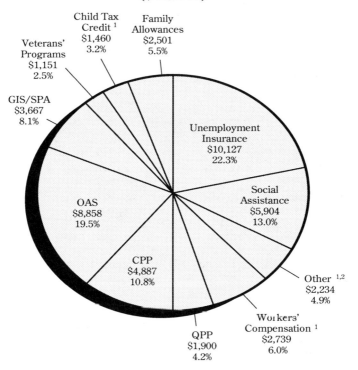

Total program expenditures: $45,428 million

1. Expenditures for Workers' Compensation, Child Tax Credit, and some provincial taxation/shelter assistance and income supplementation programs are for the 1985 calendar year.
2. Includes provincial taxation/shelter assistance and income supplementation programs.

SOURCE: Health and Welfare Canada, *Inventory of Income Security Programs in Canada* (Ottawa, 1987), p. 44.

The fourth type of income security is the needs-tested programs, which provide income to the indigent who are not covered by any of the above. These programs are administered by provincial and municipal governments and the costs are shared by the federal government under the provisions of the Canada Assistance Plan (CAP). The same cost-sharing arrangements apply to other programs, such as child welfare and work activity projects. Enacted in 1966, the CAP is the major example of federal/provincial co-operation in the social services. The contributions of the federal government to the provinces for general assistance costs only, and not for the other cost-shared programs, are detailed in Table 1.

Table 1
Canada Assistance Plan – General Assistance: Federal Payments to the Provinces/Territories ($000s)

Province/Territory	Federal Payments 1985-86
Newfoundland	$42,577
Prince Edward Island	11,205
Nova Scotia	71,641
New Brunswick	103,362
Quebec[*]	1,110,953
Ontario	739,739
Manitoba	78,414
Saskatchewan	95,367
Alberta	240,859
British Columbia	439,523
Yukon	1,083
Northwest Territories	5,482
Total[**]	$2,940,205

[*]The federal contribution to Quebec is made up of cash payments and tax point transfers.
[**]Totals may not add due to rounding.
Note: The above amounts reflect the payments made during the indicated fiscal year and may include costs incurred in previous years.
SOURCE: Health and Welfare Canada, *Inventory of Income Security Programs in Canada* (Ottawa, 1987), p. 199.

While Canada has shown imagination and commitment in developing income security programs, the fundamental assumptions underlying these programs are that Canadians will work, will earn adequate incomes, will provide for their dependants, and will save for their old age. When these assumptions founder on the rocks of high unemployment, high inflation, low wages, and the breakdown of family units, Canada's programs have proven to be inadequate.

By conservative estimate 3,535,000 Canadians – one in seven – lived on low incomes in 1987, the most recent year for which data is available. The provincial poverty rate ranged widely from 10.3 percent in well-off Ontario to 20.8 percent in economically disadvantaged Newfoundland. There are 777,000 families and 1,016,000 unattached individuals with incomes below the poverty line. (National Council of Welfare, 1989: 6)

Women are particularly vulnerable to poverty, whether as young single mothers or as seniors:

Unattached elderly women (i.e., those who live alone or in a household where they are not related to other members) run a very high risk of poverty: 40.3 percent were poor at last count. Over half (56.6 percent) of sole-support mothers raise their children on an income below the poverty line. Close to a million children under 16 – 955,000 or one in six – are in low-income families. Two-thirds of children being raised by female single parents are poor. (National Council of Welfare, 1989: 7)

Income security programs have not been connected to the more powerful policies and forces that determine the accumulation and distribution of wealth. Thus the distribution of income has not appreciably changed in the past thirty years, with the bottom fifth of the population receiving 4.4 per cent and the top fifth 43 per cent of the nations's income (Ross, 1987: 39).

The personal social services are programs designed to support individuals and families and to protect vulnerable individuals such as children. Typical programs include counselling, homemaker, home care, daycare, as well as substitute care facilities for those individuals who can no longer remain at home or live on an independent basis. They are characterized by face-to-face interaction between the service provider and the consumer. The personal social services include both statutory and non-statutory programs. Statutory services are required by legislation, such as those dealing with the prevention of and responses to child neglect and abuse. Non-statutory programs are not required by law but have been developed by both provincial ministries and voluntary agencies in response to the needs of citizens. Non-statutory programs include family counselling, homemaker, and daycare programs.

Social planning is defined here as systematic and research-based efforts to identify causes of social problems, to develop programs to remedy these problems, and to identify the social consequences of other kinds of planning activities. In addition, social planning includes the involvement of citizens in the challenge of social problem-solving. Usually referred to in the community work literature as locality development or community organization, this approach recognizes the right of citizens to be involved in and to contribute to resolving problems. Thus, social planning as conceived here does not refer only to the expert skills of city hall planners but to the participation of citizens in the social planning process.

Past Responsibilities of Municipal Governments

A comprehensive outline of the history of municipal involvement in the social services is beyond the scope of the present discussion. A number of complete accounts are available and the reader is referred to the following sources: Armitage (1988); Guest (1984, 1986); Bryden (1974); Cassidy (1943, 1945); Marsh (1943); and Splane (1965). The salient points are as follows. Prior to 1900, municipal responsibility was confined to financial assistance for the poor and indigent, and as Armitage notes this "responsibility [was] assumed *only* for the sick, elderly, young, and women with dependent children; *only* after all the family financial resources have been exhausted; and *only* where local residence was clearly established" (Armitage, 1988: 270). Even this statement requires further qualification since the range of municipal responsibilities varied between regions of the country. The provinces of New Brunswick and Nova Scotia passed legislation modelled on the English Poor Laws but the resources of the parish and township were so inadequate that "small impoverished rural parishes in New Brunswick instituted the practice of contracting out the care of their poor to the lowest bidder, but by the mid-nineteenth century public institutions for the care of the poor and destitute were operating in St. John and other centres" (Guest, 1986: 11).

In contrast, because of small and scattered populations, provincial governments in Prince Edward Island and in the western provinces (and the colonial government in Newfoundland) were responsible for relief to the poor. However, in the latter provinces, as urban and rural municipal governments came into being, they were expected to assume responsibility for the indigent. In Quebec the tradition of reliance on the Roman Catholic Church prevailed, while Ontario rejected the Poor Law approach, preferring instead to refer the indigent to voluntary organizations. Nevertheless, as Splane (1965) makes clear in his history of social welfare in Ontario, the scarcity of resources available to private charities forced municipal governments to take a share, albeit reluctantly, of responsibility for the poor.

This inadequate and haphazard mix of church, voluntary, and municipal and provincial responsibility continued until the Great Depression. As Guest (1986: 93) has noted:

The depression of the 1930s was thus a significant force for change in the development of social security programmes in

Canada. The crucial points bear repeating. The depression was so devastating in its effect that it brought home to the average Canadian the interdependence of citizens in an industrial society. Unemployment was seen less as a result of personal inadequacy and more as a common and insurable threat to the livelihood of the average citizen. Secondly, the concept of local responsibility for the relief of the unemployed was replaced first by the assumption of provincial and then of federal responsibility. From this point on, unemployment was seen as a national problem rather than a purely local or regional one.

The framework for Canadian social policies was drafted in the early 1940s by academics-cum-policy advisers/administrators such as Harry Cassidy and Leonard Marsh. Their work was based on significant research studies undertaken in the previous decade for the Rowell-Sirois Commission, the first in a long line of inquiries dealing with federal-provincial relationships, by numerous social agencies, and by Marsh and Cassidy themselves. While their proposals differed as to the relative importance placed on guaranteeing incomes by means of a system of social insurance (Marsh, 1943), a living wage policy for families to be achieved through full employment and improving public assistance programs (Whitton, 1943), and a combination of both (Cassidy, 1943), all proposals argued for an expanded role for the federal government and for a partnership in social policy between the federal and provincial governments. Subsequent legislation, while not implementing the full range of any of the above proposals, did give the primary responsibility for health and income security to the senior levels of government.

Since that time, and with some notable exceptions, municipal governments have neither been assigned a major role for social services nor, despite the intentions of the occasional reform-minded mayor, have they campaigned to include social services within their range of functions. In 1914 one such mayor, H.C. Hocken, of Toronto, spoke of a "new spirit in municipal government reflected in the establishment of public health programs and dental clinics for poor children" and "the problems we have to deal with now are problems affecting human welfare, problems of prevention and the problems looking to the betterment of people in cities" (Guest, 1986: 31). But Hocken to the contrary, municipalities have not developed social service programs and in many provinces have argued successfully for the transfer of their one major responsibility, that of providing financial assistance to the indigent, to the provincial level. The range of services provided by municipalities at the present time varies considerably and is outlined in the following discussion.

The Present Responsibilities of
Municipal Governments

Income Security

As indicated above, the federal government is responsible for the
major demogrant programs and, with the exception of Workers'
Compensation, for social insurance programs. Income-tested programs
are provided by both the federal and provincial governments. In the
provinces of Nova Scotia, Ontario, and Manitoba, the responsibility
for social assistance is decentralized to municipal or regional government in urban centres, but not in rural areas. In all other provinces
social assistance is provided by ministries of provincial governments.
While most provinces have placed social assistance programs in
ministries of social services, Quebec and Manitoba are unique in
locating this function in ministries of labour and employment. Hence,
in only three provinces do municipalities provide any form of financial
assistance and the trend in recent years has been to centralize this
responsibility at the provincial level, as has occurred in Saskatchewan,
B.C., and Alberta.

The Personal Social Services

Again the dominant pattern for providing statutory social services is
through regional offices of provincial ministries. Six provinces, Newfoundland, New Brunswick, Prince Edward Island, Saskatchewan,
Alberta, and B.C., have adopted this pattern.

Nova Scotia and Manitoba have adopted the urban/rural distinction
for providing statutory social services for families and children. Cities
in Nova Scotia have established privately organized children's aid
societies that perform these services, and Manitoba created family
and children's service centres in Metropolitan Winnipeg in 1985. Six
regional agencies were established, each with an elected governing
board of citizens and each with a number of satellite offices located
in neighbourhoods. In rural Nova Scotia and Manitoba the statutory
services are provided by offices of the provincial ministries.

In Ontario the statutory and some non-statutory services to children
and families are provided by children's aid societies. These agencies
follow the county structure of government and hence there are fifty-two
children's aid societies in the province. Although these societies are
required to include representatives of city and county governments
on their boards of directors and although municipal and county
governments contribute to the funding, they are not units of municipal
governments, nor are they responsible to them. In fact, just as
municipalities are creatures of the province and are assigned tasks
by the province, so, too, are children's aid societies. Like family and
child welfare programs in other provinces, children's aid societies are
funded almost entirely through the Canada Assistance Plan.

Quebec has established health and social service centres on a regional and local basis throughout the province. These structures provide statutory social services and out-patient health care and are governed by locally elected boards. This integrated system of health and social services is unique in Canada, and while lauded as an imaginative concept, the system has experienced difficulties in sorting out which tasks belong at the regional and which at the local level. According to one critic the provincial government has retained control of budgets, thereby making a mockery of the concept of local decision-making (Lesemann, 1984), but a comprehensive evaluation of the Quebec system has yet to be written.

British Columbia developed four integrated health and social service centres under its brief NDP regime in 1972-75, but these centres now provide only out-patient health services and in effect have become private health societies. A related development in this period was the establishment of community resource boards, which provided social assistance and family and child welfare services under the governance of boards of locally elected citizens. The community resource boards were eliminated following the election of the Social Credit government in 1975. Some further comments regarding this experiment are contained in a later section of this chapter.

Alberta is the only province to have identified a distinct role for municipalities in the provision of personal social services. Under the Family and Community Support Services Act of 1980, municipalities are encouraged to offer preventive social services. According to the Director of Calgary's Social Service Department (Blakely, 1986: 2), the basic premise underlying the Act is that

> communities can identify and act upon their own social needs resulting in enhanced, strengthened and stabilized family and community life. The current social planning activities of the Department include:
>
> 1. Social planning analysis, formation and development;
> 2. Research in regard to community needs, social issues and social trends;
> 3. Public education;
> 4. Management assistance and consultation to agencies;
> 5. Evaluation of social services; and
> 6. Community development.

Social Planning

The record of municipal involvement in social planning is neither consistent nor extensive. The range of municipal involvement includes Vancouver, which has established a department with the specific and sole charge of social planning; Halifax, with social planning assigned as a major but not the only function in a large multifunctional agency;

cities in Alberta, where social planning is the principal strategy for discharging the preventive mandate assigned to municipalities by the Family and Community Support Services Act, and where a number of municipalities employ social planners within departments of physical or urban planning. A sense of the objectives and activities of municipal social planning departments in Vancouver and Halifax can be obtained from the following quotations:

Halifax
The Social Development and Research Division is responsible for researching and monitoring urban social issues and trends, developing programs and approaches to urban social problems and consulting with the community to develop appropriate programs and services to meet new needs. Its areas of activity include training and employment assessment, pre-employment orientation, employment development, emergency housing and housing outreach, services for the mentally and physically disabled, services for single parents, senior citizens. (City of Halifax, 1983: 2)

Vancouver
The mandate of the Social Planning Department is to provide advice to the Vancouver City Council on a broad range of issues that affect the quality of life in Vancouver. Specifically this includes policy and programming in areas such as low income housing, social services policies, including a grants program of $2,000,000, cultural programming including operation of three civic theatres and several million dollars in grants and general advice on the social aspects of urban development of the city. (Beck, 1986: 1)

In Halifax the social planning function is combined with social assistance, the provision of housing, and other social service programs for the unemployed and the elderly. By contrast, while the Vancouver department is administratively responsible for some programs, it prefers a model whereby it develops programs and then turns these over to either new or established community service organizations. Both departments, however, undertake research to identify unmet needs; both advise their respective city councils on the social consequences of new industrial, shopping, or housing developments; and both review and report on the key social and economic indicators in their communities. For example, the Vancouver state of the community report is published every six months and contains information on business activities (retail sales and bankruptcies), regional and provincial unemployment figures, the incomes earned by Vancouver residents, the numbers receiving financial assistance from unemployment insurance and social assistance, and housing trends. One might envisage a useful further development including information on social factors such as the number of children in substitute care, the number of young offenders in correctional facilities, family court statistics, and the number of clients receiving services from mental health agencies.

The discussion of social planning would be incomplete without at least a passing reference to social planning councils. These councils are voluntary organizations, registered under provincial societies acts, funded mainly by allocations from the United Way and municipal governments, and responsible to elected boards of citizens. The most vibrant and competent councils are located in large urban centres, particularly in Ottawa, Hamilton, Edmonton, Winnipeg, and Toronto.

Given the recent interest in privatizing the social services, it is pertinent to question whether all social planning functions might not be appropriately assigned to the voluntary councils. There is no doubt that needs assessment, proposing ways of meeting needs, and reviewing the performance of existing programs are not restricted by auspices. These tasks can be carried out by public or private agencies. However, one essential difference derived from auspices can be identified. The telling distinction is that the municipal governments are more likely to heed the advice obtained from their own department than from an outside organization. Conversely, the voluntary council is uniquely placed to be a source of independent advocacy. Social planning councils can advocate for consumers of social services, and through briefs, conferences, films and videos, and presentations to city hall and provincial cabinets they can portray the effects of poverty and poor housing on consumers of social programs and advocate improved programs.

Thus, to state the case for social planning within municipal government is not to argue that the voluntary social planning councils are unnecessary or redundant. Quite the contrary. Municipal social planning departments can and should inform local politicians about the social impact of new developments and propose ways of meeting social problems in concert with senior levels of government. Social planning councils can represent the position of consumers and of neighbourhood organizations and can help to organize the efforts of the agencies in the voluntary sector.

Future Responsibilities of Municipal Governments

The preceding discussion described the past and present social service responsibilities for municipal governments. The remainder of the chapter is devoted to developing the position that some of these responsibilities are inappropriate and should be discarded while others are appropriate and should be accorded increased priority.

Income Security

To begin with, the provision of financial assistance is the least appropriate of all social service functions for municipal governments, and in recent years provincial governments have increasingly assumed this responsibility. Reasons such as the need for equal payments to recipients across the province, the inadmissibility of residence requirements by the Canada Assistance Plan, and the total inadequacy of the municipal tax base have combined to form powerful arguments for the transfer of financial assistance to the provincial level. Indeed, many of these reasons suggest that the federal government should assume responsibility for all income support programs. A number of submissions to a Parliamentary Task Force established to examine provincial/fiscal arrangements in 1981 recommended this change in order to eliminate inequitable payments across the provinces, to simplify cumbersome administrative arrangements, and to place the responsibility for this major function clearly and squarely in the hands of one government. In its submission the Ontario Welfare Council recommended that:

> The federal government's primary function in social welfare is the alleviation of poverty – the provision of social security. Given that roughly 90% of federal spending in the welfare field is carried out through direct transfers to persons, while only 10% is channelled through CAP, combined with the federal government's predominant role in shaping the national economy, and its ability to redistribute income by means of taxation, one can seriously question whether the provinces ought to be involved in any of the major financial assistance programmes. The federal government is financially capable of taking over this field, and there is strong logic to the suggestion that the level of government (most) responsible for the economy should also be responsible for the income maintenance side of it. (Ontario Welfare Council, 1981: 86)

A similar position was taken by the Royal Commission on the Economic Union and Development Prospects for Canada (Macdonald Commission), which recommended in 1985 that a universal income security program be established and existing programs eliminated. However, the Parliamentary Task Force concluded that the existing division of responsibility should continue and its position was reinforced in 1986 by the report of the Nielsen Task Force. In the now unlikely event that the federal government did assume responsibility for all income programs it would be necessary to develop a structure to provide emergency financial assistance. It is suggested here that the model to adopt has been implemented in the provinces of Manitoba and Quebec, where short-term assistance is provided through regional offices of the provincial departments of labour. Short-term assistance is usually required by people who are unemployed and whose unemployment benefits have either expired or have not yet been processed. In either event it makes sense for temporary assistance to be connected to the provincial offices responsible for labour and unemployment.

The Personal Social Services

A number of submissions to the Parliamentary Task Force argued that if the federal government assumed total responsibility for income security the quid pro quo would be for provinces to take over the personal social services. The position taken here, however, is that provincial ministries should only be responsible for the following functions: determining overall policies in services such as child and family welfare; allocating funds; operating specialized province-wide services; establishing standards of service and monitoring performance. The latter two functions should include the requirement that where local agencies perform statutory responsibilities that they do so using the information and record-keeping systems established by the province.

This division of responsibility assigns policy, budgeting, and standard-setting functions to the provinces, while allocating the delivery of services to community-based agencies. It is an appropriate division of responsibility between provincial governments and local communities since there is a need to balance province-wide perspectives and standards with the particular needs and resources of local communities. The division ensures that both levels of government will engage in an ongoing debate about the services needed and the structures and funds required to provide these services. Further, it avoids the establishment of extremely large provincial organizations which provide a very inhospitable work environment for human service workers. A British academic and researcher reports that:

> On social grounds bigness is on most counts a disaster. It helps to generate poor morale and lack of commitment among employees; it makes sharing in decision making and responsiveness to community interest much more difficult because of the remoteness in human relationships which it inevitably creates and bureaucracy reinforces. (Child, 1976: 447)

A review of the experiences of providing health and social services in B.C. argues for such a partnership arrangement between provincial governments and local communities (Clague et al., 1985). This review describes the development and the experiences of the Vancouver Resource Board (VRB) and four integrated health and social service centres. The VRB and the centres differed on a number of dimensions, but their similarities included integration of services, decentralization to neighbourhood or small rural community level, and the election of citizens to govern the centres. While the life span of these reforms in service delivery was short, there was sufficient experience to argue that the services can be integrated and decentralized and that citizens are sufficiently interested in the health and social services to contribute their time to governing the structures established to deliver these services. Flowing from the review, Clague *et al.* recommend that municipal governments should develop social planning departments to identify the social services needed in the community and to suggest how these services should be co-ordinated and governed. I return to these issues in a later section of the chapter.

It needs to be emphasized that local governments have shown the capacity to initiate imaginative programs in recreation and health. Such programs serve all residents without distinguishing the poor as being less deserving of public social utilities than other classes of people. While there may be less status in attending functions at public recreation centres than participating in the programs of the elite golf and yacht clubs, there is certainly no stigma. The same kind of conceptualization can be applied to the personal social services. Many families require general counselling, day care, homemakers' counselling, and home care. The argument is persuasive that if these are segregated on an income and class level, then "services for the poor will end up being poor services" (Titmuss, 1968: 143). Like all self-fulfilling prophecies, services that identify clients as being indigent, failures, and deviants will assist in confirming this status.

The challenge is then to transform the personal social services from the residual crisis-oriented service to a social development approach that focuses on the strengths of individuals. Such an approach recognizes the sustaining capacity of self-help and support groups and includes in the role of professionals the responsibility for training and teaching. An example of such a transformation is described in a study of a municipal government in the Australian state of Victoria.

> The change to a developmental approach in Fitzroy involved a redirection from thinking about welfare simply as unconnected mopping up measures dealing with personal and social problems, to a view of welfare as a process where the need to achieve physical, social and emotional well being was seen as normative and essential for each individual's growth and development. The developmental approach also took the further step that such needs should be translated into rights (for health, housing, education, recreation, etc.) and attainment of these rights therefore became the objective of social planning. (Willis, 1985: 40)

A second example comes from the region of Ottawa-Carleton, where multi-service centres have been established to provide health and social services to families in their local neighbourhood. The services include:

- emergency assistance;
- crisis counselling;
- therapy involving individuals, groups, or families;
- specialized youth or children's services;
- information, advice, and referral;
- home support services;
- primary health care for individuals and families;
- programs promoting health care;
- public health services;
- community development;
- self-help groups;
- assessment, support, and placement of the chronically ill and elderly;
- recreation programs;
- job creation and vocational counselling;
- community-based education programs. (Ottawa-Carleton, 1983: 2)

Social Planning

The social planning function is not only appropriate for municipal governments, it is a virtual necessity. As the Task Force Report of the Canadian Federation of Municipalities (1986: 115) makes it clear, municipal governments have become:

> responsible for protecting and fostering the social and economic well-being of their communities. This includes policies which promote and capitalize on the natural assets of the community, countering the undesirable consequences of urban growth, anticipating the consequences of public decisions on the lives of citizens, and resolving conflicts and maximizing opportunities for the community as a whole.

Given these responsibilities and given that decisions made by senior levels of government are experienced at the local community level, the Task Force Report goes on to argue that municipal governments must undertake continuing assessments of the social impact of political and economic decisions. Further, they must be in a position not simply to assess issues and record impacts but to contribute to social policy.

In the view of the Federation it is essential that municipal govern ments become active partners with other influential decision-making bodies in establishing policies that affect the lives of citizens. Such a stance means that municipal governments need social planning expertise combining both technical research skills and the capacity to involve citizens in identifying needs and developing programs to meet these needs. The Task Force Report clearly recognizes that the municipal arena is where the consequence of poorly connected or inadequate federal and provincial policies and programs are played out. Inconsistencies and gaps are most visible at the municipal level, where the government has no responsibility for social services. Thus, the vexing social problems of street kids and juvenile prostitution, which currently plague many Canadian cities, are most visible on city streets and to city merchants and citizens. These problems are the consequence of the failure of our economic system to provide employment not only for teenagers but for family heads and income earners, of our educational system to keep children in school, and of our family and child welfare system to promote families' well-being. A second example comes from mental health and mental retardation. Many provincial governments are committed to a policy of deinstitutionalization. While indisputably a well-intentioned and positive policy, its implementation all too often fails to involve municipalities where those discharged from provincial institutions will live and work.

A further contribution of social planning is to identify the kinds of personal social service needed in a municipality and the appropriate organizational structures required to deliver these services. The Alberta model provides one example by distinguishing between provincial responsibility for delivering services and municipal responsibility for prevention. Another alternative is to follow Ontario and Manitoba and create family and children's service centres governed by boards of elected citizens. A third approach is for municipalities to provide services under their own auspices and integrate social, health, and recreational programs. As has been noted by many observers of the social welfare scene, there is little empirical evidence to prescribe the structures and the mix of service integration patterns that are most effective. Such evidence might emerge from deliberately planned diversity at the local level. Evidence will not come from provincial blueprints that impose the same structures and service patterns on all communities regardless of size, history, and culture. If this pattern is to be changed it can only come by municipalities insisting they are uniquely placed to undertake social planning and through this process deciding on the services and governing structures required in their communities.

The case for community control of social services is exemplified by child welfare in Indian communities. The consequence of high unemployment, high alcohol consumption, the abandonment of traditional ways of caring for children, and the poorly planned and unconnected array of specialized programs provided on reserves has been that Indian children are taken into the care of the provincial ministry in a much higher proportion than are white children. In 1980, "Status Indian children were represented in the child welfare system at approximately four and a half times the rate of all children in Canada" (Johnston, 1983: 57). The evidence is that, once in care, few native children return home. This response does not help children, parents, or families and has been labelled cultural genocide by native leaders.

It is also extremely ineffective and costly: ineffective because the placements in white, off-reserve foster homes usually collapse when the children reach adolescence; costly to the tune of some $14 million each year in B.C. alone for the care of Indian children by the provincial ministry.

The point to be made is that when well-intentioned but remote levels of government plan for and not with communities the programs developed are frequently ineffective and inappropriate. From the experiences of the Dakota Objiway Band in Manitoba, the Champagne Aishihik Band in the Yukon, the Stoney Creek, Nu Cha Nulth, Spalumcheen, and many other bands in B.C., it is becoming clear that band councils can take charge of child welfare and, with adequate resources, do a better job. This experience cannot be generalized to all Canadian communities, but the example of a low-income public housing project in Toronto provides additional evidence that when residents participate in managing child welfare services the incidence of child neglect and abuse can be reduced (Barr, 1976).

Criticisms of an Expanded Municipal Role

Before we conclude this discussion of an expanded role for municipal government in the personal social services and in social planning, it is necessary to confront two criticisms of this position. The first comes from Andrew Sancton's recent case study of municipal government and social services in London, Ontario. From his review, Sancton (1986: 61) concludes:

> In the current climate, especially in London, a move to municipal control over social services could mean only one thing: Cutbacks. . . . Since social services are always consumed by a powerless minority and paid for by a skeptical majority the dangers involved in opening up the private world of the social services to the local democratic process are obvious. There is much to be lost at the hands of the cost-slashing politician, particularly the inhabitants of city halls.

In Sancton's review the existing division of responsibilities and functions in Ontario between provincial and local governments, children's aid societies and voluntary agencies, while admittedly not rational or administratively clean, provides a measure of protection for the social services. In effect, these "ramshackle arrangements" conceal the cost of the social services from the zealous cost-cutting inhabitants of city hall.

Cost-cutters, however, are not confined to city hall. Citizens and professionals in B.C. are acutely aware of the restraint measures imposed by the Bennett government in the years 1983-86. Rather than location, commitment to an ideology of residualism may be the most influential factor in deciding to eliminate or reduce social programs.

Advocates of residualism, such as Ronald Reagan, Margaret Thatcher, Bill Bennett, and Bill Vander Zalm, are convinced by their feelings and life experiences that social programs are inherently bad since they rob individuals of their self-sufficiency and initiative.

The second criticism of decentralization is that it can result in "acute localitis" (Montgomery, 1979: 59). There are several symptoms of this disease, including the tendency for a relatively small group of elites to exercise a disproportionate share of influence, and for communities to be insulated and isolated and to resist new ideas, thus becoming complacent about unacceptable social conditions. The latter symptom is graphically illustrated by a case of child abuse and neglect in Nova Scotia. In the South Mountain community located only a few kilometres from Kentville, the home of the Children's Aid Society, conditions of abject poverty, inadequate housing, and sexual abuse of children by parents, relatives, and other members of the community had existed for many years. Southam News reported in January, 1985, that "12 adults were convicted and sent to jail following 100 charges of incest, buggery, gross indecency, sexual assault and having intercourse with girls under 14" (*Vancouver Sun*, January 5, 1985). The charges were laid by a newcomer to the area who commented that incest had been an accepted way of life for 300 families living on South Mountain. To detect this symptom of acute localitis, provincial legislation must contain standards of performance in fields of service such as child welfare, and an accreditation system needs to be put in place to ensure that agencies perform in a competent fashion.

Conclusion

This chapter has developed three recommendations regarding the provision of social services by municipal governments. The first is that municipalities should relinquish the responsibility for financial assistance. Poverty and unemployment are national problems, and if they are to be resolved the commitment, the clout, and the resources of the federal government are necessary.

The second recommendation is that municipal governments become involved in the personal social services. It is not suggested that municipalities should necessarily provide social services under their own auspices, but rather that they actively engage with provincial governments to decide what services should be offered and how they should be administered. This partnership arrangement allows for the development of appropriate services to meet local needs and avoids the necessity of establishing large and cumbersome provincial bureaucracies.

The third recommendation is that municipal governments develop a capacity for social planning. Such a capacity is required in order to implement the second recommendation and to allow municipalities to contribute to debates on social policy. Social problems are played out in the municipal arena, and if municipal governments are to communicate information on the size and seriousness of these problems and plan responses to these problems, they require social planning units such as those now existing in Vancouver, Calgary, and Halifax. Concerted action by the Federation of Canadian Municipalities to establish the case for social planning would be in keeping with their recent pronouncements and would provide the leadership necessary for negotiations with provincial governments.

REFERENCES

Alberta (1980). *Family and Community Service Act*. Edmonton: Queen's Printer.

Armitage, Andrew (1988). *Social Welfare in Canada*, Second Edition. Toronto: McClelland and Stewart.

Barr, Douglas (1976). "The Regent Park Community Services Unit: Partnership Can Work," in Brian Wharf (ed.), *Community Work in Canada*. Toronto: McClelland and Stewart.

Beck, Max (1986). Director of Social Planning, City of Vancouver, Letter to the writer, June.

Blakely, S.W. (1986). Director of Social Services, City of Calgary, Letter to the writer, December.

Bryden, Kenneth (1974). *Old Age Pensions and Policy Making in Canada*. Montreal: McGill-Queen's University Press.

Canadian Council on Social Development (1986). *Community-Based Health and Social Services*. Ottawa: CCSD.

Cassidy, Harry M. (1943). *Social Security and Reconstruction in Canada*. Toronto: Ryerson Press.

— (1945). *Public Health and Welfare Reorganization in Canada*. Toronto: Ryerson Press.

Child, John (1970). "Organization and Social Cohesion," *Human Relations*, 29, 5: 443.

City of Halifax, Social Planning Department (1983). *The Future of Social Policies and Programs in Canada: A Municipal Perspective. A Brief to the Royal Commission on Economic Union and Development Prospects for Canada*.

Clague, Michael, Robert Dill, Roop Seebaran, and Brian Wharf (1985). *Reforming Human Services*. Vancouver: UBC Press

Federation of Canadian Municipalities (1986). *Policy Development*. Task Force, Reports and Resolutions, 49th Annual Conference, Hamilton.

Guest, Dennis (1984). "Social Policy in Canada," *Social Policy and Administration*. 18, 2.

— (1986). *The Emergence of Social Security in Canada*. Vancouver: UBC Press.

Health and Welfare Canada (1987). *Inventory of Income Security Programs in Canada*.

House of Commons, Parliamentary Task Force on Federal/Provincial Fiscal Arrangements (1981). *Fiscal Federalism in Canada* (The Breau Report). Ottawa: Supply and Services.

Ismael, Jacqueline, and Ray J. Thomlison (eds.) (1987). *Perspectives on Social Services and Social Issues*. Ottawa: CCSD.

Johnstone, Patrick (1983). *Native Children and the Child Welfare System.* Ottawa: Canadian Council on Social Development.

Lesemann, Frédéric (1984). *Services and Circuses.* Montreal: Black Rose Books.

Manga, Pran, and Wendy Muckle (1987). *The Role of Local Government in the Provision of Health and Social Services in Canada.* Ottawa: CCSD.

Manzer, Ronald (1985). *Public Policies and Political Development in Canada.* Toronto: University of Toronto Press.

Marsh, Leonard C. (1943). *Report on Social Security for Canada.* Reprint, Toronto: University of Toronto Press, 1975.

Matheson, Duncan (n.d.). "Financing Social Welfare in Canada: An Alternative to Cost Sharing and the Canada Assistance Plan," unpublished paper from National Welfare Grants Directorate, Health and Welfare Canada, Ottawa.

Montgomery, John D. (1979). "The Populist Front in Rural Development: Or Shall We Eliminate The Bureaucrats And Get On With The Job?" *Public Administration Review* (January/February).

National Council of Welfare (1989). *1984 Poverty Lines.* Ottawa.

Ontario Welfare Council (1981). Submission to the Parliamentary Task Force on Federal/Provincial Fiscal Arrangements.

Ottawa-Carleton Regional Municipality (1983). *Community Service Centres.*

Rice, Jim (1979). "Social Policy, Economic Management, and Redistribution," in G. Bruce Doern and Peter Aucoin (eds.), *Public Policy in Canada.* Toronto: Macmillan of Canada.

Ross, David (1987). "Income Security," in Shankar Yelaja (ed.), *Canadian Social Policy.* Waterloo: Wilfrid Laurier University Press.

Royal Commission on the Economic Union and Development Prospects for Canada (1986). *Report.* Ottawa: Queen's Printer.

Sancton, Andrew (1986). "Municipal Government and Social Services," London, Department of Political Science, University of Western Ontario.

Splane, Richard (1965). *Social Welfare in Ontario, 1791-1893.* Toronto: University of Toronto Press.

Task Force on Program Review (1986). *Report of the Ministerial Task Force on Program Review.* Ottawa: Queen's Printer.

Titmuss, Richard (1968). *Commitment to Welfare.* London: Allen & Unwin.

Whitton, Charlotte (1943). "Security for Canadians," *Behind the Headlines* (Canadian Association for Adult Education, Toronto), 3, 6.

Wills, Jenny (1985). *Local Government and Community Services.* Melbourne: Hard Pressed Publications.

9

Trevor Hancock, Bernard Pouliot, Pierre Duplessis

Public Health

Introduction

> Many would be surprised to learn that the greatest contribution
> to the health of the nation over the past 150 years was made
> not by doctors or hospitals but by local government. Our lack
> of appreciation of the role of our cities in establishing the health
> of the nation is largely due to the fact that so little has been
> written about it. (Parfit, 1986)

This chapter focuses on the public health of the community. We will
briefly examine the history and organization of municipal public health
in Canada and analyse what public health is in an urban context. We
will then review the structure and functioning of public health at the
community level. In conclusion we will deal with trends, dilemmas,
and the possible solutions we perceive.

The structure and functions of municipal public health in various
Canadian provinces will not be compared because most municipalities
in Canada do not have a public health function *per se*; in eight of the
ten provinces there is little or no local government role in public
health. Public health and local government will thus be dealt with by
looking at two basic models. They represent in themselves the breadth
of the Canadian situation, and they also explore local government
involvement in all its spectrum, from one extreme to another. The
two models are the city of Toronto in Ontario[1] and Montreal in Quebec.

Between them, these two cities with their metropolitan areas account for about 15 per cent of the Canadian population.

Health problems – contagious diseases, sexually transmitted diseases, domestic water pollution, accidents, violence, and the like – emerge more acutely in highly populated areas. In such a milieu, also, we find the bulk of health resources. As well, in the large urban areas major health policy decisions are taken for both urban and rural populations.

However, there are complications when one tries to capture the very essence of public health in the cities: the community concept, for example, is in transformation, as is the health concept (Hancock, 1986a). There are also highly complex links between health and the life of a community, which ultimately lead us to consider the health implications of such issues as transportation, urban planning, protection of the environment, economic development, and, indeed, the political process itself (Weinstein, 1980). While it is recognized that smaller municipalities may not have the same resources as Toronto and Montreal, it is nonetheless the case that the challenges and new directions for public health described here have a more general applicability.

Public Health Services in Canada

In most provinces in Canada, local governments play little role in administering or managing public health services. Only Ontario and Alberta have strong local government roles in public health, with local boards of health that have varying degrees of local political accountability. For the most part, provincial governments provide public health services directly.

Municipal public health services differ from provincial services in two important respects: they are accountable to local government (though often the bulk of their funding is from the province, which can create its own problems!), and there is an opportunity, through their Board of Health or Health Committee, for local community and political input to policy-making. Municipally based public health services have been the norm in Ontario for over a century, with only the unorganized parts of northern Ontario having public health services provided directly by the province. For the rest, the province is divided into forty-three municipal health units, each with its own Medical Officer of Health and Board of Health. The boards of health, however, are only partly accountable to local governments, as they are autonomous bodies under provincial legislation (except in Toronto), though recently a few of the boards have been replaced by health and social service committees established by regional governments.

Alberta, too, has a strong local public health tradition, with boards of health in twenty-seven municipalities. However, in British Columbia,

Saskatchewan, and Manitoba, boards of health accountable to the local municipality are found in only a few of the largest cities (Vancouver and its suburbs, Regina, Saskatoon, and Winnipeg); elsewhere the province provides public health services directly through its own regional structure. In B.C., while local boards with municipally appointed staff provide services, they are provincial services and the municipal governments contribute less than 1 per cent of the costs (Manga and Buckle, 1987).

In the four Atlantic provinces, public health is a provincial matter, with services provided by regional offices of the ministry. Although there are local boards of health in Nova Scotia, their role now is minimal, confined to some land-use issues and citizen complaints; their impact on program delivery is non-existent (Manga and Buckle, 1987).

In Quebec, municipal public health services have been replaced by hospital-based Departements de Santé Communautaire (DSCs). The DSCs, however, receive no funding from and are not politically accountable to local governments, have hardly any public health nurses providing direct services, and do not have any public health inspectors. The role of public health nurses is generally provided by staff from the CLSCs (Centres locales de Santé communautaire), a primary care agency publicly financed and more or less comparable to community health centres in Saskatchewan and Ontario, while public health inspectors work for the municipality or the provincial environment ministry. Nonetheless, the major public health program concerns in the DSCs are much the same as in the municipal public health services elsewhere in Canada. Noteworthy is the fact that some programs, though not all, may be determined by the ministry as provincial priorities.

While provincial governments, except in Ontario and Alberta, finance almost all public health expenditures directly, they also finance cities that operate their own public health services; often, the province still pays the bulk of the costs. In Ontario, for example, the provincial government pays 40 per cent of the approved costs incurred by the six Metropolitan Toronto health units and 75 per cent of the approved costs generated by all other health units. In total, however, municipal and provincial public health expenditures total less than 5 per cent of the national heath care budget (Health and Welfare Canada, 1981) and municipalities pay only a small part of this.

History and Development of Municipal Public Health

What is public health? Let us consider for the present discussion that public health can be defined as "the art and science of improving the health status of the population, of preventing sickness and promoting the efficiency of health services through the coordination of community efforts" (Rochon, 1977). Fifty years ago public health was largely confined to contagious diseases. Social misery and numerous epidemics were prevalent in Quebec and Ontario, as they were throughout Canada over the past centuries (Bilson, 1984; Hastings and Mosley, 1980; Heagerty, 1934); and historically the organization of public health was and is largely centred on municipalities. Public health services were supported by laws that empowered cities to use public health measures (drastic ones, if needed) to counteract epidemics. The origin of such laws was clearly the 1875 Public Health Act in England, which in turn owed its origins to Edwin Chadwick's 1834 report on the appalling conditions of the labouring class in Britain's industrial slums and to the effective sanitation movement his report spawned. Public health addressed infectious diseases because these were the major killers (Omran, 1971). Its apogee was reached in the 1920s with improvement of the environment, sanitation, and immunization (Desrosiers, 1984).

In the early part of this century, however, powerful diagnostic and therapeutic tools such as x-rays, antibiotics, and effective anaesthesia appeared in medicine. Clinical supremacy took over from the public health movement and better health became equated, in the minds of the public and their political leaders, with doctors and hospitals (Illich, 1977; McKeown, 1979; Starr, 1982).

By the middle of the twentieth century, then, grants for hospital construction and technology were flourishing; at the same time, congruent with the Canadian inclination for social insurance measures, hospital insurance was introduced in 1957 and medical insurance in 1968 (Vayda and Deber, 1984). During this period public health has suffered from under-financing – less than 5 per cent of the total budget for health care was and still is devoted to prevention while the structure of public health has remained virtually unchanged for almost forty years (Matthews, 1984).

Toronto as an Example

The city of Toronto was incorporated in 1834, and one of its first bylaws was to establish a Board of Health. For fifty years the Board of Health came and went as each successive wave of typhoid, cholera, or other epidemic swept the city. But in 1883 Ontario enacted the Public Health Act and City Council appointed Dr. William Canniff as the first Medical Officer of Health, to be followed in 1884 by the permanent establishment of the Board of Health. Much of Canniff's work was concerned with sanitation, sewage, and drinking water treatments, and in Toronto, as elsewhere, the Public Works Department grew out of the public health movement, as, for that matter, did urban planning, parks, housing, and social service functions (Severs, 1989). By 1910 the emphasis had shifted to pasteurization of milk and immunization against diphtheria, tetanus, and other infectious diseases. The Public Works Department was fortunate to have at its head Dr. Charles Hastings, under whose leadership it became one of the best in the world. Hastings's concerns were by no means limited to infectious diseases. He wrote reports on housing, poverty, and working conditions and established sections within the Department for welfare, social services, housing, and industrial hygiene (Bator, 1979). After his retirement in 1929, however, the Department, like public health in general internationally, appears to have gone into a decline as the biomedical model of clinical medicine gained ascendancy.

In 1978, however, a renaissance began. Based on their experience in fighting lead pollution and their roots in community activism, a reform-minded Board of Health developed a report, *Public Health in the 1980s* (Board of Health, 1978), that laid out a blueprint for a new concept of public health. Unanimously passed by City Council, the report called for better research capabilities and good health status information as the basis for program planning; improved health education and promotion resources; community development and advocacy directed toward the social and political determinants of health; and a number of administrative changes including decentralization, team management, and more community input to decision-making. Within six years almost all of these recommendations had been implemented (Hancock, 1986b).

Elsewhere in the province similar changes, though much slower, have begun to occur. In 1983 Ontario replaced the century-old Public Health Act with the Health Protection and Promotion Act, which confirmed the municipal basis of public health while establishing a broad set of core programs that all health units are required to provide at a specified level of service (Ministry of Health, 1983).

The Province of Quebec

Before examining in more depth either Toronto's or Montreal's public health system, we should first explore how the concept of the health of a community has evolved over time. Quebec offers a good illustration.

As opposed to the situation in Toronto, Montreal departed from a public health system based in the municipalities because of an important ideological shift that occurred fifteen years ago. In 1971 a special task force was appointed by the deputy minister of social affairs to further the impressive work of the Inquiry Commission on Health and Social Services, which ran from 1966 to 1970 (Gouvernement du Québec, 1970). This task force initiated a vast reform, shifting from the traditional concept of public health to what is known now as community health. Modern "epidemics," such as cardiovascular diseases, road accidents, and cancer (Smith, 1984), the task force determined, should be dealt with using new tools and new approaches.

This would involve mobilizing the overall social and community resources, not just health resources. Public health thus became community health (Ministère des Affaires Sociales, 1971).

Changes in Quebec were radical. Both public health units and municipal health services in some large municipalities were abolished. Since 1973, they have been gradually integrated into the new hospital-based public health entities known as DSCs. Thirty-two new DSCs were started within two years, integrated in designated hospitals[2] and given a territorial responsibility for about 200,000 people. The reasoning behind the decision was to integrate public health with the health care delivery system and to get prevention closer to clinical expertise (Gouvernement du Québec, 1970, 1971). In so doing, the Ministry acted as the major planning and funding agency. A departure from the 1960s was that the Ministry was no longer providing services directly or indirectly. Linking public health to hospitals had the effect not only of removing public health from municipalities but of giving control over public health to public and local corporations lacking political influence or control (Duplessis, 1981, 1982; Garon, 1979; Gosselin, 1984). Such a system is different from the other provinces in that public health is not directly linked to either a local or a provincial political body.

The mandate of the DSCs is both the protection and control of epidemics and also the evaluation of the health status and problems of the population. Added to this role were the design and implementation of community health programs and, more recently, the evaluation of both the structure and functioning of any health service in their territories (Gouvernement du Québec, 1971).

In making these changes, Quebec considerably enlarged the public health perspective to include such areas as education, occupational health, and environmental protection in a different way from what has been the case in the other provinces. The responsibilities of the DSCs could be described as planning for health, public health protection, health promotion, and capacities in occupational health.

Structure and Function of Municipal Public Health Services Today

The Toronto Department of Public Health

In Toronto, with a staff of 500-600, the structure and programs are rather different from many of the other smaller health units in Ontario. It is noteworthy, however, that other provinces are developing programs in line with the new approaches to public health exemplified by Toronto and, earlier, Vancouver (Weinstein, 1981).

The Board of Health in Toronto, unlike boards of health in most other municipalities in Ontario, includes both city councillors and

Council-appointed community members (who form the majority), as well as representatives of the public and separate school boards and provincial appointees. This composition of the Board of Health is a long tradition in Toronto and it survived a recent, politically motivated attempt to remove the community representation. The broad community representation has undoubtedly contributed to the feistiness of the Board, which led in part to the failed attempt to reduce its effectiveness.

The Board is responsible to the Minister of Health, under the Health Protection and Promotion Act, for managing public health services in Toronto; the Medical Officer of Health is the chief executive officer and is also responsible to the Minister. However, the Department of Public Health is also a department of city government (which provides over 60 per cent of the budget), the Medical Officer of Health is also a city commissioner, and the Department staff are all city employees (and members of the Canadian Union of Public Employees local) that the city "provides" to the Board of Health. (This rather unusual arrangement is also found in the Metro Toronto municipalities of Etobicoke, North York, and Scarborough; elsewhere, the Board of Health employs its own staff.)

The Board of Health, in effect, functions as a standing committee of Council responsible for managing the city's Health Department. The chair of the Board sits on Council's executive committee, the Board's reports are forwarded to Council, and the budget has to be approved like any other city department's budget. (Unlike any other city department, however, the Health Department's budget must also be approved by the Ministry of Health.)

The 1983 Health Protection and Promotion Act in Ontario mandates seven sets of core programs that health units must "provide or ensure the provision of." These are: community sanitation, communicable disease control, preventive dentistry, family health, home care, public health education, and nutrition. These services are generally delivered by the appropriate staff on a disciplinary/divisional basis. While this outline is of course specific to Ontario, it is generally representative of the responsibilities of provincial and municipal public health services nationally.

In line with the report *Public Health in the 1980s,* Toronto first developed a Health Advocacy Unit to provide additional skills in information, research, planning, education, promotion, community development, and advocacy (Hancock, 1984). With reorganization in 1982, the Advocacy Unit became the core of Central Resources, while four semi-autonomous Health Areas were established, each with a staff of roughly 110 and a co-equal management team consisting of a physician, a nurse, a public health inspector, and a business administrator. Each Health Area has a Community Advisory Board, one member of which (usually the chair) sits on the Board of Health. The management team is jointly responsible to the Ministry for the affairs of their area, as well as being individually responsible for their own disciplinary groups.

Department programs have also been revised in keeping with *Public Health in the 1980s*. Both conceptual and program planning have been described more fully elsewhere (Hancock, 1986b; Baxter, 1986), so only a brief overview will be given here.

Priority programs were identified in each of four content areas, which correspond to the four resource sections in Central Resources. They are: (1) *health information,* including health status data collection, epidemiology, research, evaluation, library and resource collection; (2) *health promotion,* including health education, media promotion and public relations, community development, advocacy, staff development and training; (3) *health protection,* including environmental health, occupational health, and emergency response; and (4)*disease prevention,* including parent and child health, school health, dental health, adult and seniors health, mental health, and communicable disease control.

The program priorities identified are of two sorts – those related to health information and health promotion, essentially supportive in nature, and those related to program delivery. The former include such priorities as developing a good health status data base, developing effective program evaluation approaches, enhancing staff skills and knowledge in primary prevention, and raising the Department's profile. The latter include environmental health, occupational health, parental and child health, prevention of premature deaths from heart disease, reduction of substance abuse and of suicide.

One of the major challenges has been the shifting of resources from traditional public health concerns to these newer priorities while continuing to maintain services still needed by the community. A dilemma faced by public health nurses, for example, is that between prevention and care. While public health has never been in the business of cure, it has been involved in a great deal of one-on-one home visiting, and the public has come to expect a high level of "hand-holding" and friendly visiting services. The process of getting out of this role in favour of more group-oriented health promotion and disease prevention efforts has not always been easy, particularly where community care services – such as for seniors or those with mental health problems – are still inadequate. Similarly, public health inspectors have had to widen their horizons to deal with chemical hazards and occupational health problems in addition to their traditional concern with microbiological problems.

One notable development has been the emphasis on community development approaches to health problems. The Department has ten full-time community health workers, two in each health area, one for multicultural health issues, and one for community mental health issues. Multiculturalism has been a major concern in a city with thirty-three heritage languages taught in schools and where the majority of the population do not have English or French as their mother tongue. Community workers have been particularly active in this area, and one result has been the establishment of a multicultural health coalition that has swiftly attained provincial and even national prominence as a leader and resource for many different cultural groups as they deal with health and sick-care system problems.

Public Health Programs in Montreal

There are eight autonomous DSCs in Montreal, but they share personnel and services when needed. They are functionally grouped in a formal association with an executive director under the authority of a board composed of the eight directors of DSCs.

In Montreal, similar program directions to those in Toronto were developed both at the DSC level and at the regional level for setting new priorities. Most of the programs and activities of the DSCs are similar to those described for Toronto under the health information and health promotion priorities sections. There are, however, direct services in Montreal DSCs only in infectious diseases (immunization programs and epidemic investigations) and in occupational health. The difficult balance in the nurse's tasks between traditional "hands-on" involvement and new community-oriented priorities does not pose such marked problems in Quebec because these nurses have been transferred to primary care settings (CLSCs) for the delivery of services. Public health thus has roots not only in DSCs but also in the large primary care network, and nurses still at work in the DSCs are oriented toward planning and not to service provision.

The Challenge for Public Health

Problems with the medical model in recent years have meant that the spotlight is turning back to public health. Facing such difficult health problems as accidents, cancer, cardiovascular diseases, AIDS, and the like, medicine is on the spot: a preventive approach may be more effective than our current emphasis on treatment. Other factors, such as an aging population and the costs of high-tech medicine, also contribute to the search for solutions in the public health sector.

In terms of cost, it is unlikely that the rate of increase can be maintained at its present pace. The costs of medicare in Canada increased from $3.3 billion in 1965 to $11 billion in 1975; for 1989 in Ontario alone, medicare cost approximately $13 billion. In Canada today, the share of governmental expenses devoted to health at the federal level is 10 per cent and at the provincial level 30 per cent or more. The proportion of Gross National Product devoted to health care was 5.5 per cent in 1960 and by the 1980s had climbed to over

8 per cent (Vayda and Deber, 1984). Added to this is the relative inefficiency of medicine, or if one puts it another way, the decrease of its efficiency curve (Jackson, 1985). Put simply, it is becoming a matter of where we get the biggest bang for our health buck.

Another factor accounting for this questioning of the health system is the demographic evolution (Duplessis and Spitzer, 1987). The proportion of elderly in the population is increasing, and with this follow costly chronic and degenerative diseases, some of which may be reduced by healthy behaviours and/or prevention or may be treated more efficiently in the community.

But if the medical model is under scrutiny, so, too, is public health. Costs, efficacy, demography, accessibility are all relevant in this field, as they are in medicine in general (Siemiatycki and Richardson, 1981). If public health is to respond effectively, it must respond to these questions as well as to those regarding its organization.

Organizational Issues for Public Health

Looking first at the Montreal model, questions arise from a few drawbacks that are worth elaborating on briefly. The first is the distance between local actions and a central co-ordinating agency. As a hospital department, the DSC is accountable to the internal structure of the hospital and not to any territorial organization; it is thus very difficult (but not impossible) to co-ordinate the work of all the different DSCs at a regional level or on issues encompassing a single territory. And the same holds true for provincial matters involving all thirty-two DSCs.

A second drawback is the gap between a DSC and its local government. In integrating the municipal health services in 1973 and in confining the mandate of public health more or less exclusively to health-related issues, other areas like environmental protection, inspection of food, water, and waste disposal were given to either local or provincial governments. And while DSCs were struggling to organize themselves to survive in their own environment, the gap between the municipalities and the DSCs became greater and greater.

A third shortcoming is the lack of community input. Unlike the primary care network of CLSCs, which was designed to be close to the community by having lay people on boards of directors, DSCs were linked to hospitals. The input from the community became minimal while the input of highly skilled professionals became dominant. Thus, needs assessment in DSCs often has a strong professional bias (Pineault, 1984).

The problems in Toronto are of a different nature. The public health service has little if any connection with the illness-care system, which – as in Montreal – consists of a set of autonomous hospitals and large numbers of independent physicians. In fact, it is misleading to think of it as a system, since there is no central co-ordination or control at the local level. The only major Metro-wide agency is home care, an autonomous agency funded by the province. Also at the Metro level is a relatively new actor, the District Health Council, but it is appointed by and reports to the Minister of Health, with no local political accountability whatsoever.

It is difficult for the six health units in Metro to agree among themselves on a common philosophy and approach to public health, never mind a concerted approach to the need for rational planning in a sick-care system strongly dominated by hospitals and physicians and ill-disposed to receive advice or criticism from their poor cousins in public health. The biggest single problem facing public health and the health care system in Toronto is thus co-ordination of programs, services, and activities. The failure to date of the six health units in Metro Toronto to co-ordinate their own activities is a major challenge for the next decade, although the Metro District Health Council is playing a useful role in bringing the health units together and developing Metro-wide approaches to heart disease and smoking, among other initiatives.

Conceptual Issues for Public Health: The "Healthy City" Concept

While the problem of poor co-ordination is perhaps generally true in Canada as a whole, a major problem for public health in the next decade will be to shift the focus of the health care system, and the debate about health, from a sick-care orientation to a health orientation (Pineault, 1984).

The "hands-on" care/community prevention dilemma has been mentioned previously. It is particularly strong in Toronto because of the Department's determination that it is not in the business of providing "hands-on" care. This has led to some friction with certain segments of the community, notably the school boards and parents, who still see the role of the public health nurse as providing first aid and head lice inspection, not teaching about responsible sexuality, alcohol and tobacco consumption, and mental health counselling.

Another problem faced by public health in both Toronto and Montreal arises from the broader understanding of health and health promotion being developed today. It is best exemplified by the recent development of the "healthy city" concept in Toronto. The Department's mission statement is "to make Toronto the healthiest city in North America."[3] Clearly, this is not achievable merely through the Department's activities, or even by the activities of the health care system as a whole. A healthy city is as much a function of housing, transportation, urban design, public works, parks, economic development, education, police, or social services as it is of the health care system, if not more so. Recognizing this, the Board of Health marked its centenary in 1984 (and the city's sesquicentennial) with two conferences. One, a national conference called "Beyond Health Care," dealt with broad issues of health and public policy in such areas as education, housing, employment, energy, and food and agriculture, to name but a few (*Beyond Health Care*, 1985). The second conference was directed more specifically at the city and sought to apply the concepts of public health policy to the city itself (*Healthy Toronto 2000*, 1984). This latter conference became the source of inspiration for "Healthy Cities," a major health promotion project in Europe organized by the World Health Organization (Ashton *et al.*, 1985), and is an example of the wheel turning full circle – the development, now under way, of a Canadian Healthy Communities project (Hancock, 1987).

In Toronto, the Board of Health established a strategic planning subcommittee in 1986. Its 1988 report *Healthy Toronto 2000* (Board of Health, 1988), which was unanimously approved by City Council in early 1989, proposed a major city-wide initiative to make Toronto the healthiest city possible (see Hancock, 1989). A set of broad health goals was identified for the city as a whole, including reducing inequities in health opportunities in Toronto by addressing problems of homelessness, hunger, poverty, unemployment, and illiteracy; creating physical environments for health through health-conscious urban planning and an emphasis on sustainability; creating supportive social environments, emphasizing community empowerment and the role of women; and advocating for a community-based health services system. The report also proposed a strategy for the Department of Public Health that was generally consistent with and built upon the Department's work in implementing *Public Health in the 1980s*.

The responsibility for the city-wide initiative has been assumed by the Healthy City Workgroup, a multidepartmental group that has been working on the implications of the healthy city concept for Toronto. The Workgroup, chaired by the Planning and Development Department, will be responsible for managing the city's Healthy City project and the newly created (mid-1989) Healthy City Office, which has a full-time staff of three. Initial plans call for two main emphases – addressing social inequities and managing the urban ecosystem – through multidepartmental initiatives and extensive community participation.

Thus, municipal public health in Toronto is developing new, broad, and multisectoral approaches to the challenge of creating a healthy city for the twenty-first century. And in doing so it is discovering the root of public health in the cities of the nineteenth century. Approaches to the development of healthy cities are of necessity multifaceted and intersectoral, requiring an assessment of the health implications of public policies. This may result in two problems, the first being "healthism" – the possibility that public health professionals will come to see everything as health and to view health as the highest (or even the only) human value. Related to this is the danger that other sections of society, in particular other departments in municipal government, may come to see public health as a threat to their own "empires," perhaps even attempting to take them over.

Clearly, the healthy city concept is neither of these things, and some care will have to be taken by proponents in pointing out that we are interested in building conditions for better health and a better quality of life for all, not in creating new empires. Our concern must be to encourage other sectors in society to see, understand, and evaluate the health implications of their actions (or omissions) but not to dictate to them. We do not need, or want, a "health police."

Toward a New Public Health

From the foregoing, it should be clear that public health, both globally and municipally, is enjoying a new lease on life. However, the road is not without obstacles, as we have seen. Public health's objectives will always be pursued by and on behalf of a given community, hence ideally within municipal limits. Facing new challenges but unchanged for more than forty years, public health in all provinces must modify its structural system in significant ways. Change will be supported and pushed forward by a new and well-trained group of community health specialists and medical officers of health who are beginning to assume key positions today (Hancock et al., 1982; Hastings, 1986). This is also foreseen by new concepts of public health not only in Canada but in most of the industrialized countries,[4] which is well reflected by the World Health Organization position (Kickbusch, 1986; WHO, 1986). We will review that briefly.

The 1974 Lalonde model (Laframboise, 1973; Lalonde, 1974), which defined health by four determinants (human biology, environment, lifestyle, and health services), has broadened to a more holistic approach (Department of Health, Education and Welfare, 1979, 1980; Blum, 1981; CASF, 1984; Hancock and Perkins, 1985). The new paradigm of health promotion envisages health as a positive value, not merely the absence of disease, and calls for the development of health-promoting public policies. These policies seek to create physical and social environments supportive of health and aim to strengthen communities, as well as help people to develop their personal health skills and reorient health services toward prevention and community-based care (Ottawa Charter, 1986). The ultimate objective is to reduce inequalities in health and to achieve "health for all," as a recent federal government policy paper suggests (Health and Welfare Canada, 1986).

This approach incorporates dimensions beyond the health care system and requires intersectoral co-ordination of policy and action in areas such as housing, food and agriculture, the environment, economy, social life, physical activities, and the lifestyle of individuals (Beyond

Health Care, 1985; Kickbusch, 1986; World Health Assembly, 1986). In terms of integrating all these determinants, cities always were and still are major actors, particularly since a second important dimension in the vision of new public health is *the community itself*. Major health problems cannot be solved if the community does not participate actively in their solutions; indeed, health promotion is defined as "the process of enabling people to increase control over and to improve their health" (WHO, 1986). This is reinforced by Rochon's definition of public health as "the art and science of improving the health status of the population . . . through the coordination of community efforts," and it is the reason for renewed interest in community development and health (McKnight, 1978; O'Connor *et al.*, 1985).

As we have seen throughout this chapter, public health is not – and never has been – solely confined to infectious diseases. Paths explored go much beyond preventive and traditional services. In Canada today, large cities integrate public health in their core activities. Although this is true in general, there are exceptions. But like it or not, cities are the major actor on the public health scene due to their strategic intersectoral decisions and the involvement of their communities. All too often, however, they may ignore the positive or negative effects on people's health when deciding on transportation, housing, land-use planning, and other areas where they are influential (Weinstein, 1980). For example, the city of Montreal refused to fluoridate its water while many other Quebec municipalities did. On the other hand, the close links between public health and municipal government in Toronto have helped to ensure that health is on the agenda when major planning issues are being considered.

Each city has the capacity to encourage or discourage behaviours conducive to health and to create environments and public policies supportive of health. In return, public health now has the responsibility to increase public awareness of issues involving urban life and health. Given that today 75 per cent of the population of industrialized nations live in an urban environment and that in the year 2025 this proportion will reach 90 per cent (Pacione, 1981), it is vital that municipal decision-makers be intimately associated not only with public health services but with the health implications of other policy decisions. This is the basic purpose of the Healthy Cities project. As was previously mentioned, "Healthy Cities" is a health promotion project in Europe that had its origins in Toronto and has now spawned a Canadian project called Healthy Communities. The project is a way of implementing the new and somewhat global WHO concepts of health promotion at a community level. Municipalities are the lowest level of government with broad multisectoral responsibilities and resources and, consequently, municipal governments are closest to the community. They are thus in unique position to act together with their communities to promote health. The Healthy Communities project, in essence, asks two simple questions of each participating city: What is a healthy city? How do you create it? Answering these questions should involve politicians, planners, civil servants, and community members in determining what the ideal healthy city would mean and in developing broad multisectoral solutions to the problems identified. The multisectoral nature of the approach is exemplified by the fact that the project is supported by the Canadian Public Health Association and the Federation of Canadian Municipalities and is housed at the Canadian Institute of Planners.

To conclude, we must point out that the broader public health approach described in this chapter is not a theoretical one. It is moving forward in Montreal, Toronto, and other municipalities in Canada, although often with structural differences as large as those demonstrated between Toronto and Montreal. Municipal leaders and public health officials have the responsibility to ensure that the structure is not an obstacle but a facilitator to bring local government and health policies closer together. The close co-operation of public health and municipal government holds out the prospect of healthier cities for all of us.

NOTES

1. In this chapter the references to Toronto refer to the city of Toronto. There is no Metropolitan Toronto public health service; instead, each of the six local municipalities has its own Medical Officer of Health, Board of Health, Health Department, City Council, and Mayor.
2. The link with the hospital might seem strange at first glance and its discussion is largely outside the subject of this chapter. However, a more interested reader can refer to the following documentation: Garon, 1979; Duplessis, 1981; Duplessis, 1982; Gosselin, 1984.
3. This was amended in 1988 to be less competitive: the mission now is "to help make Toronto the healthiest city possible" (Board of Health, 1988).
4. See, for example, Ashton and Seymour (1988), a description of the "new public health" in Great Britain and of the authors' experience in applying the concepts of health promotion and healthy cities in Liverpool.

REFERENCES

Ashton, John, Paula Grey, and Keith Barnard (1986). "Healthy Cities – WHO's new health promotion project," *Health Promotion,* 1, 3.

Ashton, John, and Howard Seymour (1988). *The New Public Health.* Milton Keynes: Open University Press.

Bator, Paul (1979). "Saving Lives on the Wholesale Plan: Public Health Reform in the City of Toronto 1900-1920" (Ph.D. thesis, University of Toronto).

Baxter, D. (1986). "Public Health in the City of Toronto. Part 2. Turning Concepts into Programs," *Canadian Journal of Public Health* (hereafter *CJPH*), 77: 185-89.

Beyond Health Care (1985). Proceedings of a Working Conference on Healthy Public Policy. *CJPH*, 76 (Suppl. 1): 1-104.

Bilson, G. (1984). "Cholera and Public Health in Canada," *CJPH*, 75: 352-55.

Blum, H.L. (1981). *Planning for Health: Generics for the Eighties.* New York: Human Sciences Press.

Board of Health (1978). *Public Health in the 1980s.* Toronto: Local Board of Health.

— (1988). *Healthy Toronto 2000.* Toronto: Local Board of Health.

CASF (Conseil des affaires sociales et de la famille) (1984). *Objectif: santé.* Québec: Gouvernement du Québec.

Department of Health, Education and Welfare (1979). *Healthy People: The Surgeon General's Report on Health Promotion and Disease Prevention.* Washington: Government Printing Office.

— (1980). *Promoting Health, Preventing Disease: Objectives for the Nation.* Washington: Government Printing Office.

Desrosiers, G. (1984). "Histoire de la santé publique au Québec," *CJPH*, 75: 359-63.

Duplessis, P. (1981). "Réflexion sur les D.S.C. dix ans après la Réforme – Partie I," *Adm. H. et Soc.*, 26, 4: 30-35.

— (1982). "Réflexion sur les D.S.C. dix ans après la Réforme – Partie II," *Adm. H. et soc.*, 27, 1: 17-22.

Duplessis, P., and W.O. Spitzer (1987). "Demography of the Elderly," in J.L. Meaking and J.S. McClaran (eds.), *Surgical Care of the Elderly.* Yearbook Medical Publications.

Garon, G. (1979). "Le département de Santé communautaire des centres hospitaliers (CH-DSC): son territoire et sa responsabilité," *Union medicale du Canada*, 108: 1095-1106.

Gosselin, R. (1984). "Decentralization/regionalization in health care: the Quebec experience," *HCMR* (Winter): 7-25.

Gouvernement du Québec (1970). *Rapport de la commission d'enquête sur la santé et le bien-être social.* Québec: Gouvernement du Québec.

— (1971). *Loi sur les services de santé et les services sociaux.* L.R.Q. c.S-5. Québec: Gouvernement du Québec.

Hancock, T. (1984). "Health as a social and political issue: Toronto's Health Advocacy Unit," in Paul D. Lumsden (ed.), *Community Mental Health Action.* Ottawa: Canadian Public Health Association.

— (1986a). "Lalonde and beyond: Looking back at 'A New Perspective on the Health of Canadians,'" *Health Promotion*, 1, 1: 93-100.

— (1986b). "Public Health Planning in the City of Toronto. Part 1. Conceptual Planning," *CJPH*, 77: 180-84.

— (1987). "Healthy Cities: The Canadian Project," *Health Promotion*, 26, 1: 2-4, 27.

— (1989). "From 'Public Health in the 1980's' to 'Healthy Toronto 2000': The development of healthy public policy in Toronto," in A. Evers *et al.* (eds.), *Local Healthy Public Policy* (in press).

Hancock, T., E.W.R. Best, and H. Le Riche (1982). "Education of the Medical Officer of Health in Canada," *CJPH*, 73: 35-38.

Hancock, T., and F. Perkins (1985). "The mandala of health: a conceptual model and teaching tool," *Health Education*, 24: 8-10.

Hastings, J.E.F. (1986). *The Ontario Health System: an overview.* Conférence prononcée lors du VIII colloque J.Y. Rivard. Montréal.

Hastings, J.E.F., and W. Mosley (1980). "Introduction: The Evolution of Organized Community Health Services in Canada," in C.A. Meilicke and J.L. Storch (eds.), *Perspectives on Canadian Health and Social Services Policy: History and Emerging Trends.* Ann Arbor: Health Administration Press.

Heagerty, J.J. (1934). "The Development of Public Health in Canada," *CJPH,* 25: 53-59.

Health and Welfare Canada (1981). *National Health Expenditure in Canada, 1970-1979.* Ottawa.

— (1986). *Achieving Health For All: A Framework for Health Promotion.* Ottawa.

Healthy Toronto 2000 (1984). Toronto: Department of Public Health.

Illich, I. (1977). *Limits to Medicine: Medical Nemesis and the Expropriation of Health.* New York: Penguin.

Jackson, R. (1985). *Les soins de santé préventifs: les questions en jeu.* Document d'étude, Conseil des Sciences du Canada ss 21-5/1985-6F.

Kickbusch, I. (1986). "Health Promotion: A Global Perspective," *CJPH,* 77: 321-26.

Laframboise, H.L. (1973). "Health policy: breaking the problem down into more manageable segments," *Canadian Medical Association Journal,* 108: 388-93.

Lalonde, M. (1974). *A New Perspective on the Health of Canadians.* Ottawa: Office of the Canadian Minister of National Health and Welfare.

Manga, Pran, and Wendy Buckle (1987). *The Role of Local Government in the Provision of Health and Social Services in Canada.* Ottawa: Canadian Council for Social Development.

Matthews, V.L. (1984). "What's Past is Prologue: Future Issues in Public Health," *CJPH,* 75: 348-51.

McKeown, T. (1979). *The Role of Medicine: Dream, Mirage or Nemesis.* Oxford: Blackwell.

McKnight, John (1978). "Politicising Health Care," *Social Policy,* 9, 3: 36-39.

Ministère des affaires sociales (1971). *Rapport du comité d'étude sur la prévention sanitaire.* Québec: Ministère des affaires sociales.

Ministry of Health (1983). *Health Protection and Promotion Act.* Toronto: Queen's Printer.

O'Connor, Anita, Maria Herrera, and Trevor Hancock (1985). "Community Development and Health in Toronto: An Update," paper presented at the Canadian Public Health Association Annual Meeting, Saint John, New Brunswick, June.

Omran, A.R. (1971). "The Epidemiologic Transition: A Theory of the Epidemiology of Population Change," *Millbank Memorial Fund Quarterly,* 49: 509-38.

Ottawa Charter on Health Promotion (1986). WHO, Health and Welfare Canada, and Canadian Public Health Association.

Pacione, M. (ed.) (1981). *Urban Problems and Planning in the Developed World.* New York: St. Martin's Press.

Parfit, Jessie (1986). *The Health of a City: Oxford 1770-1974.* Oxford: Amate Press.

Pineault, R. (1984). "The Place of Prevention in the Quebec Health Care System," *CJPH,* 75: 92-97.

Rochon, J. (1977). "La santé communautaire dans le système régional des services de santé et des services sociaux," *Annuaire du Québec 1975-76.* Québec: Gouvernement du Québec.

Severs, A. (1989). "Public Health as a Catalyst in the Growth of Municipal Departments in Early Toronto," *CJPH*, 80, 4: 291-94.

Siemiatycki, J.A., and L.J. Richardson (1981). "Le défi prioritaire en Santé communautaire: élargir notre vision pour atteindre nos véritables objectifs," *Union medicale. Can.*, 100: 1008-11.

Smith, H. (1984). "Premières causes de déces au Canada en 1982," *Maladies chroniques au Canada*, 5: 1-4.

Starr, Paul (1982). *The Social Transformation of American Medicine.* New York: Basic Books.

Statistics Canada (1985). Cat. No. 11-402-F. Ottawa.

Vayda, E., and R. Deber (1984). "The Canadian Health Care System: An Overview," *Soc. Sci. Med.*, 18: 191-97.

Weinstein, M.S. (1980). *Health in the City: Environmental and Behavioral Influences.* New York: Pergamon Press.

— (1981). "Outcome-Oriented Management at the Vancouver Health Department," *CJPH*, 72: 93-96.

WHO Regional Office for Europe (1986). "A discussion document on the concept and principles of health promotion," *Health Promotion*, 1: 73-76.

World Health Assembly (1986). "The role of intersectoral cooperation in national strategies for Health For All," *Health Promotion*, 1, 2: 239-45.

10 Richard A. Loreto

Policing

Introduction

The preservation of law and order at the community level has historically been a responsibility of local government institutions in England, Canada, and the United States (Stenning, 1988: 4). In Canada, however, the delivery of policing services designed to attain these community goals has been accomplished through the deployment of police forces established at all three governmental levels of the federal system, i.e., local, provincial, and federal. This indigenous factor in conjunction with the impact of foreign influences, from England early on and more recently from the United States, has essentially shaped the current structure and practice of local policing in Canada.

The purpose of this chapter is to examine the institutional features and contemporary issues of local policing. The approach adopted is a comparative one in that policing arrangements in all provinces are surveyed. Described in some detail are the institutional features of local policing. These encompass the history, structure, legal basis, financing, organization, and public control of the police function. As well, two key issues of contemporary policing are analysed: the impact of policing on crime; the relationship between the police and the community, the discussion of which is subdivided into three areas – community-based policing, police-minority group relations, and civilian oversight of the police. The current nature and future directions of local policing in Canada are considered in the conclusion.

Institutional Features of the Police Function in Canada

History and Current Structure

The history of local policing can be analysed from two related perspectives.[1] First, in temporal terms, three noteworthy periods of development can be identified: pre-nineteenth century, the nineteenth century, and the twentieth century. Second, an important overlay on the temporal perspective is the evolution of the municipal, provincial, and federal components of local policing in Canada. The following synopsis reflects both the temporal and structural perspectives.

Prior to the nineteenth century the common law office of constable, which had been established much earlier in England (Stenning, 1981a: 1), provided the model for local policing in British North America. The key characteristics of this office were the constable's status as a "peace officer," its local origins and autonomy from central state authority, and judicial appointment (usually by local justices of the peace). Furthermore, the constable, who was selected from among the residents of a community, was an amateur rather than a trained professional.

During the nineteenth century three significant developments occurred. The first was a shift away from judicial to municipal control of the police. Stenning (1981a: 49-55) attributes this shift to two factors, one foreign, the other indigenous. The former was the notion of police reform and professionalization inherent in the new force for Metropolitan London established by Sir Robert Peel in 1829 (Stead, 1977). The latter was the democratization of municipal government through the creation of locally elected councils. In the colony of Upper Canada this process began with Toronto's city charter in 1834 and culminated with the passage of the so-called Baldwin Act in 1849. As the democratization of municipal government spread to other Canadian provinces, it was usually accompanied by the notion of municipal control of the police.

The second development of significance during the nineteenth century was in essence a variant of the first. This was the shift within the local sphere from control of the police by elected councils to control by appointed boards of police commissioners. Once again, Ontario led the way with an 1858 statute that set up three-person police boards in its five cities (boards were optional for towns). These boards were given considerable autonomy from council control (Stenning, 1981b: I.7-I.13). The concept of a police board spread later to other provinces, although substantial modifications to the Ontario approach were usually made and boards did not completely supplant control by elected councils (Stenning, 1988: 6).

The creation of both a national and a number of provincial police forces represents the final major development during the nineteenth century. While the origins of a national force lie in the establishment of the Mounted Police Force in 1845 and the Mounted Constabulary Police Force in 1849, the organizational basis of the current federal force, the Royal Canadian Mounted Police (RCMP), was set in place during the first six years after Confederation. Early on federal policing responsibilities were divided between the Dominion Police, created in 1868, and the North West Mounted Police Force, created in 1873. The former had jurisdiction throughout the new nation with respect to federal laws; the latter policed the newly acquired western lands, effectively restricting the Dominion Police to eastern Canada (Cooper, 1981: 41).

The emergence of provincial forces was a response to the policing needs of the rural areas (Cooper, 1981: 40). The first provincial forces were created in 1870 in Quebec and Manitoba, respectively, and by the turn of the century all provinces except Prince Edward Island had done likewise. Newfoundland (which did not become a province until 1949) established the Royal Newfoundland Constabulary in 1872, while Ontario passed legislation in 1877 authorizing the appointment of provincial constables. The establishment of a force in British Columbia (1880) and the appointment of provincial constables in New Brunswick (1898) and Nova Scotia (1899) marked the zenith of the trend toward provincial policing during the nineteenth century (Statistics Canada, 1986: 29, 36, 40, 51, 74).

The impact on local policing of the creation of federal and provincial forces was twofold. First, these forces represented a deviation from the idea that policing was a responsibility subject to local control. They were set up by cabinet and subject to the administrative supervision of an appointed commissioner. Second, their jurisdiction extended beyond the boundaries of local communities (Stenning, 1981a: 40-49).

Among the many developments that have characterized the evolution of local policing during this century, three deserve some attention here: the role of the RCMP in provincial and municipal policing, the changing role of provincial forces, and the rationalization of the legislative foundations of local policing. The first two developments are intertwined and will be examined below; the third is dealt with in a later section.

Two observations should be made with respect to the continued evolution of federal and provincial policing responsibilities. The pervasiveness of structural change is the first. At the federal level the key event was the creation of the RCMP in 1919 through the merger of the Dominion Police and the Royal North West Mounted Police Force (the name change had taken place in 1904). At the provincial level the theme of structural change was more diverse. In some provinces nineteenth-century legislation authorizing the appointment of provincial constables was consolidated to provide for the establishment of full-scale provincial forces. Ontario, for example, created the

Ontario Provincial Police (OPP) in 1909. In other provinces new, usually specialized, forces were created – the Newfoundland Company of Rangers (1935), the Liquor Police Force in Quebec (1940), and the New Brunswick Highway Patrol (1980) (Statistics Canada, 1986: 29, 41, 44). Finally, Alberta (1917), Saskatchewan (1920), and Prince Edward Island (1930) completed the trend toward provincial forces initiated in the previous century.

The second observation, closely linked with the first, concerns the changing roles of federal and provincial forces. The emphasis on consolidating and expanding provincial policing services, which was the hallmark of the first three decades of this century, quickly evaporated in the atmosphere of financial crisis engendered by the Great Depression of the 1930s. Disbanding provincial forces and replacing them with the RCMP became the norm. Saskatchewan provided the impetus for this "domino effect" in 1928, followed four years later by Prince Edward Island, Nova Scotia, New Brunswick, Manitoba, and Alberta. British Columbia and Newfoundland disbanded their forces in 1950, leaving Ontario and Quebec as the only provinces with provincial forces.

The current structure of policing in Canada can be depicted along a number of dimensions.[2] At the end of 1985 total police strength was just over 51,000 officers (almost 53,500 officers if all RCMP units are included). As might be expected, there is a direct relationship between the size of the province's population and its police strength, i.e., the higher the population, the higher the level of police strength. The police to population ratio for all provinces was 1:499; it was highest in Prince Edward Island (1:707) and lowest in Quebec (1:466).[3] Moreover, while it is clear that municipal police officers represent the largest component of police strength (approximately 57 per cent), followed by the RCMP (23 per cent) and provincial forces (18 per cent), it is also evident that this pattern varies across the provinces. Municipal officers account for more than half of police strength only in the provinces of New Brunswick, Quebec, Ontario, Manitoba, and Alberta. In the other five provinces the relative size of the municipal component varies from nil in the case of Newfoundland (the Royal Newfoundland Constabulary polices municipalities but it is a provincial force in terms of accountability, control, and funding) to just under 48 per cent in Nova Scotia. The presence of the RCMP, as either a provincial force or a municipal contract force, is therefore substantial in B.C., Saskatchewan, P.E.I., Nova Scotia, and Newfoundland. The use of the RCMP to provide either provincial or municipal policing services is greatest in British Columbia, where the national force accounted for over two-thirds of police strength (31 per cent of all officers are RCMP officers working under municipal contracts). Finally, looking at the factor of police strength from another perspective, 61 per cent of Canada's police officers work for one of five forces – the

RCMP, OPP, Quebec Police Force (QPF), Metropolitan Toronto Police, and Montreal Urban Community Police.

The scope of police coverage may be examined in terms of how much of a province's population is served by each type of force. Municipal officers, the largest component of police strength, provide service to the largest share of Canada's population (approximately 51 per cent). However, this pattern varies somewhat from province to province. Municipal forces police more than half of the population in Prince Edward Island, Quebec, Ontario, Manitoba, and Alberta. Nova Scotia (45 per cent) and New Brunswick (47 per cent) are close to this benchmark. Excluding the unique case of Newfoundland, the most substantial deviation is found in British Columbia, where only 29 per cent are served by municipal forces while 47 per cent are served by RCMP municipal contract forces. A final observation regarding police coverage is that provincial forces, both the RCMP under contract as well as the OPP and the QPF, police significant proportions of the population in all provinces, ranging from 18 per cent in Ontario to 51 per cent in Nova Scotia.

Another distinction within the structure of local policing is that between municipal forces (i.e., those controlled by either municipal council or local police board) and municipal contract forces. With the exception of Newfoundland, where they do not exist, municipal forces across Canada account for just over half of all forces at the local level and approximately 85 per cent of all local police officers. Once again, the 50 per cent benchmark regarding the number of forces is not attained in all provinces. It is a characteristic of the structure of local policing in the Maritimes and central Canada, but in the West, forces established under RCMP municipal contracts are clearly the most numerous (76 per cent of forces, on average). The 85 per cent mean regarding the distribution of municipal police officers across Canada is considerably more reflective of the situations in individual provinces. Only British Columbia, where 49 per cent of total local police strength is accounted for by the officers of municipal forces, is substantially below the national norm. RCMP municipal contract forces (with the exception of British Columbia) tend to be small in size. Indeed, 93 per cent of these 190 forces have fifty or fewer officers and 46 per cent have five or fewer. The comparable figures for municipal forces are 82 and 25 per cent, respectively.

Other observations that can be made about Canada's 601 police forces at the local level are that 32.1 per cent have five or fewer officers; only 7.6 per cent have 100 or more officers; 86.2 per cent have fifty or fewer officers; Ontario and Quebec, the most populous provinces, have the highest number of forces; and Ontario and British Columbia have the highest proportion of large forces (about 15 per cent of the forces in each province have 100 or more officers).

In summary, it is clear that the federal principle is reflected in the structure of policing services. The RCMP is not only a national police force but also one that carries out (on a contractual basis) provincial and municipal policing responsibilities in all provinces except Ontario and Quebec. Three provincial forces exist (a fourth, the New Brunswick Highway Patrol, was disbanded in early 1989) and they carry out both province-wide and municipal duties. Finally, almost 400 municipal forces round out this snapshot of policing structure.

Legal Basis

The legal basis of the police function in Canada encompasses three interrelated components: the constitutional division of responsibility between the federal government and the provinces; the statutory frameworks that have evolved within these broad grants of authority to each level of government; and the unique legal status of the individual police officer, a status that contains both common law and statutory elements.

In constitutional terms the justice sphere is a classic example of shared responsibility. Under s. 91(27) of the Constitution Act, 1867 the federal government holds sway in the area of criminal law, while under s. 92(14) the provinces are responsible for the administration of justice within their boundaries. This latter grant of authority has been transplanted into practice by the creation of provincial and municipal police forces as well as the establishment of a system of courts up to the superior court level.

Notwithstanding provincial responsibility for the administration of justice, the federal government has also created a national police force. The RCMP enforces federal laws, protects federal property, and provides specialized policing programs (i.e., training, forensics, etc.) to other law enforcement agencies in Canada. In addition, it carries out both provincial and local policing duties. This mandate is set out in the Royal Canadian Mounted Police Act, which also states that the Commissioner, the administrative head of the RCMP, reports directly to the federal Solicitor General.

Provincial statutes provide the legal framework for both provincial and municipal policing. Newfoundland, Prince Edward Island, and Manitoba are the only provinces that do not operate on the basis of a police act. In Newfoundland the Royal Newfoundland Constabulary (RNC) is set up by separate statute, and the Municipalities Act permits municipalities to discharge their policing responsibilities by arranging for the services of either the RNC or the RCMP (the provincial government picks up the cost of all policing services). Prince Edward Island, which passed a police act in 1977 but has yet to proclaim it, also deals with the police function under the provisions of its Municipalities Act. The island's municipalities have the option of setting up their own forces or entering into a contract with another municipality or the RCMP. The Municipal Act is the key statute in Manitoba, where municipalities with a population greater than 750 must have their own force, although those under 5,000 population have the option of an RCMP contract. In addition, the city charters of Winnipeg and Brandon provide the statutory foundation for the forces in those two cities.

Police acts in the other seven provinces typically stipulate that policing is a mandatory municipal responsibility; establish provincial police forces; authorize contractual arrangements with the RCMP for either provincial or municipal policing services; set up provincial police commissions; outline the composition and powers of local governing authorities; state in general terms the role of the police; and specify certain standards and regulatory authorities relative to the operation of municipal (and, in certain instances, provincial) forces. Policing is a mandatory responsibility of all municipalities in Nova Scotia and New Brunswick; of cities and towns in Ontario;[4] and of municipalities above a certain population threshold in Alberta (1,500), Quebec (5,000), British Columbia (5,000), and Saskatchewan (20,000). The creation of a municipal force under the control of a local governing authority is the primary means of implementing this responsibility. However, other options usually exist, especially for municipalities below the threshold. These options could include a contract with a provincial force, the RCMP (municipal contract), or an adjacent municipal force, as well as a joint municipal force.

The police acts of Ontario and Quebec establish their respective provincial forces, the OPP and the QPF. In the five other provinces with police acts the authority to deploy the RCMP as the provincial force is provided. While Newfoundland, Prince Edward Island, and Manitoba all have contracts with the RCMP for provincial policing, the situations in the latter two provinces require further elaboration. In Prince Edward Island the Police Act, 1940 contains the statutory authority underlying the use of the RCMP as a provincial force. In Manitoba the Provincial Police Act, passed in 1920, was later amended to accommodate a contractual arrangement with the national force.

Related to the statutory component of local policing is the contractual mechanism that permits the RCMP to function as a provincial and a municipal force. Provisions for contract policing were added to the RCMP Act in 1940. With respect to municipal contracts, two approaches are currently employed. The first is a "direct policing agreement" between the federal government and a municipality; the second is "umbrella policing," i.e., the municipality contracts for the services of the RCMP as a provincial force (Statistics Canada, 1986: 16).

The final component of the legal basis of policing focuses on the individual police officer. Three considerations are relevant: the officer's legal status, geographic jurisdiction, and discretion in enforcing the law.

The legal status or jurisdiction, duties, and powers of police officers in Canada comprise an extremely complex area (Stenning, 1981a). At the core of the individual officer's legal status is the notion of a "peace officer" as defined within the context of the common law office of constable. This status has been established in Canada by statute, and the description of status can vary from province to province and sometimes from force to force. In the Criminal Code, for example, a peace officer is deemed to include "a police officer, police constable, bailiff, constable, or other person employed for the preservation and maintenance of the public peace or for the service or execution of civil process . . . ." Furthermore, the Code contains various powers, duties, and protections of a peace officer (for example, the power of arrest) (Stenning, 1981a: 63). The duties of a peace officer are defined in Alberta's Police Act to include the preservation of peace, prevention of crime and offences against the laws, apprehension of criminals and offenders, and execution of warrants (R.S.A. 1980, ch. p-12, s. 31[1]).

The geographic scope of a police officer's jurisdiction varies both by force type and to a lesser extent by province. RCMP officers exercise Canada-wide jurisdiction, while that of provincial officers extends throughout their respective provinces. In the case of municipal officers two definitions of geographic jurisdiction are evident. On the one hand, some provinces grant municipal officers province-wide scope. This is the stipulation, for example, in Quebec, Ontario, Saskatchewan, and Alberta. On the other hand, provinces such as New Brunswick and British Columbia restrict their jurisdiction to the boundaries of the municipality, with two exceptions: that the responsible Minister can direct officers to work in another municipality (at the province's expense) and that an officer can exercise his or her powers and duties outside municipal boundaries in the course of "hot pursuit."

The discretion employed by the individual officer in enforcing the law is a very important consideration. This phenomenon, which has received substantial attention in the policing literature (Wilson, 1978; Grosman, 1975; Ericson, 1982), is highly dependent on organizational and personality factors. While in some instances what an officer should do is clear-cut (for example, murder), in others it is less so (for example, drunkenness in a public place). Also, much police time is spent on so-called order maintenance and service activities where discretion is at its highest. The ultimate significance of police discretion is that different styles of policing may emerge in different geographic jurisdictions.

Finally, brief comment should be made about the legal status of RCMP officers, i.e., as peace officers, provincial constables, or municipal constables (Stenning, 1981a: 76-77). This creates a situation of potential conflict between an officer's status under the RCMP Act and his or her status under provincial legislation. Indeed, two key areas of conflict are political accountability and disciplinary procedures (Stenning, 1981a: 69-77).

Provincial Control and Supervision

Historically, provincial responsibility for policing has been part of the portfolio of the Attorney General. While this remains the case in five provinces, Ontario, Quebec, Alberta, and most recently New Brunswick and British Columbia have created the portfolio of Solicitor General to handle the police function and related public safety services. (For example, in Ontario the Ministry of the Solicitor General is also responsible for the Office of the Fire Marshal, emergency measures, forensics, and coroners.) This development may be explained in terms of two related factors. First, it is part of the general process of structural differentiation occurring within the cabinet systems of Canada's largest provinces. Second, it reflects the notion that the Attorney General's responsibility for the courts ought to be divorced from any responsibility for the police. The second factor was certainly significant in Ontario's case.[5]

According to Stenning (1981a: 58-60) provincial control over and supervision of local policing has increased dramatically since 1946. That year marked the start of an era during which policing legislation in most provinces was substantially reformed and removed from the framework of general municipal legislation through the passage of police acts. While Ontario led the way in 1946, it was over twenty years later before another province, Quebec, followed suit. Thereafter, the pace of reform quickened with acts being passed by Nova Scotia (1969), Newfoundland (1970), Manitoba and Alberta (1971), and New Brunswick and Prince Edward Island (1977).

The expansion of provincial control over local policing manifests itself in six ways, many of them rooted in the comprehensive police acts passed during the post-war period. The first is the proliferation of provincial regulations aimed at ensuring uniform standards with respect to matters such as discipline, equipment, and recruitment. Second, provinces have both controlled the creation of new forces and pursued the rationalization of police structure through policies of amalgamation and regionalization (Loreto, 1984). Third, provincial representation on local governing authorities has been either initiated or increased. The modernization of prosecution systems and the development of grant programs represent two other ways that control has been augmented in certain provinces. Finally, the creation of provincial police commissions with supervisory, advisory, monitoring, regulatory, investigative, and quasi-judicial powers is perhaps the most significant manifestation of provincial control. The quasi-judicial powers of these commissions relate to both disciplinary matters and public complaints against the police.

With the exception of the Ontario Police Commission, which was created in a crisis atmosphere in 1961 (McDougall, 1971: 211-21), provincial police commissions elsewhere were set up as a direct consequence of the policing legislation enacted between 1968 and 1977. Quebec's commission was established in 1968; others followed in 1971 (Manitoba and Alberta), 1974 (British Columbia), 1975 (Saskatchewan), 1976 (Nova Scotia), and 1978 (New Brunswick). Alberta's commission was disbanded in 1973 and its role was assumed by the Director of Law Enforcement in the newly created Ministry of the Solicitor General. In Newfoundland the associate deputy attorney general is the senior administrative official in the policing sphere, while in Prince Edward Island it is the deputy minister in the Department of Justice and Attorney General.

A final aspect to be examined is the composition of provincial police commissions. In all provinces commission members are appointed by cabinet. Commission size ranges from eleven members in Quebec to three in Nova Scotia, New Brunswick, Saskatchewan, and British Columbia. Between these extremes is the six-person commission in Manitoba (Ontario's ranges from three to nine members). An indefinite term of office is the norm except in Quebec and New Brunswick, where the term cannot exceed ten years, and British Columbia, where the term is five years (no renewal). With the exception of Manitoba and New Brunswick commission membership is full-time. Finally, the chair of the Quebec Police Commission must be a Sessions or Provincial Court judge.[6]

Police Financing

The financing of police services at the local level can be analysed in terms of a continuum in which provincial subsidization of policing costs varies from nil to 100 per cent. At the one end of the continuum is the province of Quebec, which has no cost-sharing arrangements in place. Therefore, municipalities that have their own police force must pay the full cost (the smaller municipalities policed by the QPF are completely subsidized by the provincial government). At the other end is Newfoundland, where the costs of the services provided by both the RNC and RCMP are picked up by the province. In between these two extremes a number of financing schemes exist, most of them involving the use of provincial grants.

Three approaches are evident with respect to the use of provincial grants to offset partially local policing costs. These approaches vary significantly in the degree to which such transfers are earmarked for policing expenditures. The first approach, and the one in which provincial funds are least tied to the police function, is employed in Prince Edward Island and Nova Scotia. In these two provinces policing expenditures are financed out of the general transfers made to municipalities, although in Prince Edward Island municipal forces and RCMP municipal contract forces retain court-imposed fines. The second approach, which is found in all of the remaining provinces except

British Columbia and Saskatchewan, is to give unconditional grants to those municipalities that provide their own forces either directly or under contracts. Since a municipality must have a force to receive a grant, such a transfer is perhaps better described as "quasi-conditional." The formulae for these grants vary. For example, Ontario's grant is $50 per household, Alberta's is calculated on a per capita basis, and Manitoba pegs its level of funding to a municipality's equalized assessment (up to a limit of $100,000). The third approach is to earmark provincial funds for local policing. In Saskatchewan The Police Act provides for "grants for law enforcement" that may be given at the discretion of the Minister of Justice "to cities, towns, villages and rural municipalities to assist in providing police service therein." The Minister may also make regulations regarding the eligibility, terms, and conditions of these grants (The Police Act, R.S.S. 1978, ch. P-15, s. 55). Provincial discretion is also a feature of the highly specified grants available to municipalities in British Columbia. Here the provincial government may provide funds for phasing in a new police force over a three-year period or for restructuring existing forces (i.e., a five-year exemption from policing costs). Finally, it should also be noted that the schemes allowing forces in Prince Edward Island and New Brunswick to retain revenues from fines, as well as Alberta's special grants for police buildings, lockups, summer constables, training, and the phasing in of new forces, fall within the scope of the earmarking approach.

Given the substantial role of provincial forces at the local level in Canada, an analysis of the financial basis of this method of service delivery is in order. In the early 1980s the cost-sharing agreement regarding RCMP contract policing between the federal government and eight provinces and 190 municipalities was renegotiated. The new schedule increased on an incremental basis the portion of contract policing costs borne by provinces and municipalities. By 1991 provinces and municipalities under 15,000 population will pay 70 per cent of the cost (56 per cent in 1981); municipalities over 15,000 population, 90 per cent (81 per cent in 1981) (Statistics Canada, 1986: 16). Notwithstanding the increases contained in the revised schedule, a substantial subsidy, ranging from 10 to 30 per cent of force costs depending on the jurisdiction concerned, is inherent in the RCMP's police services activity. Moreover, as an examination of the RCMP's expenditure estimates demonstrates, the impact of contract policing on the resources of the federal force is equally substantial. During 1986-87 almost 50 per cent of total RCMP personnel and 30 per cent of net expenditures were allocated to this activity.

Contract policing by the OPP in Ontario is less extensive, although the demand for such services has increased in recent years. Also, while historically the principle of full cost recovery has not been a part of the provincial approach, it has been employed in recently signed contracts and will be phased in as older contracts expire (interview, OPP). While data on the cost of contract policing in Ontario are difficult to obtain, some indication is provided by Pukacz's estimate in 1978 that contract revenues covered only 62.5 per cent of the cost of the allocated staff (Pukacz, 1978: 174-75).

Operating expenditures on policing in Canada in 1988 were $4.39 billion ($169 per capita or $82, 344 per police officer). Per capita costs varied from $105 in Prince Edward Island to $174 in Quebec. Local policing (including contracts) accounted for about 53 per cent of total expenditures; provincial policing, 30 per cent; and federal (and other RCMP) policing, 17 per cent. Salaries, wages, and benefits consumed 81.5 per cent of expenditures. The average per capita cost of local policing was $122, with only Quebec, Ontario, and Saskatchewan above the average (Statistics Canada, 1989). These national data, however, mask significant variation within provinces. Such variation reflects not only the nexus between policing costs and the social, economic, and demographic characteristics of specific communities but also the differential impact of the financing approaches described above (Pukacz, 1978: schedules 8.2, 10).

Local Governing Authorities

Police governance at the local level has evolved historically from judicial control to municipal control, i.e., either by council or by a separate board of police commissioners. The first police boards were established in Upper Canada in 1858 and since then they have spread to other provinces and exhibited a variety of structural formats (Stenning, 1988: 4-6; Stenning 1981b; Hann et al., 1985). The current approach to local police governance ranges from the absence of municipal control in Newfoundland to complete council control in Prince Edward Island, Quebec, and Manitoba. The use of boards in all other provinces represents a middle ground between these two extremes.

With the exception of Manitoba, where the city charters of Winnipeg and Brandon provide the statutory basis for police boards, local police boards are established under provincial police acts. They are mandatory for all municipalities in Nova Scotia and British Columbia, optional in New Brunswick, and mandatory for municipalities over a certain population threshold in Ontario (15,000), Saskatchewan (5,000), and Alberta (1,500). While boards are normally employed where a municipality has its own force, boards may function in an advisory capacity to the commander of a contract force. This requirement is optional in Alberta and mandatory in Saskatchewan. In British Columbia local police committees consisting of up to three provincial appointees may be set up as liaison mechanisms in those areas of the province where the RCMP serves as a provincial force. Structural linkages between

OPP commanders and local community representatives in Ontario have been described as "ad hoc" (interview, OPP). Finally, where provincial legislation mandates that municipalities of a certain size have police boards, it is usually the case that municipalities under the population threshold may set up boards subject to provincial approval (for example, in Ontario and Saskatchewan).

The composition of local boards varies from those with a majority of provincial appointees (Ontario and British Columbia) to those with a majority of municipal appointees (Nova Scotia, New Brunswick, Saskatchewan, Alberta, and Manitoba). Municipal appointees include both councillors and citizens (only councillors are appointed to the boards in Winnipeg and Brandon), and the police acts of New Brunswick, Saskatchewan, and Alberta stipulate the exact number of council members that can be appointed to a board. The size of boards is also variable. In Ontario the core size is three members, although regional boards have five members and Metropolitan Toronto's board has recently been expanded to seven. Boards in British Columbia, Manitoba, and New Brunswick have five members (the police chief is a non-voting member of New Brunswick boards), while a size range is specified in Nova Scotia (3-7), Saskatchewan (3-5), and Alberta (3-12).

Stenning (1988: 9-10) observes that the role of police boards is highly variable across Canada. In New Brunswick the board provides "direction and policy" to the force but budgetary control rests with the municipality. Ontario's boards are responsible for policing and the maintenance of law and order in their municipalities, with budgetary disputes being settled by the Ontario Police Commission. In terms of autonomy and role British Columbia's boards reflect the Ontario model; those in the remaining provinces are closer to the New Brunswick model.[7]

Police Organization

An organization is an instrument for the achievement of a specific goal or set of goals.[8] Before examining the problematic debate over the goals of policing, it is first necessary to analyse the nature of police organization, of which there are two basic levels: micro-organizational, i.e., the internal units that make up a typical police department, and macro-organizational, i.e., regional or metropolitan policing.

From a micro-organizational perspective, what has been called the traditional model of police organization (Heywood, 1980) exhibits four general features. The first is an almost literal application of Weber's ideal type of bureaucracy to the specific functions and tasks of policing. A related feature is an emphasis on specialization, especially in the largest departments. Third, internal organizational processes (and ultimately external relations) are conditioned by the "closed" nature of police bureaucracy or the phenomenon of "police culture" (Drummond, 1976). Cawley (1978: 33) notes the pervasiveness of the closed organization:

> Most police departments are organized in what might be termed a 'bottom-up' hierarchy that requires all new entrants to start at (or near) the lowest rank and move in a step-by-step fashion up the organizational ladder. 'Promotion from within' is the cornerstone of most police personnel policies. . . . Bottom-up departments tend to become closed circles in which practices pass down from one closely knit group to another. . . . [T]hey also discourage openness to outside ideas.

A final feature is a reliance on traditional operational practices, particularly with regard to patrol and criminal investigation activities.

The formality of police bureaucracy can be explained by the link between policing and the law (Heywood, 1980: 152). Its hierarchical, paramilitary character, however, reflects historical factors. In this regard modern policing's roots in Peel's twelve principles of reform as well as the use of the military as a police force prior to this century are salient (McCreedy, 1978: 61). The increasing specialization of police activities must also be viewed in historical terms. During the nineteenth century policing responsibility was gradually transferred from amateur local constables to the trained members of larger forces. This specialization at the societal level provided the impetus for greater organizational differentiation.

Early Canadian police forces, and Peel's London force, were organized to perform a single function – patrol (Wilson and McLaren, 1977: 92). The use of detectives for criminal investigation occurred later. The appearance of other specialized units represented a response to factors impinging on most modern organizations (i.e., increased scale and workload, the need for higher productivity, etc.) as well as those unique to policing. The latter included the impact of technological change (traffic patrol, vehicular patrol), the pervasiveness of particular types of crime (hence, fraud, vice, drug squads), and the need to ensure the smooth operation of the primary patrol function, which resulted in the separation of criminal investigation duties (Wilson and McLaren, 1977: 77-79, 92-97).

Today the internal organization of a large police department typically encompasses a number of identifiable line and staff functions. Line functions include patrol (general and traffic), criminal investigation, special or tactical operations, youth, and vice control. In addition, functions such as crime prevention and community relations have a line orientation (a fact that is not always reflected in the organization of a specific force). Staff functions consist of both those common to most large organizations (personnel, budget, records, communications, and property) and those specific to policing (criminal detention,

Figure 1

HAMILTON-WENTWORTH REGIONAL POLICE FORCE
Organization Chart

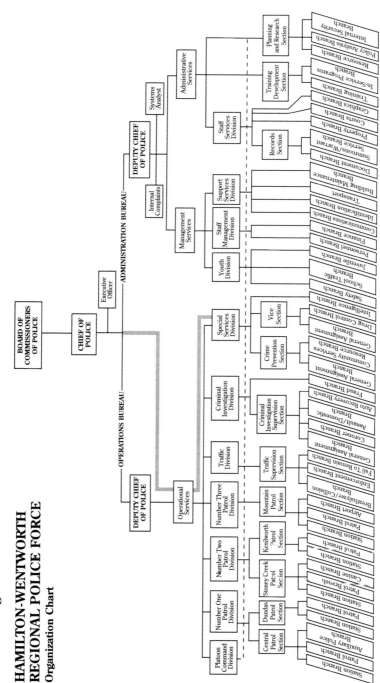

criminal intelligence, identification, and laboratory services). Planning and research, staff inspection (audit), and internal investigation are other important staff functions.

Figure 1, which depicts the organization of the Hamilton-Wentworth Regional Police Force in 1977, illustrates many of these functions. In terms of hierarchy the force is subject to the political direction of a board of police commissioners and to the administrative supervision of a chief of police. Rank structure below the chief is: deputy chief, staff superintendent, superintendent, staff inspector, inspector, staff sergeant (1st and 2nd class), and constable (1st through 4th class). Major internal subdivisions (in descending order of scale) are bureaus, services, divisions, sections, and branches. Line activities primarily come under the Operations Bureau headed by a deputy chief, and are reflected in the divisional structure of the department, i.e., patrol, traffic, criminal investigation, and special services. Staff activities are largely under the Administration Bureau, also headed by a deputy chief. Personnel, finance, records, etc. are lodged at the section and branch levels of the bureau. Planning and Research and the systems analyst report to the deputy chief. The Youth Division, a line unit, is also within the Administration Bureau.

At the macro-organizational level a relatively recent development is the concept of regional or metropolitan policing. This expands both the geographic scope and resource base of the police function through the consolidation of policing services either in whole or in part. The legal basis of regionalization is twofold. First, it is contained in the provision of several police acts regarding the use of intermunicipal service agreements and the creation of joint police boards (for example, New Brunswick, Quebec, Ontario, and British Columbia). In addition, the acts in Ontario and British Columbia permit the amalgamation of local police forces. Regional schemes undertaken in these ways normally require the approval of the provincial level. Second, the legal basis of regionalization can be found in the statutory frameworks associated with the restructuring of local government in various provinces.

Regional police forces currently exist in four provinces. With the exception of New Brunswick, where only two small regional forces are in operation, the creation of such forces has been a consequence of provincial policies primarily aimed at a more comprehensive re-structuring of local government boundaries, institutions, and decision-making processes. In Manitoba the establishment of Winnipeg "Unicity" led subsequently to the amalgamation of twelve local police forces in 1974. In Quebec the formation of the Montreal Urban Community in 1969 was followed a year later by the amalgamation of twenty-five local forces. However, notwithstanding the significance of these two forces in their respective provinces, the jurisdiction where regionalization has had the greatest impact is Ontario. The unification of Metropolitan Toronto's thirteen area municipal forces in 1957 provided the model for the nine regional forces that were set up in conjunction with Ontario's regional government program between 1971 and 1974. These regional forces are now responsible for policing approximately 56 per cent of the province's population, most of it in the highly urbanized Golden Horseshoe area from Oshawa to Niagara Falls.

Although the emergence of regional policing in certain provinces is clearly related to indigenous factors, the influence of developments in England and the United States is also important. The extensive consolidation of municipal police forces in England (and Wales) carried out between 1966 and 1969, in response to the findings and recommendations of the 1962 Royal Commission on the Police, was a touchstone for the amalgamation policy advocated by the Ontario Police Commission during the same period. Canadian policy-makers also drew inspiration from the justifications for consolidation advanced by national commissions studying the administration of the criminal justice system in the United States during the late 1960s and early 1970s. While the recommendations of these inquiries often were not implemented to any great extent, their generalized influence on Canadian thinking is very evident (Choquette, 1971).

Numerous arguments are made both in favour of and against the establishment of regional police forces. The case for regionalization, which has been largely articulated by police groups and sympathetic academic experts, is highly deductive in character and rests on a number of premises rooted in a scientific management perspective on organization. These premises include: a positive correlation between organizational scale and productivity; the primacy of crime fighting in police work (and the corollary assumption that crime is relatively uniform across local jurisdictions of varying size and socio-economic complexity); a positive correlation between the level of policing resources and the degree of crime control; a universal need for "full service" policing, i.e., the use of specialized services (for example, tactical units) and technology (for example, "911" emergency systems); and an acceptance of the traditional model of police organization with its attendant operational practices and underlying notion of professionalism.

The case against regionalization is an emerging one. Its proponents are essentially academics, particularly American public choice theorists such as Elinor Ostrom. This critique is inductive and empirical in character and reflects the theoretical insights of the human relations and open systems perspectives on organization. Moreover, its fundamental assumptions are, for the most part, direct refutations of those held by the supporters of regionalization: there is no necessary correlation between organizational scale and efficiency; crime fighting is not the primary function of policing (there are also service and order maintenance functions) and its relative importance can vary across jurisdictions; the roots of crime are complex and largely environmental, and therefore no necessary correlation exists between levels of policing resources and crime; and the absence of functional specialization and technology is not necessarily correlated with poor operational performance. Finally, critics of the regional concept embrace the structural features and notion of professionalism associated with the community-based policing approach described later.

Little systematic research exists on the regionalization concept in Canada (Loreto, 1984). Two conclusions about the Ontario situation, however, are clear. First, in conceptual and evidentiary terms, the policy on regional policing was based on a "conventional wisdom" or "orthodox" perspective on police agency consolidation rather than an analytical, empirical one (Ostrom, 1975; Dearlove, 1979; Sharpe, 1981). Second, in political terms, regional forces were created as a direct consequence of the convergence of functional (policing) and municipal interests within the executive branch of the Ontario government. Since 1974 there has been some evidence that the implementation of the regional concept has been problematic. Among the problems experienced by certain forces and documented in press reports and official studies are: escalating costs; deteriorating police-community relations; low levels of organizational integration; redundancies and deficiencies in organizational structure; poor deployment of police personnel due to inefficient management practices, statutory restrictions, and a traditional resistance to civilianization; poor performance of line and specialist units; ineffective leadership at the executive level; and the phenomenon of "levelling up" (i.e., an unwarranted expansion of police resources) in relation to the phased withdrawal of the OPP from the rural portions of the regions. Many of these problems also reflect the fact that Ontario's regional forces initially chose to perpetuate the traditional model of policing during a period of rapid societal change. The recent emergence of community-based policing among regional forces as well as changes in force leadership have helped to alleviate a number of these problems (Loree, 1988; Loreto, 1989; Tomovich and Loree, 1989).

Contemporary Issues in Canadian Policing

Crime Control

Fighting crime has always been one of the major missions of modern police forces. Yet, in recent years in Canada and elsewhere, the ability of the police to deter and to solve crime has come under critical scrutiny, especially by academics. The salience of crime fighting to police work and the impact of policing on the incidence of crime are related issues examined below. However, it is first necessary to sketch two important contextual elements, namely, the nature of crime data and crime trends in Canada during the past two decades.

Since 1962 data on crime in Canada have been collected by individual police forces and submitted to Statistics Canada under the Uniform Crime Reporting (UCR) system. In addition, data are provided on how many crimes have been solved or "cleared otherwise," the latter category referring to a situation where the offender's identity is known but a charge cannot be laid due to reasons such as diplomatic immunity, the death of the alleged offender, or the refusal of a victim to sign a complaint.[9] The use of data on crime and clearance rates is an exercise that is circumscribed by a number of important limitations. The UCR system only yields data on crimes reported to the police. Reported crime, however, is only a subset of all crime, as the fascinating results of the Canadian Urban Victimization Survey conducted by the federal Ministry of the Solicitor General and Statistics Canada in 1981 have shown (Solicitor General Canada, 1983-1988). This survey involved interviews with 61,000 Canadians over the age of sixteen in seven urban centres and represented the first systematic challenge to the utility of official crime statistics. Reported rates of crime varied substantially from actual crime for most offences: sexual assault (38.5 per cent reported), robbery (45 per cent), assault (34.5 per cent), personal theft (29 per cent), attempted theft (20 per cent), household theft (45 per cent; attempted, 35 per cent), motor vehicle theft (89 per cent; attempted, 41 per cent), break-ins (64 per cent), and vandalism (35 per cent). With the exception of victims of sexual assault or domestic violence, where fear was the principal reason for not reporting, others simply felt that either there was little the police could do or involving them was not worth the trouble.

There are other pitfalls associated with official crime data, many of which are explicitly recognized by Statistics Canada. The first is the so-called "inflation factor." Since the police are responsible for collecting data that can be used to evaluate their performance, inflation of such data, either to make a force's performance look good or to justify an increase in resources, is a possibility. Second, inter-municipal comparisons are difficult given the different environments (i.e., demographic, economic, and social), organization (for example, more police may simply lead to more reported crime), criminal justice procedures and practices, and community priorities (for example, attitudes toward law enforcement problems) that characterize local policing. Moreover, the variability of these differences over time and the non-criminal roles of the police make crime data somewhat imperfect indicators of both police workload and performance. A number of these limitations also apply to clearance rates, particularly differences in reporting practices and community priorities, and the inflation factor.

Keeping these limitations in mind, a number of observations can be made about crime in Canada. The first relates to the distribution of Criminal Code and non-Criminal Code offences between 1981 and 1985. The former are the larger category, and their share increased from approximately 75 per cent to 80 per cent during the five-year period. While violent crimes exhibited the highest rate of increase (22 per cent) they still account for a relatively small proportion of all crime in Canada (property crimes account for over one-half). Also, according to Johnson (1988: 27), the majority of violent crimes are non-aggravated assaults, and homicides and attempted murders make up less than 1 per cent of the total. Offences against provincial statutes represent the largest component of the non-Criminal Code category, but offences against municipal bylaws increased at the greatest rate (25 per cent) during the period.

Another perspective emerges from the correlation of Criminal Code offences with population between 1976 and 1985. While for most provinces increases over the ten-year period vary by crime category, three provinces – Manitoba, Saskatchewan, and Prince Edward Island – show consistently high increases. The picture in absolute terms is more stable. Provincial rankings do change by crime category but the five highest-ranked provinces are all west of the Quebec border, i.e., Ontario and the four western provinces. In relation to violent crime, Johnson (1988: 28-29) provides a municipal perspective. With the exception of Calgary, western cities have the highest violent crime rates. Victoria, Vancouver, and Edmonton report the highest rates, and six of the top ten cities are in the West. Canada's two largest cities, Montreal and Toronto, rank fourth and seventh, respectively. Finally, there is empirical evidence that population size and the level of violent crime are directly related.

Data on clearance rates show that they are higher for violent than for property crimes, and especially high for the most serious violent crimes, such as attempted murder. This observation is a familiar one and reflects several factors: victims of violent crimes usually know their killers or assailants – in 1983, for example, 81 per cent of homicide victims were slain by someone they knew (*Globe and Mail*, December 12, 1985: 1); violent crimes are more likely to occur in public places (Johnson, 1988: 27); and witnesses are more likely to be involved. The high percentage of assaults "cleared otherwise" indicates, however, the reluctance of some victims to press charges (or of witnesses to come forth).

Given this profile of crime in Canada, is it a serious social problem? Clearly, Canadian cities are safer than their American counterparts (Johnson, 1988: 27; *Toronto Star*, December 31, 1985: A4). Yet, the 1981 victimization survey also estimated that the victims of crime lost more than $431 million through damages, stolen property, and other expenses. Recently the federal government has given this aspect of the problem some priority by passing legislation designed to help victims of crime.[10] The victimization survey also probed citizens' perceptions of crime in the seven urban centres. On balance Canadians feel fairly secure, particularly in their neighbourhoods. Women and the elderly, however, express more fear about violent crime than males (who are more likely to be victims). In the case of Metropolitan Toronto, Canada's largest urban centre, fear of crime in most areas was among the lowest recorded in the survey. These perceptions of Metropolitan Toronto residents were essentially reconfirmed in a 1987 survey carried out by Goldfarb Consultants (*Toronto Star*, December 29, 1987: A15). The "gender gap" regarding fear of crime was also still evident.

Whatever one's perception of the degree to which crime is a social problem, it remains a chief concern and has primarily been entrusted to Canada's 53,500 police officers. Therefore, the more central questions are how important crime fighting is as a policing activity and what impact the police have on the suppression of crime. The importance of crime fighting to a definition of the police role has been acknowledged by many commentators (Wilson and McLaren, 1977; Wilson, 1978). Yet, the community service and order maintenance roles of the police are also recognized as legitimate, and several empirical studies of police work show that criminal matters consume only 10-20 per cent of an officer's time (Cawley, 1978; Kelling and Fogel, 1978; Goldstein, 1968; Clarke and Heal, 1980; Reiss, 1971; Ericson, 1982; Wilson, 1978).

This debate over what constitutes the essence of policing must ultimately be viewed in relation to three currents of analysis in the academic literature. First, there is a clear association between the traditional model of policing and the primacy of crime fighting (Heywood, 1980). Second, this traditional notion has persisted despite the existence of research that traces the complex etiology of crime (Ross, 1977; Skogan, 1977; Booth *et al.*, 1976; Stahura, Huff, and Smith, 1980) and demonstrates the problematic impact of additional policing resources on crime suppression (Heaphy, 1978; Clarke and Heal, 1980; Stahura and Huff, 1979; Decker, 1979). Third, now classic studies have questioned the efficacy of the cornerstones of police operations, preventive vehicular patrol and rapid response to calls (Kelling *et al.*, 1974; Ericson, 1982; Kelling and Fogel, 1978; Kelling 1980; Farmer, 1980), and criminal investigation (Farmer, 1980; Ericson, 1981).

Both this substantial criticism of reactive police operations and fiscal pressures have shifted emphasis to the concept of crime prevention, and a plethora of programs have appeared during the 1970s and 1980s. Among these are Neighbourhood Watch, Crime Stoppers, Mobile Watch, and COPS (Community Organizational Prevention System). These programs not only use advanced communications and information technology but also solicit direct citizen involvement in police work. Neighbourhood Watch, perhaps the best-known crime prevention concept, is a voluntary surveillance program in which residents alert police about the presence of unfamiliar or suspicious persons in their area. Mobile Watch is an offshoot of this program in that it encourages "truckers, private security managers and cellular phone owners to call police if they see anything criminal happening as they drive around" (*Globe and Mail*, October 22, 1987: A19). Crime Stoppers, which was launched in Canada by the Calgary police force in 1982 (it was modelled on a New Mexico program started in 1976), pays money to anonymous informants for tips that help solve crimes. At present there are twenty-nine of these programs located in the provinces of British Columbia, Alberta, Saskatchewan, Manitoba, Ontario, and New Brunswick, and some are set up on a regional basis (for example, Metropolitan Toronto, Durham, York, and Peel in Ontario). These provinces are the ones with the highest crime rates, and the results have been described as "spectacular" – 7,500 arrests, $12 million in recovered property, and $40 million in illicit drugs compared to payouts totalling $750,000 (*Globe and Mail*, June 22, 1987: A11). The fourth crime prevention program, COPS, is a computerized telephone system that can establish contact with the residents of an area at the rate of 100 calls per hour. It is being used by forces in Edmonton, Halifax, Metropolitan Toronto, and the regional municipalities of Sudbury, Halton, and Hamilton-Wentworth in Ontario. Police contend that it is valuable in "finding missing children, cutting down on burglaries and nabbing criminal suspects" (*Globe and Mail*, November 24, 1986: 8; *Toronto Star*, June 5, 1988: A14).

Evaluations of these crime prevention programs by outside observers are few in number. One such study headed by Austin Turk, a sociology professor at the University of Toronto, concluded that the Neighbourhood Watch program in Metropolitan Toronto was "more of a social club in which [those involved] can meet neighbors than an effective anti-burglary weapon" (*Globe and Mail*, May 14, 1987: A10). While any assessment at this point is tentative, Cawley's (1978: 37) caution about the nature of American crime prevention programs (a source of inspiration for Canadian forces) must be kept in mind:

> [T]here has been an abundance of 'crime prevention' programs in the past several years which have had varied successes. . . . [T]he mixed success of these programs may be traceable to a situation where the programs were initiated as a result of a national 'bandwagon' movement rather than a careful crime analysis which indicated which programs were most needed in the particular jurisdiction.

The Police and the Community

Incremental change is the hallmark of the traditional model of police organization. The dominant approach has been to add new specialist units and technical systems to a relatively static structural framework. The expected results are an increase in police capacity to fight crime and improved productivity (defined in terms of greater mobility, better telecommunications, and increased functional specialization). Yet, despite the higher volume of calls the individual officer can now handle, there has been a break in the flow of communication between the police and the public, thereby rendering crime prevention and solution more problematic.

Deteriorating police-community relations is one potential consequence of the centralization of authority, impersonality, and para-military operations characteristic of traditional police forces. This problem is especially pertinent in urban areas, given the expansion of the scale of local policing and the increasing heterogeneity of the populace. Within the parameters of the traditional model, three methods of improving police-community relations are practised (Wasson, 1977: 15-20). The first is "image-building" or the one-way flow of communication from the police to the public through mechanisms such as press releases and providing speakers for local groups. This method is often perceived as a form of "public relations" and therefore cosmetic in nature (Cawley, 1978: 37). The second method involves a two-way communication process facilitated by a community relations/services officer. This, too, has its problems in that such officers are members of yet another specialized "appendage" grafted to a fundamentally unchanged organization (Heaphy, 1978: 282-83), and strained relations and poor lines of communication may develop between them and colleagues in other line units (Dunlop and Greenaway, 1972). Third, crime prevention programs are used, but their effectiveness has not received extensive evaluation in Canada.

In recent years new approaches and mechanisms, which reflect a move away from the traditional model, have emerged. One of the most important is community-based policing. Others are found in the recommendations of various government inquiries that have examined the controversial problem of strained relations between the police and certain ethnic and racial minorities. Finally, the accountability of the police to civilian authority has evolved significantly, particularly in relation to citizen complaints regarding police misconduct.

Community-Based Policing. This concept lies at the core of the debate over contemporary Canadian policing philosophy and practice.[11] Although its impetus can be linked to the numerous team or zone policing projects initiated by both Canadian and American police forces during the past twenty years (Wasson, 1977; Schwartz and Clarren, 1977; Epstein, 1978), its historical roots encompass the communal orientation of the early approaches to the police function in the British and colonial contexts (Stenning, 1981a: chs. 1, 2; Stead, 1977). Whatever its antecedents, community-based policing is increasingly viewed by both the police and their "relevant constituencies" (Whitaker *et al.*,

1980: 15) as the approach of the future, a development that would bring the police back to Sir Robert Peel's famous dictum: "the police are the public . . . and the public are the police" (Ontario, Task Force on Policing, 1974).

While acknowledging that no clear definition of the concept exists, Murphy and Muir observe that "Community-based policing is an 'umbrella term' used to describe any approach to policing that encourages involvement with the community." From their review of the literature, five "key philosophical principles," which "establish the research elements of community-based policing and serve as a basis for further discussion of management and strategic implementation issues," are evident. They are: (1) the community plays an important role in police decision-making; (2) the objectives of policing are broad and community-defined; (3) the diverse functions that the police perform are legitimate elements of the police role; (4) community-based policing is a shared responsibility between the police and the community; and (5) it advocates "proactive" involvement with the community (Murphy and Muir, 1985: 80-95).

Goldstein also refers to community-based policing as an umbrella term embracing a number of "common elements," including: the involvement of the community in getting the job done; the permanent assignment of officers to a neighbourhood in order to cultivate better relationships; the setting of police priorities based on the specific needs and desires of the community; and the meeting of these needs by the allocation of police resources and personnel otherwise assigned to responding to calls for service. These elements are further linked to certain "common characteristics": the police have a presence in the community and are accessible, visible, and caring; crime prevention is emphasized; officers are expected to respond to the full range of community problems; officers are expected to exercise greater autonomy; the community has input into the decisions on the form of police services, especially the priority given to certain problems; and projects are designed to enable the police to develop greater familiarity with all members of the community (Goldstein, 1987: 7-10).

From a macro-institutional perspective the trend toward community-based policing is not an isolated phenomenon. Its impetus comes from developments that are very evident in other sectors of Canadian society – demands for increased accountability and responsiveness, improved service delivery within an environment of stable or declining financial resources, higher levels of personal job satisfaction, and reduced levels of citizen alienation from governing institutions. Moreover, community-based policing brings policing back to its roots as a public service that is responsive, not "professional" (i.e., detachment from the community).

Notwithstanding its inherent appeal, comprehensive and effective implementation of community-based policing faces a number of obstacles. The first is the resistance to change that is characteristic of the closed world of the traditional police organization (Tomovich and Loree, 1989: 50). The traditional model champions the primacy of centralization, specialization, rapid response to calls for service, and detachment from the community, whereas the community-based model emphasizes decentralization, generalist police roles, a proactive and multi-agency approach to service delivery, and community involvement. Second, the meaning of the term "community" is problematic and the implications of its definition have not received sufficient attention in the Canadian literature (Loreto, 1988). Finally, traditional linkage mechanisms between the police and the community, such as committees, may produce a "mobilization of bias" in favour of the professionals who have the expertise. There is some evidence of this problem in the operation of the community consultative committees set up in England and Wales during the 1980s (Willmott, 1986: 29-44).

Police-Minority Group Relations. Perhaps the most contentious issue currently facing the police is relations with ethnic and racial minorities. During the late 1980s several high-profile incidents in Toronto, Mississauga, Montreal, and Winnipeg, which involved the use of deadly force by police officers, not only exacerbated racial tensions but also spawned a number of major public inquiries into the nature of policing and other components of the criminal justice system. In Nova Scotia (the Donald Marshall case), Alberta, and Manitoba the impact of the administration of justice on Canada's native people came under critical examination. In Ontario the Race Relations and Policing Task Force was set up in the aftermath of police shootings of blacks in Metropolitan Toronto and Peel Region. Quebec instructed its Human Rights Commission to inquire into relations between the police and minority groups after a black teenager in Montreal was shot and killed while in police custody.

The context for the concern about police-minority relations has two elements. The first is the changing pattern of immigration in Canada (Linden, 1989; Ontario, Race Relations and Policing Task Force, 1989: 55-92). Between 1981 and 1986 only 36 per cent of immigrants came from Europe and the United States. As a result, Canada's "visible minorities"[12] increased from 4.7 to 6 per cent of the population (and are projected to reach 10 per cent by the end of the 1990s). In Ontario, the historic destination of the majority of immigrants, the 1986 population share was about 9 per cent (in the greater Toronto area, which attracts 40 per cent of these immigrants, the share was estimated to be 20 per cent). The second contextual element is Canada's native people, who constitute 2 per cent of the population (with a heavier concentration in the western provinces) but who are also overrepresented in the criminal justice system.

The impact of Canada's changing population on the composition of Canadian police forces has been minimal. Jain (1988), in a survey of officers on fourteen large forces at all government levels across Canada, found that visible minority representation ranged from 0.3 per cent in both Montreal and Ottawa to 3.4 per cent in Metropolitan Toronto (visible minority population shares in the three urban areas were 4.7, 4.6, and 12.1 per cent, respectively). Moreover, most of the visible minority officers were male and held the rank of constable. The Ontario task force, based on a survey of ninety-nine municipal forces and the OPP (98 per cent of police officers in the province), observed that only twenty-two forces had visible minority representation (2 per cent of officers). While the highest level of representation was found in Metropolitan Toronto (3.9 per cent) and Peel Region (4.1 per cent), it was well below the available general labour pool. The OPP's share was a meagre 0.4 per cent. Both studies singled out biased recruitment procedures as a significant cause of the problem.

The verdict of the Marshall inquiry in Nova Scotia that racism is widespread (*Globe and Mail*, January 29, 1990: A1-A2) adds to the urgency of eliminating this problem. A number of mechanisms are available. One is to create race and ethnic relations units within forces (Fleras *et al.*, 1989). These units already exist, but as the Ontario task force (1989: 165) pointed out their effectiveness may be limited:

> Six [units] were reported in the Task Force survey, some with only a single officer. Critics have argued that the units are token gestures. They are seen as weak and isolated on the periphery of police operations, powerless to serve as a genuine channel of communication and unable to alter force policies or practices.

Another mechanism is employment equity policies. The RCMP, with only 1 per cent visible minority representation, has established a national recruiting team of six officers to seek out qualified candidates from targeted groups. Both the Marshall inquiry and the Ontario task force recommended the implementation of such policies, and provision for this has been made in Ontario's new Police Services Act. Third, race relations training for police officers was strongly recommended by the Ontario task force. A fourth mechanism, currently employed by twenty-two forces in Ontario, is community consultation groups (Ontario, Race Relations and Policing Task Force, 1989: 170-73). With respect to indigenous peoples, the use of special native constables is an approach both the RCMP and the OPP have employed (the new Ontario Act authorizes the OPP commissioner, with the approval of the provincial police commission and the band council, to appoint First Nations Constables). Finally, the use of civilian-based public complaints systems is often regarded as a means of removing the distrust generated by the notion of one police force investigating another.

Civilian Oversight of the Police. The issue of civilian oversight can be viewed from two perspectives. The first is the role and structure of the local governing authority, a subject discussed earlier in the chapter. The second is the involvement of civilians in the processes for investigating and adjudicating complaints against the police.[13]

Three models of handling public complaints are apparent in Canada. These models vary in terms of both procedural complexity and degree of independence from police bodies at various government levels. The least complex and independent model is that employed in Newfoundland and Prince Edward Island, provinces without provincial police commissions. In Newfoundland, for example, complaints received by the office of the associate deputy attorney general are referred to the affected force for investigation by senior officers; further review may later be undertaken by the provincial department.

Both complexity and independence are greater in the model used in New Brunswick, Quebec, Ontario, Saskatchewan, and British Columbia. Procedurally there are two components: initial investigation by the force involved and subsequent appeals to the local board or council and the provincial commission. In Ontario and Quebec the largest forces are treated differently. Metropolitan Toronto has an Office of the Public Complaints Commissioner, an independent civilian agency with both investigatory and adjudicative authority. In Montreal a seven-person board (four police officers and three civilians) investigates complaints. The two provincial police commissions handle final appeals against other municipal forces and the provincial forces.[14]

The third model operates in Nova Scotia, Manitoba, and Alberta and is in some ways a variant of the second. The essential notion is to direct final appeals to a separate provincial body – the Police Review Board in Nova Scotia, Law Enforcement Review Board in Manitoba, and Law Enforcement Appeal Board in Alberta. Lay membership is the norm on these boards, although in Manitoba's case provision is made for the appointment of at least two former or current peace officers (in 1987 four of the board's twelve members were retired peace officers). The decisions of Manitoba's board can be appealed to the Manitoba Police Commission; Nova Scotia's board receives administrative support from the province's police commission.

Provincial systems for handling public complaints do not apply to the RCMP when it functions as either a provincial or municipal force. In 1986 an amendment to the force's Act established the RCMP Public Complaints Commission. It consists of fifteen civilians: a full-time chair and vice chair, part-time members from the eight provinces and two territories, and three part-time members at large. Final disposition of complaints heard by the commission rests with both the commissioner of the RCMP and the federal Solicitor General (*Liaison*, October, 1988: 8).

Concerns about the effectiveness of the complaints process are addressed differently by each model. These concerns include: independence from the institutions involved in policing; the membership mix of boards (i.e., civilians and police); the role of police personnel in the investigations phase of the process; the existence of multiple routes of appeal; the availability of information as well as the public nature of the process; and the adequacy of sanctions against police officers involved in wrongdoing. The new systems in Quebec and Ontario come closest to alleviating all of these concerns.

Conclusions

From its roots as a communal responsibility performed by ordinary citizens or untrained amateurs, local policing in Canada has evolved into a public function characterized by the complex interaction of intergovernmental, organizational, financial, and policy considerations. During the past forty years greater provincial control through statutory, regulatory, and funding mechanisms has clearly increased the levels of professionalization and technical efficiency. However, the fundamental challenge of the 1990s will be to balance the achievements of the past with the imperative of the future – to forge a democratic relationship with a Canadian community that is being shaped by the forces of economic, social, political, and demographic change.

NOTES

The author would like to thank officials in nine provinces who responded generously to requests for information on the topics examined in this chapter.

1. The discussion of the history, current structure, and legal basis of policing is highly dependent on Stenning (1981a). In addition, many of the observations made about the institutional features of local policing have been derived from an analysis of primary information sources, i.e., statutes, annual reports, and various publications by Statistics Canada.
2. These observations on the current structure are derived from data in Statistics Canada (1986). While this document is not scheduled for a comprehensive revision until 1991, interim updates of selected data are available in the *Juristat Service Bulletin*, another publication of the centre.
3. It is important to clarify the meaning of a police-to-population ratio. This statistic is often used by politicians, police officials, and certain interest groups as a proxy measure of police performance (i.e., economy, efficiency, and effectiveness). Yet, it is a measure that on its own is at best ambiguous and at worst meaningless. For example, depending on one's perception of what constitutes an appropriate level of policing resources in a specific jurisdiction, a low ratio may be viewed as an indicator either of effectiveness (i.e., higher density of coverage) or of inefficiency (i.e., overstaffing). Conversely, a high ratio may be construed as either efficiency (i.e., low staff levels) or ineffectiveness (i.e., insufficient coverage). The real significance of a police-to-population ratio can only be gauged in relation to other data, such as the nature of criminal activity in a particular jurisdiction, the operational strategies and tactics of a force, the level of police training, etc.
4. The situation in Ontario will change significantly when the *Police Services*

Act, which received first reading in December, 1989, is passed. This Act will replace the Police Act passed in 1946. Among the key features of the new Act are: (1) the requirement that all municipalities are responsible for "adequate and effective police services" (cabinet may exempt towns under 5,000 population); (2) mandatory police services boards for all municipalities, with a majority of provincial appointees, one of whom is designated as chair (board size may range from three to seven depending on the population size of the municipality); (3) the continuation of the Ontario Police Commission under the name of the Ontario Civilian Commission on Police Services; (4) mandatory employment equity programs for the OPP and municipal forces; (5) a revised public complaints procedure and the creation of a special investigations unit (for police incidents resulting in death or serious injury) within the ministry. (Note: the new Act received royal assent at the end of June, 1990.)

5. See Ontario, Committee on Government Productivity, *Interim Report Number Three* (Toronto: Queen's Printer, 1971): 23-25.

6. The Quebec Police Commission, which some regarded as an ineffective control mechanism, was abolished in December, 1988, and replaced by three civilian-dominated boards responsible for investigating complaints against the police (i.e., separate boards for the provincial, Montreal, and other municipal forces). See "Police Commission Termed Powerless," *Globe and Mail,* October 6, 1986: A9, and Lewis Harris, "Quebec Civilians to Dominate New Complaint System," *Toronto Star,* February 5, 1989: B5.

7. Ontario's new Police Services Act requires that all municipalities have police services boards. Size and composition are related to a municipality's population size. Municipalities under 25,000 population are to have three-person boards (head of council and two provincial appointees), and may by council resolution have a five-person board. With the exception of metropolitan and regional areas, municipalities over 25,000 will have five-person boards (head of council, a council appointee, and three provincial appointees). Regional and metropolitan boards have five members (two councillors and three provincial appointees); however, if the municipality's population exceeds 300,000, membership may be expanded to seven with cabinet approval (three councillors and four provincial appointees). The cabinet also appoints the board chair; budget disputes must be appealed to the Ontario Civilian Commission on Police Services; judges and justices of the peace cannot sit on local boards; and boards may function in an advisory capacity to an OPP contract force.

8. This discussion of police organization relies heavily on Loreto (1984) and Auld *et al.* (1978).

9. Statistics Canada, Canadian Centre for Justice Statistics, *Canadian Crime Statistics 1985* (Ottawa: Supply and Services Canada, 1986): 15-23. The analysis of crime trends presented here is derived primarily from data in this document.

10. The legislation provides for a victim fine surcharge for certain offences as well as a requirement that the courts consider "restitution in all cases involving damage, loss, destruction and bodily harm." This concept was first initiated in the United States in 1984, and programs for provincial offences in Manitoba and New Brunswick preceded the federal program. Moreover, it is a concept complementary to criminal injuries compensation programs, first started in Saskatchewan twenty years ago and now available in all provinces except Prince Edward Island (Latta, 1988).

11. Community-based policing projects either have been or are being im-
    plemented in most of Canada's major urban centres, including Victoria,
    Vancouver, Calgary, Winnipeg, and Metropolitan Toronto. In Ontario
    several regional forces (for example, Halton and Sudbury) and the OPP
    have adopted this approach. The academic and governmental literature
    on community-based policing in the United States, England, and Canada
    is substantial. The Canadian literature encompasses comprehensive
    reviews (Murphy and Muir, 1985), descriptive works (Mitzak, 1987;
    Zanibbi, 1988), and evaluative studies (Wasson, 1977; Epstein, 1978;
    Loree, 1988; Walker and Walker, 1989).

12. Jain (1988: 460) defines "visible minority" in terms of nine non-white
    groups: Chinese, black, Indo-Pakistani, West Asian or Arab, Filipino,
    Japanese, Southeast Asian, Korean, and Oceanic. Native people, another
    non-white group, are treated separately.

13. This overview is largely derived from primary documents and the
    *Proceedings of the First International Conference on Civilian Oversight of
    Law Enforcement* (1985).

14. Ontario's proposed Police Services Act essentially extends the Metro-
    politan Toronto system to the rest of the province. In addition, provincial
    responsibility for the process is shifted to the Ministry of the Attorney
    General. Quebec recently replaced its provincial police commission with
    three boards (see note 6).

REFERENCES

Auld, Hugh, Richard Loreto, Ron Smith, and Wayne Petrozzi (1978). *A Review
    of Public Safety Services in the Hamilton-Wentworth Region.* Hamilton:
    Hamilton-Wentworth Region Review Commission.

Booth, Alan, Susan Welch, and David Richard Johnson (1976). "Crowding
    and Urban Crime Rates," *Urban Affairs Quarterly,* XI (March): 291-308.

Cawley, Donald F. (1978). "Managers Can Make a Difference: Future Direc-
    tions," in Alvin W. Cohn (ed.), *The Future of Policing.* Beverly Hills: Sage
    Publications.

Choquette, Jérôme (1971). *The Police and the Public.* Quebec City: Department
    of Justice.

Clarke, R.V.G., and K.H. Heal (1980). "Police Effectiveness in Dealing With
    Crime: Some Current British Research," in Peter Engstad and Michele
    Lioy (eds.), *Workshop on Police Productivity and Performance: Report of the
    Proceedings.* Ottawa: Solicitor General Canada.

Cooper, H.S. (1981). "The Evolution of Canadian Police," in W.T. McGrath
    and M.P. Mitchell (eds.), *The Police Function in Canada.* Toronto: Methuen.

Dearlove, John (1979). *The Reorganization of British Local Government: Old
    Orthodoxies and a Political Perspective.* Cambridge: Cambridge University
    Press.

Decker, Scott H. (1979). "Allocating Police Resources and Fluctuating Crime
    Rates: An Empirical Model," in David M. Petersen (ed.), *Police Work:
    Strategies and Outcomes in Law Enforcement.* Beverly Hills: Sage Publica-
    tions.

Drummond, Douglas S. (1976). *Police Culture.* Beverly Hills: Sage Professional
    Papers in Administrative and Policy Studies, 3, 03-032.

Dunlop, Sheila O., and Denise M.A. Greenaway (1972). *An Examination of the *Metropolitan Toronto Police Community Service Officer Program. From Two Viewpoints: The Police and the Community*. Toronto: University of Toronto, Centre of Criminology.

Epstein, Joyce (1978). *Neighbourhood Police Team Experiment: An Evaluation*. Winnipeg: University of Winnipeg, Institute of Urban Studies.

Ericson, Richard V. (1981). *Making Crime: A Study of Detective Work*. Toronto: Butterworths.

— (1982). *Reproducing Order: A Study of Police Patrol Work*. Toronto: University of Toronto Press.

Farmer, David (1980). "Research and Police Productivity: The United States Experience," in Engstad and Lioy (eds.), *Workshop on Police Productivity and Performance*.

Fleras, Augie, Frederick J. Desroches, Chris O'Toole, and George Davies (1989). " 'Bridging the Gap': Towards a Multicultural Policing in Canada," *Canadian Police College Journal*, XIII, 3: 153-64.

Goldstein, Herman (1968). "Police Response to the Urban Crisis," *Public Administration Review,* XXVIII (September/October): 417-23.

— (1987). "Toward Community-Oriented Policing: Potential, Basic Requirements, and Threshold Questions," *Crime and Delinquency,* XXXIII (January): 6-30.

Grosman, Brian A. (1975). *Police Command: Decisions and Discretion*. Toronto: Macmillan of Canada.

Hann, Robert G., James H. McGinnis, Philip C. Stenning, and A. Stuart Farson (1985). "Municipal Police Governance and Accountability in Canada: An Empirical Study," *Canadian Police College Journal*, IX, 1: 1-85.

Heaphy, John F. (1978). "The Future of Police Improvement," in Cohn (ed.), *The Future of Policing*.

Heywood, R.N. (1980). "Traditional and Innovative Policing," in Engstad and Lioy (eds.), *Workshop on Police Productivity and Performance*.

Jain, Harish C. (1988). "The Recruitment and Selection of Visible Minorities in Canadian Police Organizations: 1985 to 1987," *Canadian Public Administration*, XXXI (Winter): 463-82.

Johnson, Holly (1988). "Violent Crime," *Canadian Social Trends* (Summer): 24-29.

Kelling, G.L. (1980). "The Role of Research in Maximizing Police Productivity," in Engstad and Lioy (eds.), *Workshop on Police Productivity and Performance*.

Kelling, George L., and David Fogel (1978). "Police Patrol – Some Future Directions," in Cohn (ed.), *The Future of Policing*.

Kelling, G.L., T. Pate, D. Dieckman, and C.E. Brown (1974). *The Kansas City Preventive Patrol Experiment*. Washington, D.C.: Police Foundation.

Latta, Allyson (1988). "Victims of Crime: Will the New Law Help Them?" *Perception*, XII (Summer): 17-20.

Linden, Rick (1989). "Demographic Change and the Future of Policing," in Donald J. Loree (ed.), *Future Issues in Policing: Symposium Proceedings*. Ottawa: Supply and Services Canada.

Loree, Donald J. (1988). "Innovation and Change in a Regional Police Force," *Canadian Police College Journal*, XII, 4: 205-39.

Loreto, Richard A. (1984). "Reorganizing Municipal Police Forces in Ontario: The Convergence of Functional and Local Reform Interests" (Ph.D. thesis, University of Toronto).

— (1988). "Community-Based Policing: What is the Meaning of Community?"

A discussion paper prepared under contract for the Ontario Ministry of the Solicitor General, July.

— (1989). *Organization of the Niagara Regional Police Force.* A report submitted to the Royal Commission of Inquiry into Niagara Regional Police Force, December.

McCreedy, Kenneth R. (1978). "The Changing Nature of Police Management: Theory in Transition," in Cohn (ed.), *The Future of Policing.*

McDougall, A.K. (1971). "Policing in Ontario: The Occupational Dimension to Provincial-Municipal Relations" (Ph.D. thesis, University of Toronto).

Mitzak, M. (1987). *A Selected Overview of Community Based Policing Projects in Ontario.* Ottawa: Solicitor General Canada.

Murphy, Chris, and Graham Muir (1985). *Community-Based Policing: A Review of the Critical Issues.* Ottawa: Solicitor General Canada.

Ontario (1974). Task Force on Policing. *Report to the Solicitor General.* Toronto.

— (1978). Waterloo Region Review Commission. *Police Governance in Waterloo Region.* Toronto: Ministry of Intergovernmental Affairs.

— (1989). Race Relations and Policing Task Force. *Report.* Toronto.

Ostrom, Elinor (1975). "On Righteousness, Evidence, and Reform: The Police Story," *Urban Affairs Quarterly,* X (June): 464-86.

Proceedings of the First International Conference on Civilian Oversight of Law Enforcement (1985). Toronto, October.

Pukacz, Emil K. (1978). *Report of the Special Consultant on Police and Other Services to the Administration of Justice in Ontario.* Toronto: Ministry of the Attorney General.

Reiss, A.J., Jr. (1971). *The Police and the Public.* New Haven: Yale University Press.

Ross, Marvin (1977). *Economic Opportunity and Crime.* Montreal: Renouf Publishing Company.

Royal Commission on the Police (1962). *Final Report.* London: Her Majesty's Stationery Office.

Schwartz, Alfred I., and S.N. Clarren (1977). *The Cincinnati Team Policing Experiment: A Summary Report.* Washington, D.C.: The Urban Institute/Police Foundation.

Sharpe, L. J. (1981). "The Failure of Local Government Modernization in Britain: A Critique of Functionalism," *Canadian Public Administration,* XXIV (Spring): 92-115.

Skogan, Wesley G. (1977). "The Changing Distribution of Big-City Crime: A Multi-City Time Series Analysis," *Urban Affairs Quarterly,* XIII (September): 33-48.

Solicitor General Canada (1983-1988). "Canadian Urban Victimization Survey: Bulletin." Ottawa.

— (1975-1989). *Liaison.* Ottawa.

Stahura, John M., and C. Ronald Huff (1979). "Crime and Police Employment: A Structural Model," in Peterson (ed.), *Police Work: Strategies and Outcomes in Law Enforcement.*

Stahura, John M., C. Ronald Huff, and Brent L. Smith (1980). "Crime in the Suburbs: A Structural Model," *Urban Affairs Quarterly,* XV (March): 291-301.

Statistics Canada, Canadian Centre for Justice Statistics (1986). *Policing in Canada.* Ottawa: Supply and Services Canada.

— (1989). *Juristat Service Bulletin,* 9, 4.

Stead, Philip John (1977). "The New Police," in David H. Bayley (ed.), *Police and Society.* Beverly Hills: Sage Publications.

Stenning, Philip C. (1981a). *Legal Status of the Police.* Ottawa: Law Reform Commission of Canada.

— (1981b). *Police Commissions and Boards in Canada.* Toronto: University of Toronto, Centre of Criminology.

— (1988). *The Niagara Regional Board of Commissioners of Police: Its Role and Accountability.* Niagara Falls, Ont.: Niagara Region Review Commission.

Tomovich, V. A., and D. J. Loree (1989). "In Search of New Directions: Policing in Niagara Region," *Canadian Police College Journal,* XIII, 1: 29-54.

Walker, Christopher R., and S. Gail Walker (1989). *The Victoria Community Police Stations: An Exercise in Innovation.* Ottawa: Supply and Services Canada.

Wasson, David K. (1977). *Community-Based Preventive Policing: A Review.* Ottawa: Solicitor General Canada.

Whitaker, Gordon P., Stephen Mastrofski, Elinor Ostrom, Roger B. Parks, and Stephen L. Percy (1981). "Measuring Police Agency Performance: A Critique and Proposal," paper presented at the ASPA National Conference, Detroit, Michigan, April 15.

Willmott, Peter (1986). *Policing and the Community.* London: Policy Studies Institute.

Wilson, James Q. (1978). *Varieties of Police Behavior: The Management of Law and Order in Eight Communities.* Cambridge, Mass.: Harvard University Press.

Wilson, O.W., and Roy C. McLaren (1977). *Police Administration,* 4th edition. New York: McGraw-Hill.

Zanibbi, Richard (1988). "Managing Change to Community Based Policing," paper presented to the 1988 Municipal Police Authorities Annual Conference, Toronto, May.

Conclusion: Provinces and Local Autonomy

It should be apparent by now that the key players in the direction of all of the functions discussed in this book are the provincial governments. Municipalities never had much control of certain important activities – public health, police, education. In many others, financial and legislative controls by provinces have decisively influenced the direction of policies.

Some of these policy areas originated as national policies through the federal government: the National Housing Act executed by Central Mortgage and Housing Corporation (now Canada Mortgage and Housing Corporation); the Canada Assistance Act, which helped to provide the modern basis of social welfare programs. Today the co-ordination of these programs falls on the provinces, which provide such co-ordination among the various policy fields as they can manage.

In the 1970s both the federal and the provincial governments wanted to provide some form of integrated planning to deal with what they felt was a set of interrelated urban problems. To this end a Ministry of State for Urban Affairs was established at the federal level to co-ordinate federal-provincial and municipal policies so as to avoid policy conflicts and to create a united direction to their actions. This ministry carried out extensive research to demonstrate what the policy linkages were and what factors produced the problems.

The federal initiative envisaged an elaborate tri-level consulting mechanism and a national effort at producing an urban policy. It all came to an inglorious end in 1979 when Urban Affairs was dissolved after the leading urban provinces, Ontario and Quebec, had proved reluctant to follow the federal lead. In addition, MSUA had little influence within the federal bureaucracy because it was easily outweighed in cabinet by service delivery departments such as Transport and line agencies such as CMHC.

It was also observable in the late 1970s that certain provincial initiatives at reordering the municipal framework in their own provinces faltered because there were political difficulties and financial pressures from such major reorganization. Ontario had felt that a restructured system of local government would create larger units more commensurate with the growth of demographic and economic communities. These units would have broader tax bases and more effective administrative organizations, and hence would be more capable of performing a wider range of functions and executing more co-ordinated planning. The process was interrupted when only just over half completed in 1976. The effort at reform did not complete the original intention of allowing municipalities to deal with more functions and to have greater powers of local co-ordination.

Quebec, as the other highly urbanized province, also set out to reorganize local government into larger, two-tiered urban units. On the outskirts of Montreal larger single-tier units were created as well as the Montreal Urban Community, uniting all the municipalities on Montreal Island. Urban communities were also established for Quebec City and the Outouais region around the National Capital-Hull sector. Quebec has envisaged new units to administer social services and public health in a different way from the other provinces. The net result, however, has not been an expansion of the authority of municipal government.

In recent years Ontario has discovered that provincial direction and co-ordination are required to correct local deficiencies in waste management and social services, to name only two policy areas. With respect to waste management, a deputy minister responsible for the Greater Toronto Area (i.e., Metropolitan Toronto and the regions of Durham, York, Peel, and Halton) has been appointed to ensure such control and co-ordination. This official, who reports to the provincial Treasurer, will also be taking the lead in preparing planning options to channel urban growth within the Greater Toronto Area (GTA). In fact, some see the GTA as the harbinger of a "super government" at the local level. A proposal has also been made by two committees to develop the remaining county units so that they operate along the lines of the originally restructured units, the regional governments. This has already been accomplished in one county – Lambton.

These examples are offered to demonstrate that such functions are intrinsically different facets of urban problems connected to distinct urban regions. In the larger provinces, the task of provincial guidance is too complex and bureaucratic and central congestion could be positively lessened by allowing more initiative to the third level – municipal government.

Acknowledgements

While some might suggest that producing a collection of readings is a mundane and somewhat unrewarding task, we completely disagree. Indeed, assembling a collection of original pieces by contributors from different disciplines and different parts of the country has been both time-consuming and challenging. The complexity of the task was compounded by our insistence that contributors examine developments outside their own provinces.

Despite these difficulties our efforts have been worthwhile. There is not only the satisfaction of making a significant contribution to the literature on Canadian local government but also the appreciation owed to those who assisted us. First, and foremost, we acknowledge the dedication of our contributors, who responded readily and effectively to our many demands. Second, much is owed to the staff of McClelland & Stewart, particularly Michael Harrison, and to our copy editor, Richard Tallman. Their competence and patience were indispensable in achieving the final result. Third, we wish to thank two anonymous referees. The one increased our awareness of the manuscript's deficiencies; the other, through extensive and constructive comments, charted a path for their resolution. Finally, we dedicate this book to our wives, Carol Loreto and Kathleen Price, who provided both administrative and emotional support.

Notwithstanding this substantial assistance, sole responsibility for the work rests with us.

Richard A. Loreto
Trevor Price
June, 1990

Contributors

Barbara Wake Carroll teaches in the Department of Political Science, McMaster University.

Pierre Duplessis is Director, Department of Community Health, Ste. Justine Hospital, Montreal; Assistant Professor, Department of Epidemiology and Biostatistics, McGill University; and Assistant Professor, Department of Social and Preventive Medicine, University of Montreal.

Meric S. Gertler is in the Department of Geography, University of Toronto.

Trevor Hancock is a public health consultant and Associate Professor, Faculty of Environmental Studies, York University.

Matthew J. Kiernan is with Peat Marwick Consulting Group, Winnipeg, Manitoba.

Harry M. Kitchen teaches in the Department of Economics, Trent University.

Richard A. Loreto is founder and president of Richard A. Loreto Consulting Limited, Stoney Creek, Ontario.

Bernard Pouliot is Director, Department of Community Health, Grand Portage Regional Centre, Rivière du Loup, Quebec.

Trevor Price is with the Department of Political Science, University of Windsor.

David Siegel is Chair, Politics Department, Brock University.

Brian Wharf teaches in the School of Social Work, University of Victoria, and is Dean, Faculty of Human and Social Development.

Peter Woolstencroft is Chair, Department of Political Science, University of Waterloo.

Index